STUMBLING AROUND THE BASES

STUMBLING
AROUND
THE BASES

The American League's Mismanagement
in the Expansion Eras

Andy McCue

University of Nebraska Press   Lincoln

Library of Congress Cataloging in Publication Data
Names: McCue, Andy, author.
Title: Stumbling around the bases: the American League's
mismanagement in the expansion eras / Andy McCue.
Description: Lincoln: University of Nebraska Press, [2022] |
Includes bibliographical references and index.
Identifiers: LCCN 2021038710
ISBN 9781496207036 (hardback)
ISBN 9781496232182 (epub)
ISBN 9781496232199 (pdf)
Subjects: LCSH: American League of Professional
Baseball Clubs—History. | Baseball teams—United
States—History.
Classification: LCC GV875.A15 M338 2022 |
DDC 796.3570973—dc23
LC record available at https://lccn.loc.gov/2021038710

The men who run baseball seem to have the memory span of a gnat and the ability to see ahead about 2½ inches. This most obvious fact of life, that things change, seems to be totally beyond their ability to plan consciously.

—Leonard Koppett, *Sporting News* columnist,
Sporting News, October 16, 1971

Most baseball owners were what people generally looked on as "characters." They were people who had been enormously successful in their work and as a result had a great deal of self-confidence and assurance. Call it ego, if you like.

—Lee MacPhail, baseball executive and American League
president, in *My 9 Innings*

We're all little boys. If we weren't, we wouldn't be that interested in sports. We'd be much more interested in what General Motors stock was doing.

—Charles Bronfman, Montreal Expos owner,
"A New Order Is Emerging," *Sports Illustrated*, July 17, 1978

Some—maybe most—sports franchises aren't especially well managed. Sensible, successful businessmen have been known to change once they become club owners. They do things they wouldn't dream of doing with the businesses that made them successful.

—Bill Veeck, owner of three American League teams,
in *The All-American Dollar*

The owners were a loose amalgam of highly individualistic entrepreneurs.... They're impatient, egocentric, and exasperating.... Most of them had never worked inside structures where cooperation with other strong personalities was required. They were thus very poor at cooperating.

—Bruce Johnston, U.S. Steel labor negotiator, in *Lords of the Realm*

Short was typical of new owners we would see during my tenure, owners who lacked any true affection for baseball but saw the game and the commissioner as devices to further their own business interests.

—Bowie Kuhn, commissioner of baseball, in *Hardball*

The over-riding problem is the intransigence of club owners in dealing with each other. Their inability to agree on a course of action has been dramatized by the present failure to elect a successor to Gen. William Eckert, but the same habit has poisoned baseball health for many years.

—Leonard Koppett, *Sporting News* columnist,
Sporting News, January 18, 1969

Philip Wrigley, who owned the Chicago Cubs from 1932 to 1977, had reached his own conclusion. He always referred to the game as "professional" baseball rather than "organized" baseball because "it was less organized than anything I have ever been associated with."

—Dan Ewald, in *John Fetzer*

CONTENTS

ix   Acknowledgments

xi   **INTRODUCTION**

ONE

1   The Uncooperative Partners

TWO

6   Starting Down the Road to Eclipse

THREE

10   Demographics

FOUR

14   The Boys Club—Eight Men in a Room

FIVE

29   The First Expansion

SIX

44   New Blood, Bad Blood—Ten Men at a Table

SEVEN

54   Changing the Guard

EIGHT

62   The Young Turks

NINE

75   The Luckiest City since Hiroshima

TEN

89   The Nadir

ELEVEN

101   The New Guard—Twelve Men at a Table

TWELVE
117 Expansion Three

THIRTEEN
129 Comeback and Irrelevance

141 Notes

173 Bibliography

181 Index

ACKNOWLEDGMENTS

This book began as I researched baseball's 1961 and 1962 expansion while working on my biography of the Dodgers' Walter O'Malley. Analysis did not favor the American League. I began to look at other decisions the league's owners made both before and after that expansion. The search soon revealed a pattern of reactive, poorly analyzed moves over several decades and I turned to friends, colleagues, and librarians to help me understand.

My initial thinking was greatly advanced by long and very helpful conversations with Mark Armour, Dan Levitt, and Anthony Giacalone.

As I dove into the research, I was helped by colleagues in the Society for American Baseball Research (SABR) — Ron Antonucci, David Bohmer, John Heer, Jeff Katz, Ron Selter, Andy Sharp, Steve Treder, Steve Weingarden, John Zinn, and Tom Zocco. Mike Haupert, Brian Borawski, Steve Weingarden and the members of SABR's Business of Baseball Committee and their research on baseball's winter meetings provided a consistent reference point. Mike Fuller and his excellent Seattlepilots.com website provided material not available elsewhere.

Libraries and archives were indispensable, beginning with Jim Gates, Matt Rothenberg, and Cassidy Lents at the Baseball Hall of Fame. Also, staff at the Chicago Historical Society, Chicago Public Library, the Dallas History and Archives section of the Dallas Public Library, the Sports Research Center at Cleveland Public Library, the newspaper archive room at the New York Public Library, the Burton Historical Collection at the Detroit Public Library, the Frank P. Zeidler Humanities Room at the Milwaukee Public Library, and the public library systems in Baltimore and Los Angeles. A large thank you to Susan Goldstein and the staff at the San Francisco History Center, San Francisco Public Library. And, as always, Wayne Wilson and the staff at LA84.

In academic circles, Joanne Oxley of the University of Toronto and Margaret Levenstein of the University of Michigan provided helpful context.

Baseball industry figures—Peter Bavasi, Roland Hemond, Bob Lurie, and Ross Newhan—took time to talk to me.

A special thank you to my colleagues in BASE (Baseball Authors and Speakers Exchange [https://www.baseballauthors.com])—Rob Garratt, Steve Gietschier, Dan Levitt, Rob Fitts, Rick Huhn, Jean Ardell, Dennis Snelling (who also helped with background on the Soriano brothers), and the indefatigable Bill Lamb—who read all or part of my early drafts and produced twenty-four single-spaced pages of much-needed critique. Rob Garratt and Steve Gietschier were particularly helpful at identifying organizational problems, which I hope I rectified. I would also like to acknowledge my friend of almost half a century, Marty Beiser, for using his exceptional editing skills on the manuscript.

Appreciation to my son Michael Ageno and the talented and beautiful Mary Colleen Kenney for their ideas on the dust jacket art.

At the University of Nebraska Press, my thanks to Rob Taylor, Courtney Ochsner, and Rosemary Sekora. I thank Jessica Ryan for the copyediting.

A large drop of gratitude to the *Sporting News* for its decades of coverage of the great game both on and off the field—and a tear for its demise. A bow to Leonard Koppett for his stories and columns in the *Sporting News* and the *New York Times*, which set a standard for serious sports journalism. A grateful acknowledgment of Retrosheet.org and baseball-reference.com for their invaluable databases of just about everything that happened on the field.

And, above all, my thanks and gratitude to the talented, kind, and beautiful Mary Colleen Kenney for fifty-four years of companionship and forty-four years of toleration.

September 21, 1971, was a mild, humid day with light rain in Boston. Inside the Sheraton-Plaza Hotel, where the dozen men who ruled baseball's American League were grappling with yet another self-made disaster, the air was cooler and dryer. But in their meeting room, the heated discussions endured for thirteen and a half hours. What should they do about their franchise in the nation's capital?

Bob Short, who owned the Washington Senators, wanted to move them to the Dallas–Fort Worth area. Commissioner Bowie Kuhn, who knew only too well another Senators team had left Washington a decade earlier, wanted to keep these Senators where they were. And, he had a purchase offer from Joseph Danzansky.[1] But, the owners worried, Danzansky's financing was not solid enough and the inducements offered by the Texas interests were. In the early hours of September 22, by a vote of ten to two, the Washington Senators franchise, a name that had existed in the American League since its creation in 1901, was blessed to become the Texas Rangers.

It was yet another sign that the American League had hit bottom. A quarter of the league's teams had relocated in the past four seasons. The Athletics had moved from Kansas City to Oakland in 1968. Two years later, the Seattle Pilots had to be fished out of bankruptcy court by owners in a new city—Milwaukee. These franchise moves left large cities without major league baseball. In contrast, during the demographically driven franchise relocations of the 1950s, when Boston, St. Louis, and Philadelphia lost teams, those cities retained their other major league franchise.[2]

The rival National League's average game had drawn 42 percent more customers than the American League's that season. And that was despite the Americans devising a way to inflate their attendance.

The league's representative would lose that year's World Series. It had won that year's All-Star game, but that was an anomaly. It had lost twenty of the last twenty-six games and was about to endure losses for the next eleven years.

When both leagues had expanded in 1969, under threat of a lawsuit caused by the American League's mismanagement of a team's relocation, the difference was clear. The National League had been able to ask new owners for twice as large an entrance fee as the American League. And, as they had in the previous expansion, the Nationals chose larger markets. Montreal and San Diego contained more people than Seattle and Kansas City.

This book is a study of how this proud league, parent of the mighty New York Yankees, fell into such a state, how it stumbled for decades to get out, and how it slowly emerged from its nadir only to lose its separate status as it was merged into something called Major League Baseball.

Descending to the bottom was not a simple process. It involved bad decisions by both individual teams and their owners collectively. It involved decisions cultural and demographic, social and economic. It was a downward trend reinforced several times by repeating an earlier bad choice. The key elements were a glacial approach to integration, the choice of underfinanced or disruptive new members of their club, and a consistent inability to choose the better markets among those cities available for expansion. It was the American League that wound up with the less attractive teams in the smaller markets, and thus fewer consumers of tickets, parking, beer, hot dogs, scorecards, and replica jerseys. As late as 2021, ten of the fifteen teams in the bottom half of major league attendance were in the American League, a legacy of decisions reaching back into the 1950s.

"Planning is wholly out of keeping with the American League tradition of confronting all emergencies, head on, with Panic and Patchwork," wrote Bill Veeck, who sat in American League owners' meetings from the 1940s to the 1970s and derided his fellow owners for all those years.[3]

It was exacerbated by American Leaguers' feeling that the National Leaguers looked down on them, which they did. "There was a feeling in the National League that it was superior," noted San Francisco Giants' owner Bob Lurie.[4]

To "show them," the American League owners would make reactive decisions that hurt as much as helped their own interests, which only reinforced the National League's attitude. And all this was done by men who were notably successful in their non-baseball business ventures. But success in insurance, food processing, breweries, television, drugs, hotels, entertainment, stock brokerage, real estate development, or pizza, while it provided the money to buy teams, did not necessarily translate into running the business of baseball well.

"A few years ago," *Sports Illustrated* opined in September 1963, "the argument that the National League was better than the American League was confined to a relatively small group of 'insiders' but today the evidence of that superiority is overwhelming."[5] The next month, the National League's Los Angeles Dodgers would sweep the American League's New York Yankees out of the World Series in four games in which the "Bronx Bombers" scored only four runs.

It was not like National League owners were immune from poor decision-making in this era. Their pace of integration was adequate only in comparison to the American League's. The antediluvian attitudes of owners in both leagues served to reinforce players' support of Marvin Miller and the Major League Baseball Players Association, and then to hand Miller the wrench he needed to undo the reserve clause and open the checkbooks of free agency.

The leagues governed themselves separately, cooperated when it suited them, and compromised only when forced.

The structure offered few barriers to individual team owners acting purely in their own interests. The National League was simply better at recognizing their collective interests, at screening their owners, and at recognizing the markets with the better long-term potential.

Baseball's structure was in direct contrast to the National Football League, already surpassing baseball as the country's most popular sport and doing it with an idea NFL commissioner Pete Rozelle called "League Think." "One of the key things that a sports league needs," he preached, "is unity of purpose."[6] In League Think, owners had to do what was best for the league, not for their franchise. It had been an idea originated by Rozelle's predecessor, Philadelphia Eagles owner Bert Bell, a man so trusted by his colleagues that they could argue about an issue for days and then turn it over to Bell for a decision. No baseball owner could conceive of such an idea.[7]

It had taken the American League a quarter of a century to reach this nadir. It would take time, money, better staff work, and one selfish, unethical, savvy, tyrant of an executive to get them out. And it would take changes wrought by powers then unforeseen to strip away the league's independent status and leave it with only a name.

CHAPTER ONE

The Uncooperative Partners

For the first six decades of the twentieth century, the National and American Leagues existed in strained parallel.

The two leagues had begun as rivals. The National League was twenty-five years old when the American League emerged in 1901. For two years, they fought over players, scheduling, and customers. In 1903, they agreed to cooperate rather than compete. They called it "organized baseball."

They set up a mechanism to resolve disputes called the National Commission, made up of the presidents of each league and an owner, Cincinnati's Garry Herrmann, who was thought to be fair. That system was falling apart even before the scandal attendant to a thrown World Series in 1919 broke into public view. Fearful a crooked image would damage their attendance, the owners sought to restore the reputation of their game by naming a federal judge as the commissioner of baseball. Kenesaw M. Landis was given broad powers to do what was best for the game, but he did not interpret his job to include getting the leagues to cooperate except where absolutely necessary. He would enforce their rules, settle disputes, and make rulings to force owners to conform to his view of baseball's best interests.[1] Most of organized baseball's business was still conducted in separate league meetings. The league presidents sat on an "executive council" to advise Landis, but he ignored them.

After Landis died in 1944, the commissioner's powers were circumscribed. There were more joint meetings because the owners did not want a commissioner or league president making decisions for them. An owner from each league was added to the executive council, and it was made clear to the commissioner that he was supposed to listen to their advice. Like the commissioner, the league presidents had limited powers and were fully aware they served at the pleasure of the owners.

By the late 1950s, the commissioner was Ford Frick, who had started life as a newspaper reporter, become Babe Ruth's ghostwriter, and then moved to do publicity for the National League. In 1934, when National League president John Heydler died, Frick was selected to replace him. In 1951, Frick was promoted to the commissioner's office.

Frick was widely perceived to favor his old employers, the National League owners. In the newspapers, he also was widely perceived as ineffective. When questioned as to why he had not stepped into some issue, he regularly would describe it as a "league matter," outside the purview of the commissioner's office. The reporters, eager for news on integration, franchise movement, changing demographics, television policy, or expansion, would become exasperated. They rarely seemed to understand that the role set for the commissioner was as a diplomat, who would smooth over the owners' disagreements and represent their interests to Congress. He would wear a nice suit to talk to the public, but he was not to be a leader.

In 1960, the leagues had slightly restructured the Major League Agreement that defined the relationship between the two leagues and the duties of the office of the commissioner. The powers they gave the commissioner were basically unchanged—to investigate situations that were "not in the best interests of baseball," to take corrective action where warranted in these situations, to make the final decision in disputes between the leagues or regarding players, and to set the rules for his office in the above situations.[2] That was it.

These responsibilities were all reactive, as were the responsibilities of the league presidents. Nobody was tasked with dealing with expansion, franchise relocation, television, or then-unanticipated items such as a players' union, cable superstations, or the internet. In short, nobody was responsible for thinking ahead. That was left up to individual owners willing to invest the time and effort to figure out where their collective enterprise should go and persuade their colleagues to follow.

The real power was held collectively by the owners. They set the policies the commissioner and league presidents were supposed to carry out. As with any sports league, it was a paradoxical structure. They were competitors on the field, striving to produce teams that could win more games, and therefore make more money. Off the field, whether dealing with lawmakers in Washington, cities seeking to gain or retain a team, scheduling, player demands, or national television contracts, they were partners.

In fact, the Supreme Court, back in 1922, determined that the leagues were not subject to antitrust law, thus making them a legalized cartel, almost completely free to conduct their business collectively without fear of antitrust lawsuits.[3]

Since professional baseball's antitrust exemption will come up repeatedly in this story, this deserves a fuller explanation. A short-lived rival, the Federal League, collapsed after the 1915 season. Its Baltimore team sued the National and American Leagues charging they had violated antitrust laws during the competition. In 1922, the Supreme Court ruled that the National League and the American League were not involved in interstate commerce and thus were not subject to antitrust laws.[4] In 1953, in *Toolson v. New York Yankees*, the Supreme Court sharply criticized the 1922 decision but suggested the remedy was for Congress to make it explicit that antitrust law covered professional baseball. Since then, senators and congressmen have used that possibility to leverage various issues with the two leagues, while carefully refusing to extend the immunity to other major sports.

While owners' meetings rarely discussed the antitrust exemption, it was always in the background of their thinking. Their central concern was the reserve clause Toolson had challenged. The clause was a feature of baseball's standard contract. It said the contract was for the current year and an option year. If the player refused the team's salary offer for the option year, the team could renew the contract. The owners' interpretation was that renewal covered the entire contract, including the reserve clause, effectively creating a permanent contract. Toolson had argued the clause allowed the Yankees to keep him in the minor leagues when he could have pitched successfully for another major league team. Two decades after Toolson, Marvin Miller and the players' union would argue that a one-year option was for one year, with the player becoming a free agent thereafter. They would win, breaking the reserve clause and ushering in the free agency era.

Using the reserve clause to control players and their salaries was the owners' main focus, especially as the players' union grew in militancy and power. But the owners also freely used their antitrust exemption in other ways. It allowed them to collude over admission to their ranks; the choice of where to move existing franchises or grant new ones; and negotiations with broadcast networks, cities, and others.

The idea of partnership was, at times, a hard concept for owners, schooled in competitive business fields, to accept. Any new idea always had to be examined not merely for its benefits to an owner but for possible benefits to his competition. It was possible, but not necessary, to examine the idea in terms of its benefit to the league, or organized baseball as a whole.

Their power was also circumscribed by the historic separation of two organizations in the same business, but separate. After one owners' meeting, owner Calvin Griffith lamented, "I've been sitting on committees all week and still don't know what's happening. The world thinks of us as one organization, but in reality, we are two—the American and National leagues—and one is trying to dump its problems on the other."[5]

Thus, important decisions would be made by eight, later ten, twelve, or fourteen men brought together occasionally for communal decision-making for a joint business that occupied their attention only sporadically. In 1960, for example, baseball was the main source of wealth of only four of the sixteen owners—Calvin Griffith of the Washington Senators, Bill Veeck of the Chicago White Sox, Horace Stoneham of the San Francisco Giants, and Walter O'Malley of the Los Angeles Dodgers, and Veeck was in the process of selling to a family of stockbrokers. The others brewed beer, sold chewing gum, built retirement communities, or ran an array of other businesses as their primary occupation. These were the businesses that commanded their attention and their imagination.

The owners met at least twice a year—at the All-Star game in midsummer and at the winter meetings in early December. Depending on the urgency of an issue, meetings could be added as necessary. They met as a league and then held a joint meeting with the commissioner. While fans and press might perceive problems, the issues could be given short shrift if the leadership was content. At the end of the 1961 winter meetings, Commissioner Ford Frick said, "Gentlemen, I want to congratulate you. This has been our finest meeting. We finished everything in seven minutes."[6] "Everything" included whether to continue with a second All-Star game each year, changes in the rules governing signing bonuses for amateur players, and the relationship between the majors and the financially troubled minor leagues.[7] Despite this "finest" meeting, all these issues would have to be revisited in subsequent years.

The attendance norm was two persons for each franchise, usually the principal owner and his general manager. But that practice was highly flexible. Some owners skipped regularly, others sporadically. On August 30, 1960, as the American League held a meeting on strategy for what would become the 1961 expansion, only four owners were present. The Red Sox, Indians, Tigers, and Athletics sent lesser executives.[8] When necessary, a lawyer or someone with specific expertise on an issue such as ticketing or television could be added. At times, an "owners only" meeting would be called, and the experienced baseball executives were left in the corridors.[9]

When owners attended, the experienced baseball executives were often not even heard. The table usually was set up with a chair for the league president and one for each franchise. The second person in a team's delegation sat behind his leader and spoke only when spoken to. The numbers attending and discussing did not matter. Each team had one vote and on anything important it was the owner who would "vote the franchise."

Inevitably, as in any small group, there were conflicts of both policies and personalities. As Kansas City Royals owner Ewing Kauffman summed it up: "Baseball ownership is made up of 26 egomaniacs and I am one of them."[10] And Kauffman was considered one of the more constructive owners.

Like Kauffman, Marvin Miller of the players' union would recognize the owners were not a monolithic group. There were rich franchises and less rich ones, and their interests, especially as they came to deal with free agency and rising salaries, were in conflict.[11] But there was also a strong recognition of common interests and the dangers of precedent. If limits were proposed on one owner's actions or desires, other owners had to analyze the potential impact on their own future actions. As a result, there was great deference to any owner's interests as societal changes began to affect professional baseball.

CHAPTER TWO

Starting Down the Road to Eclipse

The decline of the American League began at 215 Montague Street in downtown Brooklyn on the warm morning of August 28, 1945. The *New York Times* was reporting the first American troops had landed in Japan, signaling the end of World War II, and most Americans' thoughts were focused on their postwar lives. Jack Roosevelt Robinson, a twenty-six-year-old shortstop for the Negro Leagues' Kansas City Monarchs, traveled down from a Harlem hotel, met scout Clyde Sukeforth, and climbed to the fourth-floor offices of Branch Rickey, president of the Brooklyn Dodgers. There, under the glow of a fish tank and portraits of Abraham Lincoln and Leo Durocher, Robinson endured Rickey's probing questions and confrontational role playing. Three hours later, elated but shaken, Robinson emerged into the afternoon heat with an agreement to play for the Dodger organization.

Twenty months later, he became the first African American player in the major leagues since the Jim Crow curtain descended six decades earlier. He was the National League's Rookie of the Year for 1947 and its Most Valuable Player two years later.

By September 8, 1953, when Ernie Banks signed his first contract with the Chicago Cubs, Robinson, Roy Campanella, Willie Mays, Monte Irvin, Hank Aaron, and Frank Robinson—Hall of Famers all—had joined National League organizations. Robinson and Campanella had already won two Most Valuable Player Awards, and Campanella would gain his second at the end of the season. That victory started a streak of seven straight (and nine of ten) African American National League MVPs. The American League's first Black MVP, Elston Howard, would come in 1963, and they would have to wait eight more years for the second.[1]

In the American League, the Cleveland Indians' maverick owner Bill Veeck signed that circuit's first Black player—Larry Doby—not long after Robinson reached the big leagues. A year later, he signed ancient Negro Leagues superstar Leroy "Satchel" Paige, who proved that, even at forty-two, he could get major league hitters out. The hardscrabble St. Louis Browns signed a couple of Black players, but released them before giving them much of a chance.[2]

While the National League teams were skimming off the cream of the Negro Leagues and beginning to sign Black high school stars (Frank Robinson), American League organizations made token signings or sat on their hands. Half of the American League's eight original organizations would not produce an African American All-Star selection until the 1960s, when the National League regularly would have to leave Black future Hall of Famers out of their All-Star game starting lineups because there were too many candidates. The American League's first African American Rookie of the Year, Tommie Agee, would not arrive until 1966, nearly two decades after Robinson's debut.[3]

As usual, it was the Yankees who acted as the American League's bell cow. Part owner and team president Larry MacPhail made the business argument. After Robinson's signing he worried that a Black player would draw significant African American crowds, especially in cities such as New York and Chicago. This, he wrote Commissioner Albert "Happy" Chandler," could "conceivably threaten the value of the major league franchises owned by these clubs."[4] He worried the presence of Blacks would make his box seat customers uncomfortable. On a coarser Yankee note, it was General Manager George Weiss who told scout Tom Greenwade, "I don't want you sneaking around any back alleys and signing any n—s. We don't want them."[5] And, yet, when Hall of Fame sportswriter Wendell Smith ranked "The Most Prejudiced Teams in Baseball" for *Ebony Magazine* in 1953, he placed the Yankees fifth, trailing Detroit, Boston, Philadelphia, and Washington, all in the American League.[6]

In these years of the late 1940s and early 1950s, prejudice overcame economics. The American League was divided into one Super-Have, the Yankees, four middle-class teams, and three Have-Nots, the Senators, Athletics, and St. Louis Browns. In that era, the Yankees would scout, sign, and develop more players who made the majors than the three lower teams combined. It would have been an obvious business tactic for the poorer teams to seek Black talent aggressively. But, following the lead of the Yankees, they did not.[7]

The difference between the leagues was not merely talent. It was style. Baseball as played in the Negro Leagues placed a much greater emphasis on speed than the major leagues of the previous three decades—the era of Babe Ruth, Lou Gehrig, Hank Greenberg, Jimmie Foxx, and other large and often ponderous home run hitters. With integration, the stolen base took on a growing role in National League offenses, creating a faster, more exciting game. In the twenty-five years beginning in 1949, the National League had more stolen bases than the American League nineteen times and more triples twenty-two times.[8] But it was not all singles and steals. In the same period, they managed to out-homer the American League over half the time.

Fans responded to the Black stars, and their combination of speed and power. In 1956, the National League's average attendance per game passed the American League, which had led the previous season. The National League attendance dominance would continue for over three decades.

Until those years in the mid-1950s, performance both on the field and in attracting fans had flip-flopped between the two leagues. The American League had debuted in 1901, a quarter century after the National League. The league had been dominated by its president, founder, and chief promoter, Byron Bancroft "Ban" Johnson. He had recruited many of the owners and retained their loyalty for the league's first two decades. The upstart league quickly competed with the senior circuit for talent and fans.

In the 1920s, as Johnson's era passed, the American League came to be ruled by the New York Yankees, by far the most successful franchise in major league history. After two decades without a league championship, the Yankees won six from 1921 through 1930, and at least four in every decade through 1980.

It was the American League that had dominated the All-Star games of the 1930s and 1940s. Since the emergence of the Yankees in the 1920s, it was the American League that had dominated the World Series, winning over two-thirds of the meetings, including an unmatched Yankee streak of five from 1949 through 1953. There were those who thought the New Yorkers' dominance hurt the league's other franchises, but there was no doubt they were the biggest draw in opponents' ballparks.[9] Perceptions followed success.

By the late 1930s, the *Saturday Evening Post*'s Tom Meany was characterizing the National League as a minor league.[10] But that idea had not been internalized in either league's councils. Even seven decades later, league presidents would give Knute Rockne–style motivational speeches in All-Star game locker rooms. Interleague trading had been banned until 1959 and then was limited to specific, short periods of time. League presidents lobbied against teams that thought about trading their stars to that other league.[11] As late as 1966, National League president Warren Giles, stung by the Cincinnati Reds' year-earlier trade of American League Most Valuable Player Frank Robinson to the Orioles, boasted of blocking the trades of Maury Wills and Tommy Davis to the other league.[12]

It was not just superficial competitiveness. There were substantial differences between the leagues in managing their businesses. Even before Jackie Robinson, National Leaguers ignored the critics such as Meany. They felt their clubs were the innovators, whether it was Branch Rickey and the Cardinals developing the idea of the farm system, the Cincinnati Reds scheduling the first night game, or clubs around the league grasping the potential of radio sooner—the first broadcast game (Philadelphia at Pittsburgh, 1921), the first to broadcast all of its games (Chicago Cubs, 1927), or the first to break the New York clubs' self-inflicted ban on radio broadcasts (Brooklyn Dodgers, 1939).

National League teams invested more money in scouting and in their farm systems in the 1950s and into the 1960s. The result was more and better players graduating to the parent teams.[13]

In the early years, at every American League meeting, "there always was a discussion of ways and means of surpassing the Nationals until it became something like a religious crusade," noted Branch Rickey, then an American League executive. A few years later, Rickey moved to the National League's St. Louis Cardinals, "but I never attended a National meeting where the Americans ever were mentioned."[14]

There was also a different level of discipline. Hank Greenberg, who attended many American League meetings in the 1950s, said, "We never had a major league meeting when Del Webb of the Yankees didn't leave the meeting room and go out into the hallway where the reporters were waiting and tell them exactly what was taking place, giving his own version of it, of course, in order to get a little publicity for himself." National Leaguers kept their mouths shut.[15]

By the 1960s, perceptions had firmly shifted in favor of the National League. "For years, the National League has been regarded as the more progressive of the two major leagues," editorialized *Sporting News* publisher C. C. Johnson Spink in 1967.[16] As population shifts moved the country to the West and South, the National Leaguers had been better at geography.

CHAPTER THREE

Demographics

A s the 1950s progressed, and baseball's attendance shrank before the onslaught of television, the owners struggled to deal with a new problem. World War II had heightened the shift of population from the older cities of the Northeast and Midwest, where all major league teams were located. Southern, southwestern, and, most obviously, western cities were growing exponentially. When the National League was founded, Los Angeles was a city of a few thousand. By the American League's debut, it had barely broken the 100,000 level. By 1950, it was the fourth largest city in the country and would pass Philadelphia by 1960. San Francisco (eleventh largest in 1950) and some others had grown similarly.

One American League owner started to be bold. St. Louis Browns' owner Donald Barnes spent the 1941 season working with airlines and railroads to come up with an American League schedule that could accommodate moving his struggling team to Los Angeles. He went to the December American League meetings in Chicago fully expecting to win approval for the move. But, the day before the meetings the Japanese bombed Pearl Harbor and Barnes knew wartime uncertainties precluded any team movement. By the time World War II ended, Barnes had sold the team.[1]

The war had proven the feasibility of long-distance airplane travel, and, by the late 1950s, jet technology was cutting travel times even further. The argument that West Coast cities were just too distant to fit into a railroad-based schedule was washed away.

The major leagues spent most of the decade after World War II dithering about the obvious attraction of West Coast markets. There were sporadic reports that one of the financially weaker teams—the Washington Senators, Cincinnati Reds, Pittsburgh Pirates, St. Louis Browns, Boston Braves, or Philadelphia Athletics—would move to the West Coast, but they fizzled.

The question of how to accommodate the population shift sputtered across the 1950s. The potential of Los Angeles and San Francisco were clear to all, but a plan to capture those markets seemed to baffle the owners. There were suggestions of expanding the two existing leagues, or creating a third, or even a fourth, major league. There was talk of existing teams moving to new cities. The Pacific Coast League, the largest and most successful of the minor leagues, pushed itself forward as a possible major league conversion beginning in 1944. For almost a decade, it petitioned and prodded the major leagues to gain parity. It eventually gained the attention of Congressman Emanuel Celler and his committee examining baseball's antitrust exemption. Celler asked to see a copy of baseball's rules governing how the Pacific Coast League could be promoted. With some embarrassment, the commissioner admitted there were no such rules, and thus no possibility of conversion. Embarrassed, the major leagues responded with some changes to the Pacific Coast League's status. There were higher prices for Pacific Coast League players sold to the majors and more restrictions on who major leagues teams could draft, but the Pacific Coast League remained a minor league.[2]

By 1953, the flip side of demographic shifts made itself felt. In three successive years, franchises from older two-team cities that were stagnant or losing population moved to what they hoped were better markets. But the decisions were not always thoughtful. In 1953, it was the National League's Boston Braves going to Milwaukee, a slightly larger city. Thirteen years later, the team, citing poor attendance, would move again, this time to Atlanta, a growing city in the South. In 1954, it was the American League's St. Louis Browns moving to a much bigger city, Baltimore, where the team would find success on and off the field. But Baltimore, the twelfth largest metropolitan area in the United States in 1960, was the one city in the U.S. Northeast that had been conspicuously ignored by the majors for the previous half century. In 1955, it was the American League's Philadelphia Athletics moving to Kansas City, the twenty-seventh biggest market in the country in 1960. It was a city on baseball's western edge, but still closer to Boston than Los Angeles. It was a move that passed over larger markets not only in Los Angeles and San Francisco, but Houston, Dallas, New Orleans, San Antonio, San Diego, Seattle, Buffalo, Memphis, Denver, Atlanta, Minneapolis, and Indianapolis. Like the Braves, the Athletics would move again thirteen years later—to Oakland in the San Francisco Bay Area.

While talk of expansion and franchise shifts had been rampant, planning on these topics had been almost nonexistent. Throughout the mid-1950s, the

Sporting News, generally the voice of the baseball establishment, kept calling for market research and thought. Commissioner Ford Frick agreed.[3] Committees were formed and drifted into irrelevance only to be formed again a couple of years later.

Philip Wrigley, owner of both the Chicago Cubs and the international chewing gum company, sought to bring the practices of private industry to his hobby. "Industry hires experts and spends a great deal of time and money to compile figures on population shifts and what sort of people are living where," he told *Sporting News* editor J. G. Taylor Spink in 1954. "Baseball is trying to sell a product, too. But what has it done about finding the best market for it? The game still is operating just as it did in the horse and buggy days."[4] Of course, Wrigley was a National League owner.

Most owners would think about baseball's demographic issues when prodded by a reporter's question or given a committee assignment by other owners. But nobody was in charge of thinking strategically about baseball. There was, however, one man who both served on baseball's executive council and ran his team as his sole business.[5] Walter O'Malley was also a man inclined to think strategically.[6]

By 1956, O'Malley had spent a decade trying to get the Dodgers a new ballpark in Brooklyn. New York City had not been accommodating. He had tried flattery, emissaries, political maneuvering, and increasingly less subtle stratagems. He moved some home games to Jersey City, New Jersey. He sold the real estate under his ballpark, Ebbets Field. His search for leverage was not working, and he began looking around. In early 1957, while returning from accompanying his team on a tour of Japan, he stopped to reconnoiter a place he had heard about called Chavez Ravine in Los Angeles.

In February 1957, he bought the Los Angeles Pacific Coast League franchise and its ballpark from Philip Wrigley of the Cubs. Under baseball rules, the franchise purchase gave him the rights to the Los Angeles market. Los Angeles officials rushed to the Dodgers' Vero Beach training facility to woo him. New York officials dithered some more. That spring, New York Giants owner Horace Stoneham told his National League colleagues he would be moving his team to Minneapolis. O'Malley suggested their two teams could move their rivalry to the West Coast and put Stoneham in touch with San Francisco officials.[7] By October, O'Malley and Stoneham both had firm offers from their West Coast cities, and nothing but vague promises from New York.

After years of dithering by both leagues, O'Malley and Stoneham moved boldly to snap up the two most attractive markets in the country for the National League. The National League's attendance surged as the optimistic predictions about West Coast fans proved true. The American League knew they had to respond.

For the eight men who ruled the American League, their options were clouded by the looming quid pro quo. The National League clearly would want back into New York City, still the largest market in the country. Within weeks of the Giants' and Dodgers' departures, New York City set up a committee to lure a National League team. By July 1959, its efforts had evolved into an attempt to create a rival league. For owners, especially in the American League, the next year and a half would be dominated by questions of expansion, realignment, and markets.

CHAPTER FOUR

The Boys Club—Eight Men in a Room

As they watched the National League snap up the tempting markets of the West Coast, the American League, as it had been for over half a century, was run by eight men who would decide the how and why of league expansion. They were all white, mostly wealthy, and most had made their money outside baseball.

The New York Yankees claimed the seat at the head of the American League table as their due for their perennial place in the standings. Larry MacPhail, Dan Topping, and Del Webb had bought the team from the estate of Jacob Ruppert in 1945, paying only $2.8 million. MacPhail ran the team for three seasons before flaming out in a drunken, public scene after the 1947 World Series. Topping and Webb bought out his share and divided team management.

Topping was Mr. Inside, overseeing General Manager George Weiss and the operations of the team. Webb was Mr. Outside, dealing with the league, the commissioner's office, and baseball politics. Despite their contrasting backgrounds, they worked well as a team.

Daniel Reid Topping, born in 1912, was the grandson of two of the most successful robber barons of the late nineteenth century—John A. Topping and Daniel G. Reid.[1] "You weren't born with a silver spoon in your mouth. You were born with a gold one," MacPhail told him.[2] He went from an elite prep school to the Ivy League. He played sports in a gentlemanly way—football and baseball to be sure, but his focus soon turned to golf where he had success on the amateur circuit. He enjoyed golf, but acknowledged his limitations, agreeing with a British golf writer who said Topping had "a long drive, a genial smile and little else."[3] But mostly, he lived the life of the wealthy playboy, toying with jobs in banking and then advertising. He married six beautiful women—his most famous bride being Norwegian Olympic skater and actress Sonja Henie—and kept the unions short.

As he aged, he began to settle down. He enlisted as a private in the Marine

Corps during World War II. He quickly became an officer and was Captain Topping by the time he bought into the Yankees.[4] He was always tanned and sharply dressed. One reporter said he had an "air-conditioned look."[5] He became that elusive figure the press loved—the millionaire "Sportsman," to be contrasted with those whose interest in the game was monetary. "He always knew where his next yacht or private plane was coming from," wrote Red Smith, but added, "Dan Topping had class, which is something money cannot buy."[6]

In the 1930s, Topping invested in professional football's Brooklyn Dodgers, named after the National League team, and who fittingly played their games in baseball's Ebbets Field. The team was intermittently successful on the field but eventually was a financial failure. In the meantime, it led to useful connections. He met then-Dodgers' executive Larry MacPhail while negotiating for the use of Ebbets Field and when MacPhail began to look for monied partners to fund his bid for the Yankees, he approached an interested Topping. Topping, in turn, led MacPhail to Webb on a golf course in California and the partnership was formed.

Topping worked out of the Yankees' offices and attended most home games. George Weiss dealt with trades, salary negotiations, and the minor league system, the issues where the reporters clustered. Topping handled the more mundane areas—stadium operations, ticketing, and working with pro and college football teams as well as boxing promoters interested in renting Yankee Stadium.[7] He set up a pension plan for salaried employees. But his most important role in the organization, a role he shared with Larry MacPhail's son, Lee, was to smooth the edges of George Weiss. Married to Weiss's efficiency in putting together a team, minimizing salaries, and maximizing profits was a talent for annoying virtually everyone he dealt with. Topping, with an easy manner and patrician pedigree that hid multiple cases of ulcers, served as a release valve for players, press, and others who had to deal with Weiss—and a check on some of Weiss's more ruthless moves. When the Yankees fired Casey Stengel after the 1960 season, it was Topping who stood at the press conference podium.

In general, Topping left league affairs to Webb, but he could get involved when an issue got close to his interests. In 1955, he angered Washington Senators' owner Clark Griffith by his aggressiveness in supporting Arnold Johnson's bid to buy the Philadelphia Athletics and move them to Kansas City.[8] Topping, Webb, and Johnson had multiple business dealings. In 1953, Johnson bought Yankee Stadium and its real estate, a sale that recouped all of Topping's and Webb's investments in buying the team. Both men were on the board of Johnson's Automatic Canteen Co. of America.

In 1960, as the possibility of expansion arose, Topping first insisted that the National League could not re-enter New York City, as it was the Yankees' territory. Later, he argued that the American League had to be allowed into the Southern California market pioneered by Walter O'Malley's Dodgers. He lost on the first issue but got his way on the second.

Dueling with Commissioner Ford Frick, the National Leaguers, and his American League colleagues was more Webb's bailiwick. Until they met on the golf course and decided to bid for the Yankees, Webb's and Topping's backgrounds were sharply divergent.

Webb was born in 1899 in Fresno, California, the son of a small-time contractor. He learned carpentry from his father and dropped out of high school to pound nails and pitch semipro baseball for a decade. In 1927, his team played an exhibition at San Quentin prison and Webb said he caught typhoid fever from an inmate. He went from 200 pounds to 90 over the next year and a half. As a consequence, he gave up pitching and, on the advice of a doctor, moved to the hot, dry climate of Phoenix, Arizona, in 1928.

There, the spare, six-foot, four-inch Webb returned to carpentry. He was helping build a supermarket when his paycheck bounced and the contractor disappeared. Webb went to the store owner and convinced him to front the necessary funds and let Webb put together a crew to finish the store. It worked and Webb soon expanded to build other grocery stores as well as hotels. By the late 1930s, Del E. Webb Construction was doing $3 million in business every year. He opened an office in Los Angeles to expand to the West Coast and was perfectly positioned when World War II created the need for multiple military training facilities in the more predictable and drier weather of the Southwest.

He won a $3 million contract to expand Fort Huachuca near Tucson, Arizona, for the army and came in on time and budget. With further expansions, he would eventually do $22 million at the fort. With his reputation for performance established, his company built dozens of facilities—air fields, Marine bases, and a concentration camp for Japanese American internees. He expanded his efforts into a brewery, a clothespin factory, and producing movies with Bing Crosby. By his fifties, the itinerant carpenter was worth at least $100 million.

He did not project that way. He had a "monotonous and somewhat tedious" manner of speaking. A *Sports Illustrated* profile described his "level-eyed, laconic western charm, somehow suggestive of sagebrush and wide-open spaces." But, it noted, he liked "large and gloppy ice cream desserts," after his regular steak and baked potato dinners. He usually ate in the coffee shops of his hotels rather than fancy restaurants.[9]

Webb spent most of his time running the construction business and flying in his private plane around the country, where he maintained hotel suites in New York, Phoenix, and Los Angeles, each with its own full wardrobe. He belonged to fourteen country clubs so he always had a chance to indulge his passion for golf.[10] He was organized and involved, focused on his profits, although colleagues and friends said he was less interested in the money than in the power his wealth gave him. Thus, he would never be involved in the day-to-day management of the Yankees, although Topping would consult with him on major salary negotiations and other large decisions. Yankee Stadium would see him on Opening Day, the World Series, and Oldtimers' games.

Webb projected a somewhat ambivalent attitude toward his ownership. "I invested in the Yankees strictly from a business viewpoint,"[11] he said early in his ownership career, a time when reporters were fascinated with his background in semipro ball. He would later soften that stance in public, but his reputation as a dedicated capitalist was cemented. It grew with anecdotes such as the time MacPhail decided Yankees players needed to dry their uniforms outdoors during spring training. He knew Webb owned a clothespin factory and placed a large order, only to be surprised when Webb billed him at the full price.[12]

Webb was sucked quickly into the politics of the American League. His first venture came in 1950 when Commissioner Albert "Happy" Chandler began investigating him for gambling connections. Webb had built the Flamingo Hotel, the first of the luxury casinos in Las Vegas. It was owned by gangster Bugsy Siegel and after Siegel was murdered in 1947, Webb wound up owning a piece of the resort. Despite Chandler's concerns, the commissioner's investigation went nowhere. Webb would go on to build several more casinos in Las Vegas. A 1977 investigation found that "behind the public image, his Del E. Webb Corporation of Phoenix has been an active business partner with mob figures for three decades."[13]

When Chandler ruled against the Yankees in some personnel cases, Webb's irritation over the investigation blossomed into a successful campaign to oust Chandler. Inevitably, that led to involvement in choosing Chandler's successor. Webb pushed for someone with a legal and business background and bowed to the selection of Ford Frick, but he was now fully involved in the upper councils of the game.

His business interests drew him in further. While Del E. Webb Construction was now a national business, his roots remained on the West Coast and he pushed for an American League team to be moved to Los Angeles. He could not persuade his colleagues to allow Bill Veeck to move the St. Louis Browns there in 1953, but that was probably because of Veeck's reputation among the owners. He did push hard for his business associate, Arnold Johnson, to be allowed to buy the Philadelphia Athletics in 1954. Critics whispered his sole interest was to win contracts to build stadiums in places such as Los Angeles and Kansas City. Veeck charged that Webb would change his vote in league meetings to feed his corporate interests.[14] He ultimately would build Anaheim Stadium for the expansion Los Angeles Angels. Webb said he was just looking to capture better markets for his league.

When expansion talk heated up with the Continental League in 1960, Webb was the obvious point man for the American League.

Tom Yawkey entered baseball in 1933 as a "Manhattan Sportsman," and he left the game forty-three years later as a "Sportsman Owner."[15] In his early years owning the Boston Red Sox, he would be known for spending lavishly to buy the best talent. In his later years, he would be known as the lenient sportsman who deserved to win a World Series, but never did.

He was born Thomas Yawkey Austin in February 1903. His father died that September and Tom's mother entrusted him to her brother, William Yawkey, a part owner of the Detroit Tigers. His mother died when he was fifteen. His uncle adopted him and rearranged his name to Thomas Austin Yawkey. Tom would inherit multiple millions from the Yawkey family, mostly when he reached thirty.[16]

Like Topping, Tom Yawkey took the prep school to Ivy League route, through the Irving School in Tarrytown, New York, to the Sheffield Scientific School, the engineering and science program at Yale. He was preparing for a life running the family interests in mining, lumber, and other ventures. After graduation, he would spend the rest of his life enlarging those assets while developing a strong interest in conservation.

Yawkey had fallen for baseball as a boy when his uncle brought Ty Cobb and other luminaries to the family dinner table. He played varsity baseball at Irving and intramurals at Yale.

On his thirtieth birthday, the trust governing his inherited millions handed over the money. Less than a week later, he translated some of it into his dream—buying the Red Sox. Over the next fifteen years, Yawkey spent millions buying stars from money-losing franchises such as the Philadelphia Athletics. He spent more millions completely rebuilding twenty-year-old Fenway Park. He was famed for high salaries and a casual approach to discipline.[17] He loved to take batting practice and infield at Fenway after the varsity was done, crowing at hitting a ball off the Green Monster and banning cameras who might take his picture while he enjoyed himself.

At Yale, Yawkey had a reputation for "fast cars, pretty girls, drinks, laughs."[18] He married soon after graduation but that ended in a divorce in 1944, leaving one adopted daughter. He soon remarried, to Jean Hiller, a New York fashion model. They would be childless. In the late 1940s, he was told that his manager, Joe McCarthy, did not think it was right for the owner to be in the clubhouse.[19] Yawkey, who now was older than his players, stopped going, but never lost his desire for close, increasingly fatherly, relationships with the players.

He also presided over the slower league's slowest franchise to integrate, waiting for 1959 to bring up the team's first African American. It was not so much Yawkey himself, but clearly racist managers and general managers who Yawkey allowed full sway to run the team.

The racism, selflessness, high salaries, and disciplinary laxity showed in Yawkey's profits. By the end of 1959, he had owned the team for twenty-seven seasons, only nine of which had made money. The cumulative loss was $2.4 million.[20] Summed up by Dominic DiMaggio, an All-Star for the Red Sox in the late 1940s and later a millionaire businessman: "The difference between the Yankees and the Red Sox was that the Yankees always were run as a business. They made sound business moves. The Red Sox, under Yawkey, were a hobby. He always kept friends around too long and made decisions according to who he drank with."[21]

Yawkey had sat at the American League table since 1933, over a decade more than any of his colleagues. As a rookie, he kept his mouth shut at his first winter meetings. His pocketbook did the talking as he bought All-Star players for All-Star prices. Soon, he was involved. He was working on umpire-related issues and, during World War II, would serve on a league owners panel concerned with postwar planning.

During the 1950s, he supported Happy Chandler in Chandler's unsuccessful battle to remain commissioner and moved from support to opposition on interleague play.[22] He fought player salary increases and advocated unsuccessfully for expansion.[23] With Webb, he first opposed Calvin Griffith's moving the Senators to Minnesota, citing the need for a team in the nation's capital. In the *Sporting News*, Shirley Povich characterized Webb and Yawkey as "the two most powerful owners in the league effort."[24]

For virtually all that decade, he represented the American League on baseball's executive council, the commissioner's first line of advisors. For forceful owners such as Webb and Topping, he was the perfect representative. As the *Sporting News* editorialized, he was "a man who thinks first of baseball and then of his own club.[25]

The rising voice in the American League came from Detroit—and was slow in coming. John Fetzer was wrestling with a dysfunctional franchise. He had been the major contributor of the $5.5 million paid for the Tigers in 1956, taking a third of the shares. He wanted to focus on his main business interests, so he became chairman of the board, while letting Fred Knorr take the presidency and the spotlight. Knorr and Kenyon Brown led partnerships that each owned another third. These groups sniped at each other through the newspapers. The presidency rotated annually. The team offices were filled with holdovers from the Briggs' family ownership who proved resistant to change. Ownership was proving to be a ripe target for fans and reporters as the Tigers won fewer games each year.[26]

In 1959, veteran executive Bill DeWitt was brought in as president. His disagreements with manager Joe Gordon went public.[27] The franchise appeared lost and floundering. In October 1960, Fetzer stepped in and bought another third of the team, giving him control. He assumed the presidency and DeWitt left to become general manager of the Cincinnati Reds. "It is extremely difficult to administer the affairs of a club by group ownership. Baseball is too complicated. The team should be run by one individual who has the authority to make decisions," Fetzer said.[28] He began to show up at league meetings.

The other five franchises in the American League had issues that limited the influence of their owners or whoever represented them in league meetings.

The Indians were controlled by William Daley, a man who showed little interest in anything beyond being a superfan and seeing his name in the paper. Nate Dolin, a Cleveland associate of Veeck in his various ownership ventures and a minority owner of the Indians, solicited Daley and his mentor and partner Cyrus Eaton to join a group to buy the Indians. Eaton, a man with extensive interests in steel, railroads, and coal, said he did not need anything like that. Dolin responded: "Mr. Eaton, you can make a $100 million deal and you'll get four lines on the financial pages of the *Plain Dealer*. When Mr. Daley becomes head of the Indians, every time he sneezes, he'll be on the front pages." It was an anecdote Daley loved to tell.[29]

When he took over majority control of the Indians in 1956, Daley harked back to his boyhood as an usher at League Park and promised he would leave day-to-day operation of the team to the professionals.[30] Unlike owners before and after him, he generally kept that promise. He also promised to keep the team in Cleveland, but by 1959 he was threatening to leave town if attendance did not improve.[31]

The short, balding Daley was born in Ashtabula, Ohio, in 1893. He got his law degree in 1917 but by 1931 was president of Otis & Co., a major Cleveland investment banking firm. He was on the board of numerous corporations and closely associated with Eaton. Daley was a devout Catholic. Both of his sisters became nuns and his older brother was a monsignor in the Cleveland diocese. He and his wife were notable for their generosity to charities, especially Catholic charities.

While Daley concentrated on Otis & Co., the Indians were run by vice president Dolin and the general managers. By 1960, that meant Frank Lane, a voluble man always available to talk to reporters or make trades, which he often viewed as a means of generating publicity as much as building a team. He served as general manager of the White Sox, Cardinals, and A's as well as the Indians. He always created fan interest with his trades, and sometimes improved the teams although never far enough to win a pennant. Like Bill Veeck, he advocated revenue sharing and other ideas unpopular with the powerful owners.

While he could get work as a general manager, Lane's manner and his views on revenue sharing were not widely respected in the upper corridors of the game. He was too gauche, too talkative.[32] Behind the scenes, the Indians' ownership was also fractured by questions about a move to Minneapolis or Seattle, or a sale to Houston interests. Acrimonious board meetings came to nothing when the costs of breaking the Cleveland stadium lease were calculated.[33] At league meetings and on league committees, minority owners such as George Medinger and Dolin represented the Indians. As minority owners, and since they did not attend all meetings, the impact of their voices was muted, although Dolin was credited with a positive role in the final negotiations to get the American League into Los Angeles.[34]

In Baltimore, the partnership that had bought the moribund St. Louis Browns and moved them in 1954 was similarly fractious. Clarence Miles, the attorney who led the partnership during the move, was soon gone. James Keelty, who became president in 1955, remained in that post for four years despite consistent rumors he was on the outs.[35]

The divisions on the team's board stemmed from disagreements over the role of Paul Richards, the team's general manager and field manager, as well as the team's erratic improvement and falling profits. Richards, hired during Miles's tenure, was forever a "my way or the highway" kind of a guy. Some board members were uncomfortable with the bonus money he was spending on young players and his lack of interest in management and procedure.[36] Two board members concerned about Richards, Joseph Iglehart and Zanvyl Krieger, had been buying shares and owned nearly half the stock, controlling the board.[37]

The board, indicative of its divisions, went outside the organization, and the partnership, to bring in Lee MacPhail from the Yankees as an internal diplomat as well as an executive. In November 1958, MacPhail joined the team as general manager, supposedly just to take some of the administrative duties off Richards's hands. A year later, MacPhail became team president. But board members from different factions joined him at baseball functions and Iglehart's influence was reviewed positively.[38] When MacPhail replaced Keelty, the excuse was the pressure of Keelty's real estate business, but that had not kept him from road trips and spring training in previous years.

Bill Veeck of the Chicago White Sox was beloved by fans who appreciated his populist style, promotions, and iconoclasm. He brought fans to the ballpark, where he would circulate, talk, sit in the bleachers, and share a beer with fans. He saw a game as another form of entertainment rather than Armageddon, although he did appreciate that fans found home team victories more entertaining.

He also was beloved by sportswriters, for whom he was blunt and funny in a world of serious euphemism. At his funeral, they shunned the seats set aside for the press and sat with his other fans.[39]

Veteran sportswriter Paul Zimmerman wrote of how Veeck mesmerized reporters during interviews. "As I was talking to him I knew that whatever I was going to write was going to be inadequate because there was no way I could cover this man in one column or a magazine piece or even one book, unless it was a real fat one. What really made a memorable impression was that I lost my critical perspective totally within the first ten minutes. Scared me because

I was no longer a journalist—I mean, I was just an admirer and I never had my critical instincts so completely wiped out so quickly."[40] The reporters elected him to baseball's Hall of Fame soon after his retirement.

Born in 1914, Veeck was raised as minor baseball royalty. His father became president of the Chicago Cubs when Bill was five. He spent his summers around Wrigley Field and his teen years hating the rich kids in his prep school. After a brief stint in college, and after the death of his father, he spent most of the 1930s working in the Cubs' front office and getting a thorough grounding in administration and stadium operations. He even helped plant Wrigley's iconic ivy.[41]

In 1941, Veeck put together a package of other people's money and, by paying off its $100,000 in debt, took over the minor league Milwaukee Brewers. There, he began to build his reputation. To Brewers fans, he offered humorous promotions, roster maneuvers, and stunts designed to raise a laugh and some awareness.

He read the league rules looking for loopholes. He raised or lowered a fence to the advantage of his hitters. He sanded down the basepaths to slow down the other team's baserunners. (He said his were too slow to make any difference.) He juggled game start times to give his team the advantage. And then he rubbed it in. As league owners met to pass new or clearer rules to restrain him, Veeck showed up for the meeting in a football helmet and fencing mask.[42]

He also showed a barbed wit aimed at other teams and their executives. When Milwaukee faced a poor Kansas City team on the road, he entered their ballpark and began handing the local fans $1 bills as refunds because they had to watch such a bad team, a joke that infuriated Kansas City general manager Roy Hamey, soon to be a Yankee executive.[43]

In late 1943, Veeck joined the Marines. He was trained as an artilleryman and sent to Bougainville in the Solomon Islands where a gun's recoil damaged his right foot, which became badly infected. Ultimately, his leg was partially amputated, the first of over thirty amputations and other operations on it over the rest of his life, some of them because he did not follow doctors' orders, or common sense.

With the war over, Veeck turned his thoughts to owning a major league team and in 1946, he put together a syndicate to buy the Cleveland Indians. He assembled the team that won the 1948 World Series. There were promotions almost every game and the 1948 team set a major league attendance record that would stand for fourteen seasons.

The stuffier baseball executives grumbled he was making a travesty of the game. Veeck said he was entertaining people, giving them what they wanted. He was happy to expand on his Milwaukee reputation for thumbing his nose at the owners' club. He told Arch Ward of the *Chicago Tribune* that he "apologized for not insulting any one at his first league meeting. 'I've got to get warmed up,'" he said.[44]

Veeck sold the Indians in 1949 to provide funds for a divorce settlement but soon put together another syndicate to buy the St. Louis Browns. But even Veeck's promotional talents were not up to saving the dismal Browns. These were the years he sent a midget to the plate as a pinch hitter. He also had the fans run a game, using cue cards to make decisions about tactics such as bunting or stealing while the Browns' manager sat ostentatiously in a dugout rocking chair.

He clearly had not learned how to play well with others. In 1952, he proposed a television-revenue-sharing measure for road games. In the Veeck manner, he did not try to build a coalition of the league's other have-nots. Instead, he presented it as an attack on the Yankees. He lost the vote seven to one.

Eventually, he settled on a move to Baltimore as the solution to his financial problems. In both 1953 and 1954, he asked for permission. In both cases, he was stymied by the votes of his fellow owners, who eventually forced him to sell the team to Baltimore interests. That opposition was led by the Yankees.

The Yankees, Del Webb, Dan Topping, and George Weiss were an irresistible target to Veeck. It was very personal. He once crushed a hat Del Webb was wearing. When the White Sox won the 1959 pennant, he gave Yankee officials the worst seats in the house.[45] "Hating the Yankees isn't part of my act. It is one of those exquisite times when life and art are in perfect conjunction," Veeck summarized.[46]

His ability to irritate was not confined to the Yankees. He wrote articles in national publications such as *Look* and *Sport* telling other owners how to run the game. He gave speeches on "the future of baseball."[47] He pointedly refused to wear a tie, which only emphasized the stuffed-shirt image he was trying to pin on his colleagues. He shared dozens of ideas with sportswriters before raising them around the owners' table. He implemented others, such as putting players' names on the back of their jerseys, without consultation. He integrated his teams long before the rest of the American League.

The reaction could have, should have, been expected. Yawkey regularly called him a "God damn Socialist."[48] Supporters pointed out his methods were counterproductive. "If you were as charming to the other owners as you are to cab drivers or doormen, they'd be eating out of your hands," Hank Greenberg said to his friend.[49] Charlie Finley summed him up, "He really taught us how to rock the boat."[50] His lone-wolf methods doomed his ideas to be ignored or ridiculed, leaving him with little influence beyond what the fans and the reporters liked.

In 1959, he rejoined the American League owners club by constructing a syndicate to buy the Chicago White Sox. His manner had not changed. He was still running creative promotions and still bad-mouthing his colleagues.

Veeck claimed he skipped routine owners' meetings, but *Sporting News* coverage indicates that was only half true.[51] In 1960, Hank Greenberg represented the White Sox at all the meetings until his own bid for the expansion Los Angeles franchise took his time. Veeck did attend the meetings where the crucial decisions about whether to expand and who would win the franchises were decided.

The Kansas City Athletics franchise was in a vacuum as the American League approached its first round of expansion decisions. Arnold Johnson, who had bought the team in 1954 and moved it to Kansas City, died in March. His wife had put the team on the market and was listening to offers. Management, and representation at league meetings, was usually by general manager and vice president Parke Carroll.[52] As a former Yankee minor league executive, he was inclined to go along with Webb. As a temporary official of a secondary franchise, Carroll did not carry much weight. Major meetings could draw officials of Johnson's trust, but they were completely unfamiliar with baseball.[53]

What weight he did carry was tainted by Johnson's relationships with the Yankees, Webb, Topping, and Johnson had extensive investments, but the major one was the Automatic Canteen Co., where Johnson was the vice-chairman and Topping served on the board of directors. In 1953, he worked out a complicated deal to buy Yankee Stadium then sell it to the Knights of Columbus, who then leased it back to Johnson who in turn leased it back to the Yankees. When Johnson bought the A's a year later, with Webb and Topping's support, eyebrows were raised. They stayed raised for the next five years as Carroll presided over a series of trades that were perceived as trading bright, young talents to the Yankees for journeymen and prospects doomed to failure.[54]

The roots of Calvin Griffith's ownership of the Washington Senators went back to 1911, when Clark Griffith became the team's manager and largest shareholder. Clark Griffith was a star pitcher in the late nineteenth century, moving on to manage several American League teams. At his death in 1955, he owned 52 percent of the team.

Calvin Griffith, who would inherit half of Clark's shares and control of the team, was born Calvin Robertson in 1912. His father, a minor league player, died when Calvin was two and his mother took him and his six siblings to live with her brother Clark in Washington, D.C. Clark eventually gave Calvin and his sister Thelma his surname while helping his sister raise the Robertsons. Thelma got the other half of Clark's Senators shares.

Calvin was trained to run the team. He sold peanuts and worked in concessions at Griffith Stadium. He was a successful pitcher in high school and at George Washington University. Beginning in 1935, Calvin spent the next seven years at Senators' farm teams in Chattanooga, Tennessee, and Charlotte, North Carolina, doing all the front office jobs while also serving as manager and, at times, playing catcher.[55]

In 1940, he was summoned to Washington, D.C., to serve as Clark's assistant, moving into trades, contracts, and press relations. By the time Clark died, Calvin was thoroughly grounded in operating a major league baseball team. He was also thoroughly committed to taking care of his family. Thelma had married a Senators pitcher named Joe Haynes, who became assistant farm director, joining brother Sherry Robertson. Brother Billy took over stadium operations and Jimmy ran concessions.

In addition to the team, Calvin inherited racist practices from his adopted father. Clark was very happy to rent out Griffith Stadium to Negro League teams but wouldn't let them use the home or visitors' showers and locker rooms. He successfully courted Black fans, but never allowed an African American player on his teams, although he extensively recruited multiracial Cuban players because they were cheaper. Cheaper was a big factor with both Clark and Calvin, whose only source of income was the Senators. In later years, Calvin's team would lead the majors in salary arbitration cases.[56] The baseball joke was that swimming was invented the first time Calvin came to a bridge toll.[57]

Calvin was not highly rated by his fellow owners. He was inarticulate and prone to malapropisms. "I can't tell you exactly what I intend to do, but I can tell you one thing: It won't be anything rational," he once said.[58] Griffith also did not understand the time value of money, accepting a buyout offer with less up-front cash with the interest-free remainder paid over years.[59]

He began leading the Senators delegation to the winter meetings in 1955, complaining the team could not get a team in the highest minor leagues because other franchises had more than one, but he never pushed the issue.[60] However, his unwavering focus in league affairs was to gain permission to get his team out of Washington.

In this he would have a sympathetic ear in American League president Joe Cronin, who happened to be Calvin Griffith's brother-in-law. Born in San Francisco just after the great earthquake and fire of 1906 wiped out the finances of his Irish immigrant parents, Cronin's baseball skills brought him to the Washington Senators in 1928. He established himself as a player, and then a manager, leading them to an American League pennant in 1933. After the next season, Clark Griffith sold his contract to Tom Yawkey for $250,000, and Cronin took his bride, Calvin Griffith's sister Mildred Robertson, to Boston where he would spend the rest of his career.

He soon became a favorite of Yawkey's, remaining manager through the 1947 season and then serving as general manager until his elevation to the league presidency in 1959. Cronin "was a family man, a devoted churchgoer, a gentleman who wore suits and watched his language in front of women," wrote his biographer, Mark Armour, "Joe Cronin did not have a rebellious bone in his body."[61]

A Hall of Fame player and a successful manager, Cronin's years as general manager were, at best, undistinguished. "A warm, friendly man, Cronin shared one of Yawkey's worst faults—he didn't know how to fire anyone. The result was a dreadful clutter of deadwood at almost all levels,"[62] wrote Boston sportswriter Al Hirshberg. He presided over a Red Sox farm system that did not sign or develop much in the way of major league talent and a scouting staff that could not seem to find African Americans of talent.[63] The last in the majors to integrate, the Red Sox's first Black players appeared in Cronin's last year as general manager. At last, Yawkey perceived the problem but felt an obligation to see that his friend wound up with a respected job that would provide for him the rest of his life. When American League president Will Harridge announced he was stepping down, Yawkey had his solution.[64]

The role Cronin assumed in January 1959 was not a strenuous one. League presidents oversaw umpires, promoted the league, settled protests and disputes, and made up the schedule. Like the commissioner, league presidents were not expected to think ahead or plan. They were more glorified assistants than chiefs of staff. The role, wrote Bob Addie of the *Washington Post*, was "something like the popular conception of the Vice President of the United States—someone to send out for cigars and ice during a party."[65]

Still, Cronin could recognize that the American League was falling behind the Nationals. He saw the gains the National League had made in jumping first to the West Coast. Doing something about it was another matter and it would dominate his first years in office.[66]

CHAPTER FIVE

The First Expansion

The American League had taken a called third strike over the West Coast. The National League had swooped into Los Angeles and San Francisco, the best markets available. The resulting numbers were striking and the talk of expansion heated up.

In 1958, the Giants had their best attendance year in a decade and the Dodgers broke the record for their seventy-five-year-old franchise. The National League's attendance advantage over the American, which had been a bit over 600,000 in 1957, leaped to 2.9 million. As the Dodgers and Giants opened new stadiums in the coming years, the gap would get bigger. The Giants broke their franchise attendance record in 1960, the opening year for Candlestick Park. The Dodgers broke the National League record in 1960 and the major league record in 1962, when Dodger Stadium opened.

For the next two decades, the American League would stumble to catch up, reacting rather than acting. An American League team would not regain the major league record for a season's attendance until 1990.[1]

Since Donald Barnes in 1941, the American League owners had recognized the potential of the West, and California especially. Owners in both leagues already were conscious they were in a race.[2] In mid-1953, Yankee owner Del Webb had proposed moving the league's two weakest teams, the St. Louis Browns and Washington Senators, to California.[3] That fall, he fought the transfer of the Browns to Baltimore, but his advocacy was tainted as he was labeled an agent of Los Angeles interests, an action that drew Commissioner Ford Frick's censure.[4] Frick also tried to tamp down public discussion of relocations and expansion, feeling there was too much speculation and too little serious consideration of the issues.

Walter O'Malley's and Horace Stoneham's moves to the West Coast produced a brief lull in the chatter. The American League had established a

Realignment Committee to look into possible expansion, but its main possibilities had been snapped up by its rival. It lacked clear direction or obvious targets; committee membership changed often and did little. As Joe Cronin took office as American League president in early 1959, he noted the league had not seriously discussed expansion for the past two years and that the committee had produced "no solid, concrete proposals."[5]

Complicating the American League's position was Calvin Griffith's desire to leave Washington, D.C. He cited poor attendance, blaming much of it on the capital's African American population.[6] Initially, he expressed an interest in the West Coast cities, but with the National League's moves, his eye turned to Minneapolis–St. Paul.[7] He regularly raised his desire through the late 1950s and was regularly turned down.

To the owners' minds, eliminating a major league team from the entertainment zone of senators and congressmen opened both leagues up to retribution against their antitrust exemption and to possible challenges from future leagues. Indeed, in 1958, a bill before the U.S. Senate, which would have affirmed the antitrust exemption died quickly after Griffith asked for permission to move.

Griffith had the sympathy of some American League owners, and he also had the full support of Joe Cronin. As general manager of the Red Sox, he had been constrained to vote as his owner wished, and Tom Yawkey was firmly in the school that the league needed a team in Washington. As league president, Cronin was able to lobby for his brother-in-law.

While the American League fiddled, New York burned for the return of the National League. The city's efforts would force the pace of expansion and provide strong ownership groups for some of the new teams.

Facing re-election and worried about charges his administration had "lost" the Dodgers, New York mayor Robert Wagner in December 1957 created a committee to bring National League baseball back to the city.[8] One of the committee members was a lawyer named William Shea. After a year of failing to woo the financially weaker National League teams, such as the Cincinnati Reds, Philadelphia Phillies, and Pittsburgh Pirates, Shea got in touch with Branch Rickey, now in semi-retirement. Rickey had an idea for a third major league, which he called the Continental League. He envisioned it would build up its operations by signing high school and college players, as well as other free agents. Rickey at first pledged there would be no stealing players from existing franchises as earlier rival leagues, including the American in its earliest years, had done. One of the franchises could go to New York, Rickey suggested. Shea figured the Continental League was leverage on the existing leagues, if nothing else.

Rickey knew building up teams by signing amateurs and others without major league contracts would require serious money for scouts, player bonuses, and front office staff. Eventually, the franchises would need minor league operations and stadiums. It would also take time to build up the quality of play needed to encourage fans to buy tickets, which would lead to early losses. Thus, he needed ownership groups with deep pockets. He began to put together some impressive possibilities. The Continentals' New York franchise was led by Joan Payson, a former minority owner of the Giants and heiress to the Whitney fortune, which went back to the *Mayflower*. Her brother owned the *New York Herald Tribune* and was ambassador to Great Britain as well as a founder of the country's first venture capital firm, J. H. Whitney and Co. Her grandfathers had both been cabinet members.[9] It also included Dwight Davis Jr., son of the founder of tennis's Davis Cup, and George Herbert Walker of the merchant banking firm of Brown Brothers Harriman.[10]

The Houston franchise was fronted by Craig Cullinan Jr., heir to the Texaco fortune, but next to him were Bud Adams and R. E. "Bob" Smith, two wealthy oil men, and the political powerhouse that was Roy Hofheinz. In Minneapolis it was merchant banker Wheelock Whitney and representatives of the Dayton family (Dayton's department stores and later Target), Pillsbury, Hamms Brewing, and the *Minneapolis Star-Tribune*. In Toronto it was Jack Kent Cooke, with wide media interests. The Denver group was headed by Rickey's protégé Bob Howsam, but the key player was Howsam's father-in-law, Colorado governor and former senator Edwin Johnson. There also were Continental groups in Dallas, Atlanta, and Buffalo, but they did not have the connections or the money of the others.[11]

The Continentals began to scare the big boys. Johnson persuaded his friend and former Senate colleague Estes Kefauver to introduce a bill that would limit the number of players a major league club could have under contract. In later versions, it would have allowed Continental League teams to draft players from Major League farm clubs and ended the antitrust exemption. The political argument was that a player not good enough for a team like the Yankees could help the hometown Senators if he was not tied down. It also just happened to tie in with Rickey's plans for finding players, although it was a break from his earlier promises not to take players from the established leagues.

And then there was Billy Cannon. The Louisiana State University running back had won the Heisman Trophy in 1959. He agreed to a $10,000 contract with the Los Angeles Rams of the National Football League, but then leaped at a $110,000 offer from the Houston Oilers of the fledgling American Football League.

Baseball's owners already were concerned about growing competition for amateur talent within their ranks and had instituted various ineffective attempts to limit bonus payments.[12] Now, they could see another well-financed group of competitors on the horizon. After all, the Oilers' principal owner was Bud Adams of the Houston group in the Continental League. Even if the Continentals were not going to try to steal players already under contract, the current bonus war for amateur baseball talent would only become more costly if new, wealthy interests joined. Bud Adams, if nobody else, was clearly willing to join such a war.

The Continental League would fail, but only after it provided the leverage for which William Shea had been hoping.

While Shea and his committee were still hoping to lure an existing National League team, Philip Wrigley persuaded the National League to form an expansion committee and fund a survey on expansion cities, demographic changes, and ballparks. The next day, the American League followed along, adding its own members to the committee.[13] But the debate remained unfocused. There was talk of further franchise moves, or maybe expansion to nine or ten teams in one league or both. Or maybe there could be a third league, but when Rickey volunteered the Continental as that third league, Frick turned him down.[14]

In late June, major league owners' confidence was shaken when the Senate narrowly defeated Senator Kefauver's bill to end the antitrust exemption and allow the Continental League to draft their players. Their lobbying experts had told them the bill would be defeated easily. Soon, the owners were taking a more accommodating position with the Continental League.[15]

On August 2, 1960, the Continental League leaders and the two established leagues' expansion committees met at the Conrad Hilton Hotel in Chicago. After an all-day meeting, a decision was announced. Both leagues agreed to add two teams quickly and perhaps four more down the road. "All expansion business will be done under Continental League franchise holders," announced the National League's Walter O'Malley, who chaired the meeting. Although Rickey was committed to the Continental League, this was the outcome Shea had desired. The Continentals best ownership groups were dazzled at the idea that at least four of them would be joining the big boys.[16]

Webb, the head of the American League's expansion committee, and Cronin kept their mouths shut during the announcement and the implications of that silence were not noted immediately. The American League's key goal in this expansion process was to get into the Southern California market. In addition, the debate among American League owners about Griffith's proposed move to Minneapolis had advanced to the point where it was clear that the move would be allowed only if a replacement franchise went to Washington. But the Continental League had no ownership groups in either Los Angeles or Washington.[17] Rather than deal with the issue up front, Webb and Cronin chose to ignore the promises of the Chicago meeting. When the American League eventually revealed its expansion cities and owners, Webb tried to explain to Rickey but was met with the latter's assessment: "The dictionary definition of perfidy has now been confirmed."[18]

O'Malley soon announced the National League would add two teams in 1961 or 1962. Late that month, Cronin announced that the American League also would expand to ten teams in 1962. The *Sporting News* editorialized that "the American League's unwillingness to rush pell-mell into expansion is a mark of prudence."[19] The timetable may have been prudent, but the American League owners hadn't decided on such basics as the selection method for ownership groups. They knew their desired cities were Los Angeles and Washington, D.C., but had no idea who might own those franchises or how to choose among multiple applicants now that the already organized Continental League groups were benched. Instead, they spent a great deal of time reaffirming their belief that Southern California should be an open market.[20]

O'Malley, head of the Nationals expansion committee, was already interviewing Continental League ownership groups about their proposals and some American League owners were pressing Webb to dump prudence and speed up the process.[21]

On Sunday, October 9, as Webb's Yankees fell into a tie with the Pittsburgh Pirates after four games of the World Series, George Kirksey of the Houston Continental League group ran into Webb at the Waldorf-Astoria in New York. Webb questioned him about the Houston commitment to the American League. Kirksey said he told Webb he favored the American League, but Craig Cullinan, who was the big-money man, leaned toward the National.

Webb called together the American League expansion committee to press for a commitment on Houston on the morning of the tenth.[22]

O'Malley quickly outflanked him. Two days after Webb's call, National League president Warren Giles announced the Houston group had applied for membership in the National League, joining New York, which had applied October 1.[23] Less than a week later Giles reported that New York and Houston had been accepted as members, to begin play in 1962.[24] As with the Dodgers' and Giants' moves three years earlier, the National League had wrapped up the two most attractive markets.

Outmaneuvered and angry, Webb and his colleagues were clearly in reactive mode and riddled with divisions as they moved toward the 1960 winter meetings.[25] The Kansas City Athletics were in leadership limbo after the March death of Arnold Johnson. Rumored buyers, including Dallas investors, were thought to be interested in moving the Athletics elsewhere. The Cleveland Indians were anxious to move and saw expansion as removing potential alternatives.[26] Griffith was looking to move the Senators. The Orioles wanted to move to a stadium closer to Washington. Hank Greenberg, a Chicago White Sox executive, was pushing to own an expansion team in California. Rumors of a split between Webb and Yankee co-owner Dan Topping circulated as longtime general manager George Weiss and field manager Casey Stengel were fired.

The American League prudence praised by the *Sporting News* was a bygone concept and Webb's rhetoric and actions were more like a ten-year-old challenged on the playground. Ten days after the National League coup, Webb announced that if the National League was going to expand for 1962, the American League would do it in 1961, a year sooner than announced barely eight weeks earlier. They would also up the ante by adding two more teams by 1964—and maybe make that move by 1962. The situation was getting personal. Asked if he'd talked to O'Malley about the Los Angeles market, Webb snapped, "I don't see why. O'Malley said all the while he wanted to meet with us and then without meeting us at all he came up with a couple of clubs."[27]

The *New York Times*'s Arthur Daley aptly summed up the American League's move as "needless impetuosity," noting this timetable gave the new owners barely four months to put together a management team, players, a ticketing and sales group, and a minor league system.[28] While the National League was working with organized ownership groups in New York and Houston and a deadline eighteen months away, the American League wasn't set on what cities

it would go into, much less who potential owners might be. The league owners also allowed Griffith to move his Washington Senators to Minneapolis–St.
Paul. That confirmed the American League's options were limited to Los Angeles and Washington. Griffith's move had been approved by a six to two vote.
That majority had been won only when an amendment that another American League team had to be placed in Washington was added to the motion.[29]
Washington had an aging stadium and no obvious ownership group.

In public, Webb wasn't committing to any cities, although he hinted strongly
that Los Angeles would be one of the chosen.[30] He made no mention of the
secret commitment to Washington, D.C., and no acknowledgment that, like
the nation's capital, Los Angeles had no organized ownership group trolling
for a team. Nor did he admit these cities lacked time to get organized.

The Los Angeles question was fraught with problems, especially now that
the Nationals had staked a firm claim to get back into New York. O'Malley was
ambivalent. At times he offered to leave Los Angeles open to the American
League.[31] At others he opposed.[32] His critics, such as Webb and Bill Veeck,
believe he deeply opposed any intrusion and acquiesced only at the bitter
end.[33] There is no doubt he had problems reconciling his personal interest
in monopolizing Southern California with his league's interest in regaining a
presence in what was still the nation's largest market and leading media center.

It was clear the American League owners had not analyzed the Los Angeles
situation realistically. Dan Daniel, an orotund New York writer who generally
reflected the New York Yankees point of view in the *Sporting News*, wrote,
"The situation hardly was a credit to baseball and it did not flatter the perspi-
cacity of the magnates of the American League who were not loath to admit
the weakness of their position."[34]

Ultimately, O'Malley was a pragmatist who understood expansion was a
struggle for markets and that the price of the National League's return to New
York was the American League's entrance into Los Angeles. With New York
and Houston in the National League fold, he had done his best for his league.
Now was the time to make the best bargain he could for himself.

On November 17, the American League affirmed that one of the expansion
teams would go into Washington, D.C. As for the other city, they would try to
get baseball rules amended to allow the American League into Los Angeles.[35]
Dallas–Fort Worth, the largest market available outside Los Angeles, was left
in the dust—and angry about it.[36]

At that meeting, the American League owners also set November 28 for the draft to stock the two expansion teams. Finally approved, the Washington franchise at last could select its manager, general manager, and other officials, wait for the eight existing teams to produce their lists of players exposed to the draft, and then have fewer than eleven days to study their choices. The presumed Los Angeles ownership, which had not been chosen, would have even less. Heading the Washington franchise was retired Air Force general El-wood "Pete" Quesada, the head of the Federal Aviation Administration and a friend of President Dwight Eisenhower's from his service under Eisenhower during World War II.

The American League had barely begun to grasp its problems with the Southern California market. O'Malley had been dropping hints about his terms since the summer. He noted he had absorbed costs in opening the Los Angeles market that the American League would now benefit from. He had paid Philip Wrigley $3 million for the rights to the Los Angeles market and was paying $450,000 in indemnities to the Pacific Coast League for grabbing its biggest city. He had been forced to spend substantial sums to defeat a ballot measure that would have overturned his stadium contract with Los Angeles. He was investing $16 million to build Dodger Stadium and his biggest worry was financing that investment. He also argued that any American League ex-pansion into Los Angeles should not take place until Dodger Stadium was completed in 1962.[37]

Frick was coming into line. For months, he had been saying that both New York and Los Angeles were open territory.[38] He consistently dismissed the Yankees' arguments that they had become sole owners of the New York terri-tory, noting they had shared it with the National League for decades. In fact, both the Giants' and the Dodgers' franchises had predated the Yankees by nearly twenty years. But now, he temporized. Los Angeles was open only if the American League could make a deal to compensate O'Malley for the expenses of opening a new territory to Major League Baseball. He noted the $450,000 indemnity to the Pacific Coast League and also the $150,000 spent on mak-ing the Coliseum into something usable for baseball. He did not mention the other costs cited by O'Malley. Of the American League, Frick said, "They want to pay nothing, to do nothing. I won't stand for it."[39]

Los Angeles Times sports editor Paul Zimmerman noted stiffly that the American League had bypassed multiple opportunities to move to Los An-geles, especially with the Browns in 1954 and the Athletics in 1955. They had waited until O'Malley proved the market and now were paying the price for their timidity.[40]

Two days later former Detroit Tigers slugger Hank Greenberg, consistently reported as the leading contender for the Los Angeles franchise, said he was dropping out. American League president Joe Cronin said it was because of Frick's comments.[41] Bill Veeck, a friend and sometime partner of Greenberg, said the straw that broke Greenberg's back actually was the American League's plan for franchise fees and the cost of buying players to stock the new team, the same reasons Greenberg gave Branch Rickey.[42] But, Veeck said, Greenberg's desire for the franchise had already been undermined by Frick's insistence on compensation for O'Malley.

With the American League bid in trouble, Webb flew to Los Angeles for a meeting with O'Malley, who then journeyed to New York for a conference with Webb, Frick, and the two league presidents. Before the meeting O'Malley outlined what he said were his terms: no American League expansion for 1961, and not in the Coliseum; ultimate stadium location at least fifteen miles from Dodger Stadium; owners "genuinely interested in baseball and not just temporary publicity seekers" (a provision that would give O'Malley veto power over anybody he did not like); and some undefined payments to the Dodgers for pioneering the territory.[43]

The newspaper speculation, and interviews of prospective owners, went on for weeks. Candidates emerged and disappeared, several presumably because they had provided financial or political support for the ballot initiative challenging O'Malley's contract with the city. Eventually, Gene Autry, former country-western crooner, and owner of radio/television stations and hotels, emerged as the leading candidate. Autry and his radio station partner, Bob Reynolds, spent the morning of December 6 in O'Malley's suite, working out terms. The next day, a day Autry joked would live in infamy, the American League owners awarded his group the Los Angeles franchise by a vote of six to two, concluding three days of intense negotiations at the Park Plaza Hotel in St. Louis.[44] "The action of the American League in acceding to many of Walter O'Malley's wishes is an indication of the respect our circuit has for the man," Yankees co-owner Dan Topping said, with tongue perhaps moving toward cheek.[45]

Technically, the negotiations turned on major league rule 1(c), which defined how a new team could enter a city with an existing franchise. In reality, it was a matter of reaching compromise on various issues. Movement began when the National League's John Galbreath, owner of the Pittsburgh Pirates, asked everybody to take a step back and look at the broader interests of both leagues—specifically the desire of the American League to get into Los Angeles and the National League to return to New York. His intervention, quickly supported by several other centrist owners, cooled off the rhetoric and allowed Webb, O'Malley, and the others to find solutions for the individual concerns. The American League's opposition centered on Yawkey, Veeck, and Griffith.[46] For the American League, all the negotiations had to be carried out with the knowledge that Frick would vote with the National League if an agreement could not be reached.[47]

O'Malley had conceded on allowing the Angels to begin play in 1961 and had vetoed some candidates before Autry was chosen, but the American League accepted his other conditions.[48] The terms, brokered by Galbreath, American League owners John Fetzer of the Detroit Tigers and Joseph Iglehart of the Baltimore Orioles, and Frick, would go a long way toward easing O'Malley's concerns about paying for Dodger Stadium. The Angels would play the 1961 season in Wrigley Field, rather than the Coliseum. Then they would become O'Malley's tenant at Dodger Stadium for at least four years, with an option for three more. The terms strongly favored the Dodgers. The rent would be 7.5 percent of revenue, with a minimum of $200,000. Concession revenue for Angels' home games and maintenance costs would be split. Parking revenue would be O'Malley's. The Angels would also pay $350,000 to cover O'Malley's investment in Pacific Coast League indemnities and legal costs in Los Angeles.[49] They agreed that if they moved to a new ballpark after their Dodger Stadium years, it would have to be at least fifteen miles from Dodger Stadium.

The Americans took an ounce of revenge as the meetings ended. The new National League franchises in New York and Houston wanted to begin building their organizations by fielding minor league teams in 1961, allowing some development before taking to major league diamonds the following year. The minor leagues and the National League had already voted to approve the idea. In what the Sporting News's Cliff Kachline called "a retaliatory blow," the Americans found a wrinkle in the rules that allowed them to table the motion.[50]

The expansion process was a prime example of how major league owners could use the exemption from antitrust law to legally act like a cartel. A basic principle of any cartel is to control both the number of members and their identity. The two leagues approached expansion with differing goals. In a mirror image of each other, the American League wanted into the greater Los Angeles market and the National League wanted back into New York. That set up the clear basis for a trade.

But, within the cartel, the two leagues also had competitive goals and could operate as independent entities. Each wanted the best markets they could get and the strongest ownership groups. In that competition, the National League had clearly outpaced the Americans. Their cumulative market additions had more people and more potential for growth. Their ownership groups had deeper pockets.

That did not stop the American League from crowing. They considered their 1961 start date a coup and a clear advantage that their teams would have major league stadiums—Washington in Griffith Stadium and Los Angeles in that city's Wrigley Field.[51] Even a year later, the National League expansion teams would be playing in retreads such as New York's Polo Grounds and a temporary ballpark in Houston while the Colt .45s waited for the Astrodome, American League partisans argued. The spin conveniently overlooked the Los Angeles Wrigley's minor league provenance.

As multiple sports writers noted in a *Sporting News* survey, the rest of the world doubted.[52] "The A.L. is going to California without a ball park to call its own. This alone was considered three strikes for any C(ontinental) L(eague) hopeful," wrote Murray Robinson of the *New York Journal-American*. The *St. Louis Post-Dispatch*'s Bob Broeg noted the American League's lost opportunity. "Dallas–Fort Worth would have taken to its proud Texas bosom a thin franchise with much more affection than a sickly stepchild will be accepted in either Los Angeles or New York, where they've got big league ball and parimutuel diversion, too."

Looming over all was the actual size of the league's "new" markets. New York and Houston added 17.4 million to the National League population base, according to the 1960 census. Los Angeles and Minneapolis–St. Paul gave the American League an additional 9.4 million. The difference was almost completely due to New York's greater population than Los Angeles's. The Twin Cities and Houston were virtually identical in size, but Houston would prove to have much greater potential for growth. By 1980, it would be nearly 50 percent larger.

As Broeg noted, the American League owners' fears of the consequences of letting Calvin Griffith leave Washington had prevented them from taking the

Dallas–Fort Worth market, clearly the most attractive area on the table. While Washington was marginally larger than the Dallas area, it was a different city in 1960 than it is today. There were virtually no corporate headquarters. Only lobbyists, looking to impress members of Congress, were likely to spring for season tickets. The city's population was dominated by lesser-paid civil servants and poorer people in service jobs. Dallas, with the oil business and the banks and other institutions supporting it, was booming, with a 49 percent population increase in the previous decade.

The owners' go-along-to-get-along practices also ensured that fans in Congress would continue to see a bad team. They could have followed the suggestion that the promising young team Griffith had begun to assemble could remain in Washington. Griffith could have been given an expansion franchise in Minnesota while the players formed a new franchise in the nation's capital. Instead, they again chose to let one of their eight-man club do what he wanted.[53]

Los Angeles was viewed as being an addition to parallel the National League's return to New York, despite its much smaller size. But the Los Angeles market was simply not as open to a new team as the New York area was. Again, the American League had stumbled in the markets race.

New York had thousands of recently disenfranchised National League fans, many of them with anti-Yankee attitudes. The Yankees, in fact, had been stunned that their 1958 attendance had dropped despite the Dodgers' and Giants' departures. Aside from recent immigrants from American League cities and the nationwide following of the Yankees, Los Angeles had no American League connections.

The Yankees were still winners, but they were almost boringly consistent, and their fans could be blasé about it. Their 1958 attendance had dropped despite another pennant, the fourth in a row, the ninth in a decade. Los Angeles was agog over the Dodgers, the team that had given the city "major league" cachet and won the 1959 World Series. As with any expansion team, the Angels were destined to be losers for several years. The Mets could turn lovable losers into a marketing tool, but the Angels just looked pale.

The Angels were doomed to spend their first five years in either a "minor league" park—Wrigley Field—or in a sparkling new stadium named for their rivals. In fact, the Angels never uttered the words "Dodger Stadium," referring to the ballpark only as Chavez Ravine, the area where the stadium had been built. From the beginning, Gene Autry knew he would have to find a new host city so that his team could develop its own identity. That is why he had no objection to being forced to locate his future park at least fifteen miles from Dodger Stadium. He was talking to suburban cities even while the Angels were playing in Wrigley Field. He moved to Anaheim as soon as his agreement with O'Malley allowed.

But five years was a long time to wait to begin building your own identity. In New York, the Mets would play their first two seasons in the Polo Grounds, the old home of the Giants. It was falling apart, but it was clearly "major league" and redolent of history. They avoided the alternative that faced the Angels, playing their games in a ballpark with a minor league history or one named for their cross-town rivals. Autry understood the dangers of playing second fiddle, but felt he had to stick it out.

The long-term effect was obvious. The Mets made their first playoffs and won their first World Series, in their eighth year. The Angels made their first postseason appearance in their nineteenth year and won their first World Series twenty-three years after that. The amazingly incompetent Mets outdrew the Yankees in their third season and did so for the next twelve years, despite the Yankees' winning the American League pennant. Since then, the better-performing team has generally led the New York attendance race. In sixty-one years, the Angels have never outdrawn the Dodgers.

The American League's stumbles in finding their expansion franchises continued into the draft. Their National League counterparts would have a year of scouting and planning before drafting any players. While both leagues used the draft to extract the most money possible for the least talent lost, the American League engineered a quickie holdup while the National League took its time lifting the expansion owners' wallets.

And then the American League bungled the heist. Each American League expansion team was required to pay $2.1 million for the players it would draft. This was roughly 40 to 50 percent of the price for recent American League franchise sales, although existing franchises included more and better players, minor league systems, established brand names, equipment, and real estate. Executives surveyed by the *Sporting News* estimated it would take $5 million total to get a new team off the ground, very much in line with recent sales prices.[54]

The original November 28 date for the American League expansion draft was ten days past before Autry's group was chosen. The Washington franchise had been allowed to participate in the majors' annual minor league draft that day and gained more time when the Angels' situation caused the expansion draft to be reset to December 14. The Angels did not benefit. They had eight days, including two weekends, to put together a staff and prepare for the draft.

Autry, at least, had some advantages. His connections within the Los Angeles sports scene quickly brought him recent Milwaukee Braves manager Fred Haney as his general manager and recent San Francisco Giants manager Bill Rigney as the field manager. Casey Stengel, miffed at his recent firing by the Yankees, was only too happy to provide rundowns on Yankee prospects and O'Malley turned over the Dodgers' scouting reports on American League minor leaguers.

A flip side of the Americans haste to expand was that the existing teams did not have much time to think through the list of those they would protect. The Angels, with the aid of knowledgeable veterans such as Stengel, Rigney, Haney, and the Dodgers, were able to pluck some bright young talents, which gave them a head start on the new Senators.

The Senators' and Angels' planning was complicated by the arcane rules the American League set up for the draft. Each team had to draft exactly ten pitchers first, then two catchers, then six infielders, followed by four outfielders and then six more without regard to position.[55] No existing team could lose more than seven players, and no expansion team could take more than four players from any one existing team. Rigney would later claim the American League had not informed the teams of the latter complication, although the information appeared in the November 30 edition of the *Sporting News*.[56]

On the chilly morning of December 14, Haney, Rigney, Senators manager Mickey Vernon, general manager Ed Doherty, and farm director Hal Keller climbed to Joe Cronin's sixth-floor office in Boston's IBM Building. The draft meeting was limited to six people to try to keep secret which fifteen players from each existing team's roster had been exposed to the draft.

The day began smoothly enough, with the Angels' choice of Eli Grba kicking off the pitchers' portion of the draft. But when it came time for the infielders, things got messy. The Angels drafted Coot Veal from Detroit when they had already picked their limit of four from the Tigers. Cronin said nothing and both expansion teams took outfielders from teams whose limits had already been reached. In the miscellaneous players phase, Cronin finally stepped in to enforce the rules. He ordered players dropped or moved. Still, by the time they thought they were done, the Angels had taken more than four from two teams, and the Senators were over the limit from another. Two existing teams had lost more than the seven-player limit.

To smooth over the mess, Cronin ordered four trades. The last of these sent White Sox outfielder Joe Hicks (389 future major league plate appearances with a .221 batting average) from the Angels to the Senators in exchange for Dean Chance (who twice won twenty games and the Angels' first Cy Young award).[57] When announced to the reporters, there was no mention of the mid-draft rearrangements by Cronin, nor the four concluding trades. All was papered over. The Angels did not really know who Chance was.

As Bill Veeck summarized nearly a decade later, the National League had "gobbled up such gold mines as Milwaukee, Los Angeles, San Francisco, New York, and Houston, while the American League was moving into Baltimore, Kansas City, Minneapolis, and an inferior situation in Los Angeles."[58]

CHAPTER SIX

New Blood, Bad Blood—Ten Men at a Table

T
he American League's two new franchises brought two differing
ownership groups and the established franchises continued to experience turnover as the league moved through the early 1960s. Out West,
the Los Angeles Angels featured a former singing cowboy who would stay
with the game for three decades. Back East, it was a former general front-
ing buttoned-down merchant bankers who would be gone before the decade
was out.

Orvon Gene Autry was born in Texas in 1907 but grew up on a small Oklahoma ranch.[1] He worked for his uncle baling hay to earn the $8 for his first
guitar, plucked from the Sears, Roebuck catalog. As a teenager, he sang and
played at local events but hoped for a more reliable career. He learned Morse
code and won a job as a part-time station agent for the Frisco Railroad.[2] While
working overnight shifts, he took a correspondence course in bookkeeping
and played his guitar to pass the hours.

One night, the nationally known humorist Will Rogers dropped by to send
in his newspaper column. He saw the guitar and asked Autry to play, told him
he had talent, and urged him to get on the radio. Autry used his railroad pass
to go to New York but soon was back in Oklahoma, playing at a small station
and grabbing any kind of gig he could find. He had made one solid connection in New York, with American Record Corp., a little-known company with
a big portfolio: It pressed records to be sold under brand names such as Sears
Roebuck & Co. Autry began recording for American and his records began to
sell throughout Sears' rural territories.

In 1930, Sears called him to Chicago where they put him on a national program based out of their company-owned radio stations, WLS.[3] Autry, reveal-
ing the business sense that would mark him all his life, won a percentage of

all the merchandise—guitars, boots, and other paraphernalia—sold by Sears under the Gene Autry name.

In 1934, his American Records connections brought him to Hollywood, where Republic, a smaller studio that cranked out B westerns, had a need for a singing cowboy. Autry fit their bill and he soon gained a national following as the archetypal cowboy hero—he always played straight, never shot first, invariably won, and only kissed the girl once in more than ninety movies.

And he made a lot of money, much of it with his shrewdness. Against the usual studio practice, Autry insisted on retaining the rights for all merchandise sold under his name, including the Sears deal. He kept several months each year free for touring, and then he organized the tours, booking the venues and the other acts. He kept all the normal manager's and promoter's profits for himself. By 1940, he was one of the top box office stars in Hollywood, and number one among western stars.

In 1942, he enlisted in the Air Force. His income from record sales remained, but other ventures faded, and he began to think he might have to make a living beyond performing. Late in the war, he bought a radio station, and later a television station, in Phoenix. But his singing and acting years were not over. In 1949, his wife convinced him to record a Christmas novelty song Autry did not like. "Rudolph the Red-Nosed Reindeer" would sell millions of copies, and still bounces from December Muzak systems around the country. He would produce and star in television shows through the 1950s introducing the straight-shooting, non-kissing persona to a new generation.

Despite that, Autry was adjusting his career. In 1952, he partnered with Robert Reynolds to buy Los Angeles radio station KMPC. Eventually, Golden West Broadcasting would own six radio stations and three television properties. He would go briefly into the hotel business (with San Francisco's Mark Hopkins among others) and owned cattle ranches, oil wells, and music and television production facilities.

In 1960, KMPC lost the rights to broadcast Los Angeles Dodger games. Autry went to the American League's expansion meetings to try to tie up the new team's broadcast rights. Instead, he and Reynolds wound up with the franchise.

Autry was a man who largely bought into the image he projected in his movies. He wore boots and western-cut suits, projected a calm, modest demeanor, and restructured business deals when it became clear they were not working out too well for the other guy.[4] But, he also had another side, admitting fairly late in life to a drinking problem. He also fathered no children, presumably because of a bout with gonorrhea as a young man.[5] He was fidgety when sitting.

He had played shortstop in his youth on sandlots and company teams, claiming he could field and hit, but had no speed. His interest in professional baseball first surfaced in 1951 when he teamed up with Rogers Hornsby in an unsuccessful attempt to buy the San Francisco Seals of the Pacific Coast League.[6] At KMPC, he and Reynolds built their programming around sports, which gave them the friendships that quickly brought Fred Haney, Casey Stengel, and Bill Rigney to the Angels for the expansion draft.

With the Angels, he kept his hands off his general managers and managers. With the players, however, he was a constant source of encouragement. He would often call the clubhouse after a game to offer congratulations on a win or console them on a loss. "I'm a lousy owner. I hate like hell to let anybody go. When a guy's a personal friend, you can't just treat him like *anybody*," he said.[7] In later years, "Win one for the Cowboy" would become a mantra throughout the organization.

Autry, through the 1960s, was a bit of a cypher in league affairs. He missed meetings and made sure his general manager was with him when he did go.[8] As the battles with the Players Association heated up, he became much more involved and very militant. He hated Marvin Miller, cited his own (negative) experiences with unions in Hollywood, and urged the other owners to resist player demands.[9] But on other matters, he was generally quiet.

On owners' committees and nonunion matters, the Angels were more likely to be represented by Reynolds, a minority owner born in 1914. He shared Autry's Oklahoma roots and his "quiet-spoken, easy-going" manner as well as the look of a "Western movie hero." Reynolds had won a football scholarship to Stanford.[10] A tackle, he played in three straight Rose Bowls, going the full sixty minutes in each contest, the only man ever to have done so. After graduating, he went into the oil business in Texas despite being hounded by G. A. Richards, the owner of the Detroit Lions, to play professional football. Eventually, Reynolds agreed to play if he was also given a job at one of Richards' radio stations. After two years, he quit football and became a full-time salesman at KMPC. By 1942, he was the station's general manager. Upon Richards death, he persuaded Autry to join him in buying KMPC. The men went on to became business partners in many ventures. Reynolds was named the Angels' president while Autry became chairman of the board.

The expansion Washington Senators ownership was even more hands off than the Angels, with the team's general managers generally representing the club at the meetings.

Ownership had been formed with ten equal partners and Elwood "Pete" Quesada as president on a two-year contract. Quesada was a retired Air Force general whose Ninth Tactical Air Force had aided the Allies drive across northern France during World War II, earning him the friendship of his commanding general, Dwight Eisenhower.[11] His baseball years proved considerably less elevated as he irritated his partners as well as the club's manager and general manager.[12]

When Quesada's contract ran out in early 1963, and it appeared a group led by Nate Dolin and Bill Veeck would buy a dominant share bloc, three of the remaining original ten stepped forward to keep the team under local ownership. James Marion Johnston Jr. and James Lemon (not the Senators player), two merchant bankers, each took 30 percent, and George Bunker, an aerospace executive, pushed his share up to 20 percent.[13] Two smaller partners remained with 10 percent shares. In 1965, Johnston and Lemon bought out everyone else.[14]

Johnston and Lemon had been equal partners in a merchant banking firm, but it was Johnston who took the public role with the Senators. Born in 1895 in Chapel Hill, North Carolina, Johnston attended the University of North Carolina and then the University of Illinois, although his loyalties remained in Chapel Hill. To this day, the James M. Johnston foundation provides scholarship help to students there. He enlisted in the fledgling Air Force in 1917 and flew fighters in France before returning to work in the brokerage business in New York. In 1920, he moved to Washington, D.C., where his father had substantial financial interests.[15] In 1925, Lemon joined him in the firm that became Johnston, Lemon & Co.

In his first public venture as owner, Johnston showed a choked-up grip on the bat and talked modestly in his soft North Carolina accent of his days on the sandlots of Durham. He won some amateur golf tournaments around Washington but choking up on the bat in public was completely out of character. Johnston, a top bridge player, was a conservative fellow and a conservative dresser, often wearing the same tie for a week.[16] He and Lemon preferred to keep a low profile. In Johnston's obituary, the *Washington Post* noted, "reporters found them friendly, gracious and hospitable, but generally unproductive of news stories."[17]

Johnston took the title chairman of the board, with Lemon becoming vice president. (After Quesada's departure, Johnston had sworn the team would never have a president.) Whatever the title, he believed his role was to support the baseball people he hired and stay out of running the team, or the league, although there was a direct phone line from the team's offices at DC Stadium to Johnston's desk.

While news from the American League owners' meeting of 1960 focused on expansion and the new owners it brought, the decision with the greatest impact occurred quietly. Kansas City Athletics owner Arnold Johnson had died that spring and the trustees of his estate spent the year sorting through the bids. The other owners asked Joseph Iglehart of the Orioles to check out Charles O. Finley, the leading bidder. His conclusion: "Under no conditions should this person be allowed into our league."[18] But Finley's bid was the highest and the trustees felt their fiduciary duty compelled them to accept. The owners went along.

Finley did not sound like a problem at first. He had smarts, management skills, and a clear understanding of how markets worked. Like Veeck, he was simply incapable of playing well with others. Unlike Veeck, he had no modesty and limited social skills. The *Wall Street Journal* would come to characterize him as "pro sports' most persistent owner-meddler."[19]

Finley had been trying to buy a baseball team since he had made enough money to afford one. He had lost out to Arnold Johnson for the A's in 1954, to John Fetzer for the Tigers in 1956, to Bill Veeck for the White Sox in 1958, and to Gene Autry for the Angels in early December. "I was so hungry for a ball club I could taste it," he said.[20] He won approval just a dozen days after Autry.

Charles Oscar Finley had been born in Birmingham, Alabama, in 1918, the middle child of a steelworker.[21] The family moved to the steel mills of Gary, Indiana, when he was fifteen. Finley did yard work and sold magazines from an early age. After high school, he worked in the steel mills while starting college. When World War II broke out, he tried for the Marine Corps but was rejected because of an ulcer. He went to work at a nearby munitions plant and quickly rose to a supervisory role.

Guided by his father-in-law, he started to sell insurance on the side. Overwork brought on a diagnosis of tuberculosis, which put him in a sanatorium for two years. There, Finley had his epiphany. Garrulous, he chatted with his doctors about how his lack of income hurt his family. They told him they faced the same problem when they were sick or injured and Finley realized there was a market for disability insurance for doctors. After he got out of the sanatorium in 1948, he studied actuarial tables and came up with a plan better than anything else on the market. He sold his first policy to the Lake County Medical Society in the Gary area.

Finley hit it big when he convinced a national insurance firm to offer group medical disability insurance for doctors. Soon, he branched off as Charles O. Finley and Co. and had his millions for a baseball team by his midthirties.

In Finley's mind, this was all attributable to "S + S = S," or "Sweat plus Sacrifice equals Success," a mantra Finley endlessly pressed on his employees whether in insurance or baseball. There was little doubt Finley worked hard and that "Sacrifice" meant keeping expenses to the minimum. In later years, when he called San Francisco Giants owner Bob Lurie, he would always call collect.[22]

Finley's business dealings could skate the edge, marked by products that did not match promises, bills unpaid or paid late, promises broken, and lawsuits galore. He told the story of one of his boyhood business ventures, selling eggs that had been cracked or shown up as being fertilized. To Finley, the only drawback of the product was that it prevented repeat business.[23]

Finley tried to assume Veeck's mantle. "Veeck and I are supposed to be kooks. We couldn't care less," he said.[24] Veeck actually wanted nothing to do with Finley. "Finley does things without class," summed up the original Baseball Barnum.[25]

He soon irritated his American League colleagues. "I've never seen so many damned idiots as the owners in sport. Baseball's headed for extinction if we don't do something," he said early in his reign.[26] Finley was soon spouting public cynicism about his business partners. "Do not go into any league meeting looking alert and awake; slump down like you've been out all night and keep your eyes half closed, and when it is your turn to vote, ask to pass. Then you wait and see how the others vote, and you vote the same way. Suggest no innovations. Make no efforts at change. That way you will be very popular with your fellow owners," he said.[27]

Charlie Finley was constitutionally incapable of following this advice. His ideas ranged from interleague play, colorful uniforms, and other possibilities to three-ball walks and a designated-runner rule, which, at least so far, have not come close to acceptance. He was dismissive and disruptive in meetings and beyond obnoxious in private conversations. Bowie Kuhn, then just a National

League attorney, described an overheard conversation between Finley and American League president Joe Cronin.[28] "It was a long, obscene call. Finley was abusive, disrespectful and coarse, painstakingly and repetitively so." He would be an unwelcome voice around the American League table for twenty years.

Finley, meanwhile, would take shrewd advantage of an old concept that had finally won approval from the owners—a draft for high school and college players. The draft idea had worked well for professional football and basketball, but baseball's owners had resisted. Branch Rickey, working for the talent-poor Pittsburgh Pirates in the early 1950s, was one of the first to push the concept.[29]

The resistance was based on two ideas. Some, like Finley and the American League's expansion teams in Washington and Los Angeles, were willing to spend money to build up weak teams. Finley was scooping up players such as Catfish Hunter, Blue Moon Odom, and Joe Rudi with bonuses regularly in the $100,000 range. The breaking point came in June 1964 when the Angels, competing with Finley, agreed to pay Rick Reichardt $205,000.

Baseball executives knew that clubs able to pay the growing amounts, such as the Yankees and Dodgers, had an advantage in acquiring talent.[30] The haves, led by Walter O'Malley of the Dodgers, argued that a draft was "socialism" and incompatible with baseball. "In the last five years, five different clubs have won pennants in our league. If that isn't competition, I don't know what is," he said, noting the draft in the other major sports had done nothing to stop dynasties such as basketball's Boston Celtics or football's Green Bay Packers.[31]

Other owners were worried a draft would expose their precious antitrust exemption to congressional critics.[32] Baseball's lobbyist, Paul Porter, was a constant presence in the meetings to discuss early versions of the draft proposal.[33] Eventually, legal advice eased these worries.[34] In fact, it was their antitrust exemption that allowed the owners to act in classic cartel mode. They were trying to control their costs by limiting the options of the commodity they were trying to buy.

At last, at the winter meetings of 1964, the issue came to a vote. Opposition at earlier meetings of general managers and owners had come from the Athletics, Senators, Angels, and Yankees in the American league, joined by Los Angeles and two other National League teams. Seeing, however, that they were going to lose thirteen to seven, the opponents backed down and made the vote unanimous.[35]

When the inaugural draft was held the following June, Finley used the first overall pick on Arizona State outfielder Rick Monday, a sixth-round choice on Sal Bando and a twentieth-round pick on Gene Tenace. The next year, with the second pick, he chose Reggie Jackson. In 1967, it was Vida Blue. These players would be core pieces as Finley rebuilt the A's.

In Cleveland, poor attendance and a decrepit stadium continued to weaken the franchise. William Daley checked out Seattle in 1964 and a move was never far from his mind. He had cut the team's budget to the bone, gutting what had been a productive farm system. Attendance followed the budget down and profits were chancy at best.

His initial pledge to keep the team there had been abrogated with the poor attendance. Names of cities such as Dallas, Houston, Toronto, and Minneapolis had been thrown around.[36] Two of those were still available in the mid-1960s and reports added Seattle and Oakland, cities the American League desired to cut into the Nationals' vast advantage in West Coast attendance.[37]

The strong man in Cleveland was now Gabe Paul, the largest shareholder (20 percent) and the team's general manager. He was frustrated with the budget limits imposed by Daley and the board of directors, and he was willing to put more of his own money into the team.

Paul had been born in Rochester, New York, in 1910. By the age of ten, he was cutting school to work at the ballpark—bat boy, ground crew, vendor. As a teenager, he wangled a job covering high school sports for the local paper and turned that into a job as the Rochester correspondent for the *Sporting News*. In 1927, the Cardinals sent Warren Giles to run their newly acquired Rochester farm team and Giles wanted to meet all the newspaper reporters covering the team. He was stunned by Paul's age but soon had him working for the team. When Giles became general manager of the Cincinnati Reds in 1936, he took Paul with him. He put Paul in charge of press relations and Paul's ability to work with reporters, and his reputation as a consumer of hot dogs, would stand him in good stead over the years.[38]

When Giles moved up to National League president in 1951, Paul succeeded him as the Reds' general manager, laying the foundation for the National League's pennant-winning team of 1961 and gaining a reputation as a premium whiner about league schedules.[39] He also showed his gift for promotion by organizing the ballot-box stuffing campaign that put seven Reds into the 1956 All-Star game starting lineup.[40] It also led to the vote begin taken away from the fans.

But then, Paul made what he considered the worst mistake of his life: he joined the expansion Houston club in the National League. He was supposed to run the team but found owner-president Roy Hofheinz very much wanted to do things his way. Paul left before the team played a game and quickly joined the Indians.

"He was very intelligent, a great promoter, and a guy who knew how to get next to people with money," said Cleveland sportscaster Pete Franklin. "Gabe was the ultimate baseball survivor." Echoed Cleveland attorney David LeFevre, who once tried to buy the Indians, "I want to stand next to Gabe Paul when they drop the atomic bomb."[41]

Paul could not find the partners to join him in buying out Daley and some of the others. In 1966, Daley realized Paul was not going to find the investors and he sold to Vernon Stouffer, head of Stouffer Foods Co., who had been a minority shareholder. Stouffer bought out all the other shareholders except Paul and pledged to fill the board with fellow Clevelanders and keep the team there. As with Daley a decade earlier, the newspapers rejoiced at the pledge.[42] Paul got a ten-year contract and generally represented the team at owners' meetings.

Stouffer Foods had grown out of a stand his parents had opened in downtown Cleveland in 1922. It served buttermilk from the family's dairy farm and Lena Stouffer's much-admired Dutch apple pie. Born in 1901, Vernon Stouffer graduated from the University of Pennsylvania's Wharton School in 1923. The next year he persuaded his parents to invest in Stouffer Lunch, a modest restaurant that served sandwiches for a quarter.

Even in the middle of the Depression, Stouffer's grew. By 1937, there were restaurants in Detroit, Pittsburgh, and New York. The company started a "Top of" chain, with restaurants offering rooftop locations with spectacular views of their cities. It was "the kind of place you could go with your grandmother," said Richard Klein, a professor of urban studies at Cleveland State University. They featured "satisfying but unremarkable American stalwarts with a touch of European flair."[43] They were often Lena Stouffer's recipes and Vernon Stouffer swore by them. In later years, when visiting a company facility, he would go to the kitchen to sample before heading for the managers' offices. He kept a second, test kitchen in his apartment and enjoyed experimenting with new recipes.

What made Stouffer something more than a regional restaurant chain was its pioneering work with frozen foods for the consumer. It started in 1946, when customers began asking the manager at a suburban Stouffer's Lunch to freeze their dinners so they could take them home for reheating. Stouffer ran the idea past his dubious mother, who insisted the frozen dish had to taste the same as the fresh. He was elated when "Mother didn't know the difference."[44] It would establish such brands as Stouffer's Lasagna and French Bread Pizza as well as Lean Cuisine.[45]

By 1966, Stouffer Food Co.'s sales stood at $79 million. It operated forty-six restaurants and twenty hotels in twenty different markets and employed 8,000 people. It provided frozen food to institutions and airlines as well as individual consumers. It also managed food facilities for clients.[46] And it was all run out of Cleveland.

Another major change was happening around the owners' table without a franchise changing hands. Tom Yawkey, never a social man, came to the owners' meetings less and less frequently.[47] In 1960, he liquidated the Boston American League Baseball Co. and made it a privately owned entity in the Yawkey business empire.[48] It was part of a general withdrawal. Now, he rarely appeared in Boston before May and watched games by himself in the owner's box. He lashed out at the press after a critical story in the *Saturday Evening Post*.[49] He was drinking heavily and had begun to "act like a rich guy and pretend to work," according to one associate. A Red Sox history characterized his attitude as "abject neglect."[50] His years on the executive council had ended in 1958 and, even when he did attend, his voice carried little weight. He would not attend an owners' meeting again until 1966.

The Old Guard and its power brokers would continue to change.

CHAPTER SEVEN

Changing the Guard

As the Yankees faded, Detroit's John Fetzer emerged as the most powerful voice at the American League table. He was the owner who took the Yankees' place as the American League owner on the executive council. He was the owner who others respected and clustered around.

The respect grew directly out of his personal history, and his personality. Born in 1901, Fetzer grew up in West Lafayette, Indiana. His father died when he was two and the most influential man in his life was Fred Ribble, the husband of Fetzer's older sister. Ribble worked as a telegrapher for the Wabash Railroad. Ribble's two passions were Detroit Tigers baseball and extending his knowledge of electrical communication to the new field of radio. Fetzer would latch firmly to these same interests.

Fetzer's modest baseball skills remained on the sandlots of Indiana, but he showed talent for engineering. At nine, Ribble had given him his first telegraph receiver and taught him Morse code. While at Purdue University, Fetzer built his own ham radio set and began regular exchanges with Westinghouse radio engineer Frank Conrad in Pittsburgh. Soon, they discovered, others along their transmission route had begun building their own crystal sets so they could listen in. One day, Conrad put a record player near his microphone and broadcast a song. Conrad's work would help Pittsburgh's KDKA become a pioneering radio station in the country.

While he wandered in and out of colleges in his twenties, Fetzer found his initial niche building radio stations. In 1923, while attending Emmanuel College in Berrien, Michigan, he built a radio station for the college as payment for his tuition.[1]

The station struggled financially and Fetzer eventually bought it for $2,500. He and his wife worked all the jobs, from announcing to selling ads and booking entertainment, but it continued to struggle. In 1930, he moved it to the much larger city of Kalamazoo and station WKZO thrived. He slowly began to add other stations. He was in one of the few businesses that grew consistently through the Depression.

He built up his standing in the industry by inventing a directional antenna that allowed stations operating on the same wavelength to avoid interference. By World War II, he was well known in the radio industry and running its self-censoring operation. After the war he moved into television.[2]

Fred Ribble was not the only long-lasting influence on Fetzer. His mother was deeply spiritual, and his father's early death would give Fetzer a lifelong interest in genealogy and his family background. He would write one book on his family's history and a second that combined reminiscences, more genealogy, and spiritualism. Chapter titles include "Creation and Re-Creation," "Creative Presence," "The Fruits of Understand," and "A New Order."[3]

Fetzer dressed and acted like a buttoned-down Republican businessman. "In striped pants, he'd look like a disciplined professional in the State Department," wrote the *Detroit News*'s Watson Spoelstra.[4] But, as his books revealed, he had a deeply metaphysical streak. He could impress Japanese officials with his grasp of Zen Buddhism.[5] Childless, he would leave much of his fortune to the Fetzer Institute in Kalamazoo, whose mission is "helping to build the spiritual foundation for a modern world."[6]

As he took a more active role, Fetzer's presence and ideas were beginning to make an impression on other owners. After the tense 1960 meeting that resolved issues with the National League over expansion, Commissioner Ford Frick had high praise for Fetzer, who "appealed to the more combative representatives" of the American League to seek compromise and put his "logical persuasiveness and business sense to work."[7] Fetzer's influence would grow.

His background in television and radio made him the obvious point man as baseball struggled to figure out its national TV policy.

In the mid-1960s, as the National Football League prospered with its new television contract, the owners were feeling pressure to clean up the mess that was baseball's television presence. After congressional action to allow an exception to antitrust rules for sports league television contracts, the National Football League had shown the way by negotiating a $28 million two-year contract with CBS that tripled each team's payout.

In contrast, baseball's television policy was a hodgepodge of holdovers from radio—and protectionism. Each team had its own agenda for local broadcasts. Nationally, there had been a "Game of the Week" rotating through the three major networks since 1953, but it could be blacked out in the home team market, or the visiting team market, or minor league markets. The blackouts, and the use of Dizzy Dean as an announcer, had left these telecasts with a relatively small and largely rural audience, unattractive to big advertisers.

With his experience, Fetzer was made head of the owners' television committee and came up with a plan that was ahead of its time. He broached the idea in March 1964 and by August, he was in New York pitching the networks with the idea for a *Monday Night Baseball Spectacular*, a national telecast each Monday evening. Since most major and minor league teams used Monday as a travel day, there would be fewer scheduling conflicts and potential blackouts. For the networks, Mondays presented few sports programming opportunities.

The networks did not bite. CBS said its Monday evening lineup was too strong to break up. Critics suggested baseball had not given the networks enough time to study the proposal and take the temperature of possible sponsors. "Fetzer picked the right night for baseball but the wrong night for television," said one network TV executive.[8] Just six years later, ABC would launch *Monday Night Football* to enormous success, but NFL commissioner Pete Rozelle had built up that idea for several years by scheduling Monday night games and selling them in small packages to prove the concept and the audience.[9]

While the Monday night idea wound up back in Fetzer's desk drawer, it did lead to the first truly national broadcast contract. ABC agreed to a two-year contract starting in 1965 for a Saturday afternoon telecast and the owners agreed to the revolutionary idea of dividing the $12 million equally among the eighteen participants. It was an idea similar to one Veeck had pushed in the early 1950s, but the diplomatic Fetzer didn't insult his fellow owners and make it an attack on the Yankees. The idea was adopted.

For ABC, the contract was not a success for it truly was not a national contract. The Yankees had an exclusive contract with CBS to televise games nationally and the Phillies had a regional television contract that made their games unavailable. ABC dropped the contract after one year. But NBC stepped into the breach and with the end of the Yankees and Phillies contracts in 1966, the relationship would be extended for thirty years.

Most important, Fetzer had learned to package. The networks were not particularly interested in the "Game of the Week" concept. There were lots of other attractions for viewers on summer Saturday afternoons. They were, however, highly interested in the All-Star games and the World Series and

Fetzer insisted on selling the rights as a package and using the Saturday after-noon telecasts to keep baseball in the public eye.

Ratings shot up for 1966 as viewers appreciated the color telecasts and Fetzer's committee made some important concessions. The network was given flexibil-ity to change its schedule to show crucial games late in the season. Teams were encouraged to limit their Saturday regional broadcasts to time slots that did not compete with NBC. By 1968, baseball agreed to limit blackouts to the home cities of the participating teams, and NBC agreed to provide a backup game to those markets.[10]

The television negotiations added to Fetzer's standing. "The owners relied heavily on him to come up with an acceptable television contract," said Lee MacPhail. "There were several who were somewhat reluctant to relinquish their individual rights. But John convinced them it was for the good of all." The television committee work also allowed Fetzer to build a relationship with Walter O'Malley, the National League's man on the committee and the most powerful voice in that league. At joint meetings, they would quietly trade notes to move issues ahead.[11]

"He doesn't say much and, by design, he stands in the background, but there's no question that John Fetzer is the most powerful force in baseball," said the *Chicago Tribune*'s Jerome Holtzman.[12]

The most consequential ownership change of the period between the first two rounds of expansion was the Yankees sale to CBS in 1964.

Both Del Webb and Dan Topping were losing their enthusiasm. They had already gained enormous profits from their original $2.8 million investment. Their sale of Yankee Stadium in 1953 had more than covered their purchase costs and the steady run of pennants and World Series appearances had con-tinued to generate cash. There were reports they were not getting along and rumors that they understood the team's farm system had been declining since their dismissal of George Weiss in 1960.[13]

They had reached a secret sale agreement with Lehman Brothers in 1962, but that was put on hold while Webb and Topping waited for a ruling from Washington on the tax implications.[14] While they waited, CBS president Wil-liam S. Paley approached Topping to see if the Yankees might be available. Topping explained why they were not but said he would call Paley if anything changed. In July 1964, it did. Lehman Brothers got tired of waiting and called off the sale. Topping immediately contacted Paley.

Within four weeks, they agreed that the network would buy 80 percent of the stock for $11.2 million, with Webb and Topping each retaining 10 percent. Topping would stay on to run the team. CBS would be allowed to buy the remainder within five years, which they did, raising their bill to $14 million.

CBS, which prided itself on being the "Tiffany Network," was interested in diversification, but then only in the best properties in a given arena. The Yankees were on their way to their fifth straight pennant and fifteenth in the last eighteen seasons. While $11.2 million was significant money for most corporations, it was less than 20 percent of what CBS had earned on another of its diversification efforts, the musical *My Fair Lady*.[15]

News of the sale did not come from Yankee Stadium or from CBS headquarters at 52nd St. and Madison Avenue in Manhattan. It was released on a Thursday in Chicago by Charles O. Finley. Typically, Finley was mad about it. This time, he got support from another new voice from Chicago, White Sox owner Arthur Allyn.

Both said they had not been contacted until the vote was decided. Cronin said he had made phone calls and sent telegrams but had not been able to find them until after the necessary two-thirds majority had been established by the other owners. That was not a sufficient explanation for Allyn and Finley, who raised questions both procedural and profound.

Allyn noted the owners had met just three days earlier without a whisper of a deal. According to the league constitution there was supposed to be fifteen days' warning before any meeting and a wire or telephone vote could only be held with unanimous approval.[16] Cronin refused to call another meeting, said he hadn't been told about the sale until that Thursday and that the league's lawyer had assured him the wire vote was "sufficient and legal."[17] The Twins' Calvin Griffith said Cronin had told him he had organized the wire vote because "that's what CBS asked me to do."[18]

The questions about the mechanics exposed a lack of confidence in the way the American League did things. The *Sporting News* editorialized sympathetically with Allyn's and Finley's concerns that the issues deserved a league discussion.[19] Cronin did not help his case when he said earlier changes had been approved by similar votes.[20] Finley noted the close ties among owners that raised suspicions. The Yankees had obvious financial reasons for approving the sale. The Angels' and Tigers' owners had television stations that were CBS affiliates. The head of CBS Sports was the brother of the Orioles' president, and another Orioles board member was on the CBS board of directors.

The Indians, perennially interested in moving, were not going to cross the league majority. Two others had reasons to protect the besieged image of Joe Cronin, who was on the long list of candidates to succeed the retiring Ford Frick as commissioner. Cronin was a longtime Red Sox executive, a friend of Yawkey's, and brother-in-law of the Twins' owner. The new Senators owners had a former Yankee running their team.[21] While some of these objections seemed paranoid, others rang true.

Reporters quickly jumped on the story, with Finley supplying documents and the Yankees, CBS, and, above all, Cronin caught in a sea of reactive denials.[22] *Sporting News* readers unanimously joined the reporters in panning the sale.[23]

More profoundly, the sale added an urgent dimension to the owners' concerns about television. One National League owner piled on, echoing questions about what the sale would mean for baseball's relationship with national television networks.[24] How could they devise and then negotiate a lucrative package with the networks if one of those networks had a major executive sitting in the discussions?

The heated debate got Congress riled up again. Various congressmen and senators began to talk about baseball's antitrust exemption and whether the Justice Department should examine the sale. They, too, were suspicious of the networks' power. The Justice Department did begin to look into the situation, but it was not an "investigation" they were careful to say.[25]

Like most of the impassioned talk, the non-investigation went nowhere. The hearings went nowhere. The Yankees and CBS, concerned about the publicity and the possibility of the investigation, asked Cronin to redo the vote. There was fifteen days' notice. There was a discussion at the meeting. CBS president Frank Stanton came in to answer questions. Tom Yawkey caused a kerfuffle when he suggested the sale be approved subject to a favorable ruling by the federal government. Lawyers quickly wrote some mush wording to salve Yawkey's concerns. The vote was still the same, eight to two.[26]

In the short term, the sale went ahead. In the longer term, there was a belief the years of Yankee preeminence were over. "The owners have blown the whistle on this domination," Allyn told a Senate hearing, "It was unheard of before that the Yankees were not members of the executive council of baseball."[27]

Arthur Allyn's emergence in the CBS-Yankees affair was a symptom of how the old guard was changing. In 1961, Bill Veeck, battling serious health issues and his endemic restlessness, had decided it was time to sell the White Sox. Among other ailments, coughing fits were causing blackouts and Mayo Clinic doctors told him to retire. And, as usual, his enthusiasm for ownership had run its course, and he was ready to go on to the next thing, whatever it was. A decade earlier, Veeck had taken an idea of Nate Dolin's and persuaded the Internal Revenue Service that an owner buying a team should be able to treat the player contracts that came with the purchase as a depreciating asset. After all, the player was getting older. Thus, an owner was allowed to write off from his taxes a portion of that declining value for the first five years of ownership.[28] As the five-year deadline approached, Veeck and many other owners would find the financial attractions of owning a team disappearing like the value of the contracts.

Veeck's solution was already in his boardroom. The Chicago brokerage firm of A. C. Allyn & Co. had helped finance Veeck's purchases of the Indians, the Browns, and the White Sox. In the latter case, Arthur Allyn Sr. had taken some stock in the team. When he died in 1960, those shares were split between his sons, Arthur Jr. (born 1913) and John (1917). The Allyns had slowly added to their holdings and were willing to buy the rest of the Veeck syndicate's shares, a total of 54 percent of the team. Within a couple of years, they would buy out the minority holders.

Arthur Jr. had a somewhat difficult relationship with his powerful father and spent his early years establishing his own identity. He dropped out of Dartmouth, got a job as a chemist at a dog-food manufacturer, and then took his last few dollars and moved to California. There, he joined California Packing Co., where his genetic interests led him to leading the research department. As the war ended, he went off on his own, starting Pacific Vinegar Co., where he was president when his father finally persuaded him to join the family business in 1949.[29]

While the brothers were equal partners on the team's stockholders' list, it was Arthur who took the public role. That was anomalous for a man who liked to keep to himself, enjoyed building his own television sets, studying genetics, and adding to his world-class collection of 150,000 butterflies. When he inherited his shares, Arthur Jr. had attended two professional baseball games in his life—in 1929 and 1958. And when he did go to games as an owner, he often sat by himself in the bleachers.

His personality mixed "a bashful smile, a soft voice and a crushing candor," said one profile. "People in baseball are not very interesting," he summed up.[30]

As he entered the world of baseball owners, he shared his early impressions: "Frick is lazy, and neither Cronin nor (NL President Warren) Giles knows the meaning of the words 'yes' and 'no.'"[31] He was also blunt in going against baseball's holy writ. Major league baseball, he said, was a business and, like other businesses, it should be subject to antitrust laws.[32]

In talking with both reporters and his colleagues around the American League owners table, Arthur Allyn would remain equally forthright with his opinions. He was also idiosyncratic. He and Finley had teamed up in the CBS-Yankees affair, although Allyn was not the league's biggest disruptive force. Finley retained that role. But Finley, Allyn, and the emergence of another group of younger owners presaged a movement to change the way the leagues and baseball as a whole managed its business.

CHAPTER EIGHT

The Young Turks

The evolving dynamics of the American League crystallized around the new commissioner, William Eckert. But it soon morphed into a broader attack by a group of newer American League owners who came to be called the Young Turks. Their ultimate failure would delay reforms for another couple of decades.

The unhappiness was triggered by John Fetzer's biggest mistake.

In August 1964, as the news of the Yankees' sale to CBS swirled, Commissioner Ford Frick confirmed what baseball had been talking about for the past few years. He would retire at the end of his current term, in September 1965. The National and American leagues embarked on a stumbling search to replace Frick, and Fetzer was at the center of the stumbles.

The commissioner's office had been established four decades earlier to redeem baseball's image tarnished by the Black Sox scandal. Their first choice was a grandstanding federal judge named Kenesaw Mountain Landis, who reclaimed the image but irritated owners with an often-high-handed style. After he died in 1944, the owners turned to Kentucky senator Albert "Happy" Chandler but gave him fewer powers than Landis. Chandler was ridiculed by the New York press for his supposed lack of sophistication, but it was his treatment of owners that ended his term prematurely. He questioned Del Webb's Las Vegas connections and soon found himself out the door. Frick had replaced Chandler in 1951.

By the mid-1960s, nobody doubted a baseball game's integrity, but the sport existed in a much more tangled world of corporate ownership. Frick prided himself on enforcing the rules. What he never seemed to grasp was that the environment of baseball was changing and that the commissioner had a role in leading as well as following the existing rules. Television was just one area of growing importance. New markets were opening up as demographics changed. Franchises had not moved for five decades when Frick took office, but now seemed to move with regularity—and disgruntled members of Congress were threatening the cherished antitrust exemption.[1] Many owners felt the need to do more with national marketing and promotions, which had always been left to individual teams. Labor troubles lurked on the horizon.

The National League's Walter O'Malley suggested that, with a year to make their choice, the owners agree on a job description before discussing candidates, a way of bringing some focus to the kind of leadership owners wanted.[2] Like O'Malley, observers such as Leonard Koppett knew the game's environment was changing but the owners were not. Baseball's "problems are vastly more complicated, events are moving more quickly, and immense sums of money are involved in television rights, pension plans, franchise shifts, and now draft rights. In many of these matters, it is unavoidably essential to have one man to negotiate through, a man whose decisions can be regarded as binding and a man who can grasp the complexities and act accordingly, even if some of his 'employers' don't show the same degree of understanding," Koppett wrote.[3]

While all agreed the new commissioner would have a large role in improving the image of the game, they differed on the other qualities needed. Did they want an executive with extensive baseball experience? Did they want one with a corporate management record? Or maybe someone with a national reputation and contacts in Congress? Ignoring O'Malley, they set up a system to make a list of candidates before deciding what the successful candidate would do, a task they never got around to.

At a November 1964 meeting, Frick joined the debate by suggesting the owners consider strengthening the commissioner's powers, returning some taken away when Landis was replaced. And the owners set up their first process: Every franchise would submit its own list of candidates by March 1965.[4] The rumor mill produced dozens of names and 156 nominees were proposed by sixteen franchises.

In late March, they set up a committee to sift through the nominees. Fetzer represented the American League and Pittsburgh's John Galbreath the Nationals. But sifting was a low contact sport. The committee members were not to interview the candidates or discuss them with people who might know them. One owner-critic noted his colleagues on the committee were not asked to know more than could be gleaned from Dun & Bradstreet or Who's Who.[5]

By late July, the Sporting News reported Fetzer and Galbreath had cut the list to around fifty before the owners brought it down to sixteen.[6] It was a mish-mash of old baseball hands such as Cronin, MacPhail, National League attorney Louis Carroll, former Players Association lawyer Robert Cannon, and national personalities such as former vice president Richard Nixon, Bill Shea of New York Mets fame, two Supreme Court justices, and Air Force general Curtis LeMay.[7]

By late October, the list had shrunk to seven and changed radically. Only Cronin, Carroll, and LeMay remained, joined by Gabe Paul, former secretaries of the U.S. Army and Air Force and Bing Devine, a former Cardinals general manager now working for the New York Mets.[8] In a day-long meeting at Chicago's Edgewater Beach Hotel, some owners tried to force a decision while others wanted delay. The Indians' Gabe Paul, the Orioles' Jerold Hoffberger, and the White Sox's Arthur Allyn joined in trying to force a decision, but failed.[9] As the process dragged on, Frick agreed to stay on as long as necessary.

On November 17, the owners announced that they had unanimously chosen retired Air Force general William D. Eckert to replace Frick. It later came out the vote wasn't unanimous as Calvin Griffith had held out for his brother-in-law Cronin.[10] Owners later claimed Eckert had been on the original list of 150, nominated by Gussie Busch of the Cardinals, but acknowledged his name had emerged late.[11] Fetzer had done the owners' first interview.[12] Eckert's name certainly had not been bandied about on the baseball rumor mill, and sportswriter Larry Fox gave him the nickname that stuck: The Unknown Soldier.

Eckert, fifty-six, had attended West Point and served thirty-five years in the Air Force, retiring in 1961 to become a consultant and lobbyist. He had an MBA from Harvard and had spent much of his career in Washington, D.C., overseeing logistics and acquiring new weapons systems. He had retired as the Air Force's comptroller. The owners evidently thought the years in the capital meant congressional connections but Eckert had done his work within the Pentagon and made his contacts with defense contractors. Despite his years in Washington, the *New York Times* could not find enough in its files to write a profile the day he was chosen.[13]

Eckert admitted he was not much of a fan, using the football analogy of "calling the signals" at his first news conference.[14] He later conceded he had attended only a few games during his lifetime.

The owners did recognize his ignorance of the business they were choosing him to lead. As early as July 1965, they had decided on a beefed-up support staff for the commissioner's office.[15] Lee MacPhail would become Eckert's chief of staff, using his twenty years of front office experience to handle the inside-baseball decisions and leaving Eckert free to deal with broader issues. An experienced reporter, Joe Reichler, was hired as a full-time press relations assistant. Staffers for amateur/college and Latin American relations would be added.[16]

They also had bowed to Frick's call to restore some powers to the commissioner's office, reviving a baseball rule that banned owners from suing the commissioner. They also allowed the commissioner to decree that an action could be "detrimental to baseball" even if it complied with major league rules.[17]

Said one hopeful owner on the day Eckert was chosen, "Just because we never knew too much about him before doesn't mean he won't make a good commissioner."[18]

He did not. Eckert lasted barely three years.

He proved decisive in some early, small decisions. He brokered a deal to stop Venezuela and the Dominican Republic from stealing players from each other during the winter leagues. He settled a fight between Paul Richards and Houston's Roy Hofheinz over a contract settlement. He banned Atlanta's illegal signing of Tom Seaver and set up a bidding system for the pitcher's rights. He resolved a spat with Japanese baseball that allowed the resumption of major league teams' postseason tours. He allowed minor league teams to raise their roster limits when major league owners opposed the measure.[19]

It was in boosting baseball's image that Eckert stumbled. At first, there were just warning signs. The acerbic New York sportswriter Dick Young wondered if Eckert could say "hello" without referring to cue cards.[20] Koppett, a more thoughtful New York sportswriter, summed up his first impression: "If he can't come across as forceful or interesting or informed or provocative or amusing or austere in face-to-face meetings, his capacity to sell baseball in the bitterly competitive battle for attention is not promising. Such an evaluation may be premature, unfair, wrong. Nevertheless, it is the first impression he made, and he will have to live it down."[21]

The stories began to circulate among both owners and reporters. At early press conferences, it became clear he did not realize the Los Angeles Dodgers had been in Brooklyn barely a decade earlier. At a speech, he reached into his pocket for the ever-present cue cards and grabbed the wrong stack, telling a baseball audience that he wanted to thank them for their contributions to American aviation. At an early owners' meeting, Eckert referred to the Cincinnati Cardinals. "It was so embarrassing we let it pass," said Gabe Paul.[22]

The unrest built quickly in the spring of 1968. Dr. Martin Luther King Jr.

was assassinated on April 4, four days before the regular season began. Baseball had to decide if, and how, to acknowledge King's legacy as the funeral was scheduled for Tuesday, April 9, and President Lyndon Johnson declared that day a national day of mourning. Some teams announced cancellations and rescheduling. Others said they would go ahead only to have the visiting team back out. There was clearly no central direction and some owners seemed more concerned with attendance than respect. In the end, nobody played on April 9, but the impression of incoherence was strong as Eckert left the decisions up to leagues and individual teams.

Barely, two months later, on June 6, presidential candidate Senator Robert Kennedy was killed. Despite two months to reflect on the King experience, Eckert dithered again. He ordered the Yankees (New York was the site of the Saturday funeral) and Senators (Washington was the site of the Saturday evening burial) to cancel their games that day. But, he "asked" other teams to postpone or move game times to avoid overlap with the ceremonies. Most owners went along, but then the players started to revolt. The Major League Baseball Players Association, with a new executive director named Marvin Miller, sent a telegram to Eckert, Cronin, and Giles asking for a day of remembrance. At least three teams voted not to play, and when two of those teams were forced to play under threat of forfeit, stars such as Rusty Staub and Maury Wills did not appear.

The criticism was loud, national, and reflective of the nation's divide over those charismatic victims. As Joe Trimble wrote in the *New York Daily News*: "Like the money-changers in the temple, baseball's buck-chasing owners tried to carry on 'business as usual' this tragic weekend and their tactless approach was backed up, with only minor restraint, by THEIR commissioner (emphasis in original)."[23]

As the winter meetings started in December, the owners were confronted with Miller's demand that players get a greater share of the new television contract. Otherwise, the players said they would stage a strike during spring training in 1969. As they gathered for dinner and cocktails on the night before the meetings ended, Jerry Hoffberger and some of the younger owners, already unhappy with Miller's move and the state of the game, fanned the flames. The old guard did not resist.[24]

The next day, barely done with the third year of Eckert's seven-year contract, the owners asked him to step outside their conference room. When called back, he was told he had resigned. As Dick Young wrote, "William D.

Eckert brushed aside the blindfold and the cigarette. He walked to the dais, stood erect and alone, 10 feet tall, and announced his retirement."[25]

With the shouting dying down, the Yankees' sale to CBS was creating quiet ripples around the American League owners' table.

In Baltimore, it led to the emergence of Jerold C. Hoffberger, who would speak loudly at that table over the next decade and a half.

Hoffberger had been born in Baltimore in 1919, the son of a family with extensive business interests centered on the National Brewing Co. After prep school and the University of Virginia, Hoffberger served in the army during World War II and then emerged to take his place in the family businesses. He became president of the brewery in 1947, and his work there would bring him into baseball as well as a host of civic commitments around the city.

Over the next two decades, he would lead National Brewing from 150th among American Breweries to fifteenth.[26] Part of that growth was adding breweries in Detroit, Orlando, and Miami, but part was due to a strong attachment to baseball as a marketing vehicle. National, and its flagship National Bohemian beer, sponsored the Washington Senators broadcasts. When the Orioles moved to Baltimore for the 1954 season, National began sponsoring their broadcasts as well. Hoffberger joined Bill Veeck's bid for the Tigers in 1956 and the Detroit brewery later had its Altes brand sponsor the Detroit team.

Hoffberger took those relationships very seriously. He sparked a fight with the stadium authority in Baltimore when it sold space on Memorial Stadium's scoreboard to a rival brewer. He threatened the National-sponsored television broadcasts would never show home runs disappearing into the outfield seats near the scoreboard but instead would provide shots of first base.[27] When National Brewing lost the Orioles sponsorship for the 1957 season, he became interested in influencing the relationship by being an owner of the team.

In the late 1950s, he slowly began to accumulate shares.[28] But he never requested a seat on the board, even when the size of his holdings entitled him to one. National Brewing regained the sponsorships, beginning in 1962.[29] Joseph Iglehart and Zanvyl Krieger continued to be the main players on the board, and the owners who were most likely to join team president Lee MacPhail at the owners' meetings. By late 1964, Hoffberger, Iglehart, and Krieger each owned between 25 and 30 percent of the team's shares.[30]

But Iglehart also was a substantial shareholder of CBS and major league rules prohibited cross-ownership.[31] Iglehart chose to sell his Orioles' stock, with pieces going to both Hoffberger and Krieger. The National Brewing owner acquired a majority of the stock by 1965. National Bohemian and the brewery's newly introduced Colt .45 malt liquor were firmly anchored as Orioles radio and television sponsors.

As the Los Angeles Dodgers' general manager and later the president of the San Diego Padres and California Angels, Buzzie Bavasi sat in many an owners' meeting with Jerold Hoffberger. He saw him as a man focused on how baseball helped his business, "His interest was financial more than anything else," Bavasi said years later. "I think he was concerned about the finances of the Baltimore club rather than anything else and did everything to protect his own interests. I'm not sure that he knew enough about baseball to concern himself about the game itself, but he was a good financial man."[32] At one owners' meeting, Walter O'Malley would dismiss Hoffberger by telling him, "I haven't got time for beer salesmen today."[33]

Hoffberger was clearly interested in marketing—an area he felt the Orioles were lacking. In his early days as owner, he called in the sober-sided Lee MacPhail, the Orioles' president, and suggested he add a little color—a sport coat in Orioles colors and a red convertible. MacPhail demurred.[34] Instead, Hoffberger brought in the advertising director from National Brewing to head marketing, and Frank Cashen went on to a successful career as a major league general manager.[35] He also gave Hoffberger a trusted subordinate within a management team that ran this unfamiliar business for him.

Hoffberger delighted in his new public role. He enjoyed a ducking in the clubhouse showers during the beer- and champagne-soaked pennant-clinching celebration after the Orioles captured their first-ever title in 1966.[36] Although he would be a committed opponent of the Players Association, he would work hard to maintain good relations with his players, getting to know their families and socializing with them.

In many ways, Hoffberger was a classic, liberal Democrat, supporting the presidential campaign of John F. Kennedy and the State of Israel. From the 1956 run at the Tigers, he had established a strong relationship with Veeck and talked with him regularly after taking over in Baltimore. Based on his experiences selling beer, he was a great believer in Veeck's critique of baseball's public relations and marketing efforts.[37] He would push hard for greater efforts at the national level as well as upgrading the marketing push in Baltimore.

Topping would remain at the head of the Yankees until 1966, when he sold his remaining 10 percent and moved to Florida. His replacement was CBS's representative on the Yankees' board of directors, Edmund Michael "Call me Mike" Burke, a man who had moved from a middle-class Connecticut household to New York chic, hobnobbing successfully in the Hamptons and elsewhere.

Born in 1916, Burke spent his early years between his lawyer father's house in Enfield and his grandfather's tobacco farm just across the Connecticut River. As a high school freshman, he was living in West Hartford and playing on the varsity basketball team. Then, he was discovered playing under an assumed name for a local semipro team and disqualified. He was rescued by the local prep school, Kingswood, which had decided to upgrade its athletic program by recruiting from the local public schools. Burke was tapped and said, "For me, Kingswood was life's major turning point."[38] His considerable charm quickly overcame his Irish background and he was soon spending weekends at classmates' country homes complete with golf courses and eleven-car garages. He was successful as both a football player and, after near dismissal, as a student. He won a football scholarship to the University of Pennsylvania. In the Ivy League, he was a part-time player as a junior and a part-time starter as a senior.

After graduation, he appeared briefly with the Philadelphia Eagles of the National Football League before going into the marine insurance business. In 1942, at a social occasion, Burke ran into Col. William Donovan who was forming the Office of Strategic Services (OSS), the forerunner of the U.S. Central Intelligence Agency. Donovan recalled a daring punt return Burke had made at Penn and recruited him.

In Italy, the Balkans, and France, Burke's OSS adventures would earn him a Navy Cross and a Silver Star. He drank with Ernest Hemingway at the Ritz Hotel in Paris. His exploits would serve as the basis for a brief run as a Hollywood technical advisor and screenwriter after the war, resulting in the forgettable *Cloak and Dagger*. OSS service would also make him fast friends with the next rich man to give him a boost up the ladder. His partner in the clandestine operations had been Henry Ringling North of the family that ran Ringling Brothers Barnum and Bailey Circus.

After his abortive jaunt to Hollywood, and some thin times trying to become a writer, Burke returned to what was becoming the CIA. He was stationed in Europe charged with finding and training Eastern European natives to return to their Russian-occupied homelands and foment rebellion. It did not work.

In 1954, he was approached by Henry North's older brother to run the circus. It had $3,000 in the bank while owing approximately $1 million. Burke's two-year tenure was unsuccessful in turning around the circus's fortunes and North wound up abandoning the tents, and Burke, to move to indoor arenas.

Burke's lack of success as a CIA provocateur and circus executive did not stop CBS from hiring him. Through contacts at *Forbes* magazine, he was introduced to CBS president Frank Stanton and wound up working in the television department. He spent a year learning the ropes, five years in Europe looking for programming CBS could use, and then returned to New York to look for ways for the company to diversify beyond television, radio, and music. One of those projects was the Yankees. In 1966, he dropped his other CBS duties to run the baseball team full time.

Burke hired Lee MacPhail away from the commissioner's office to run the baseball side and dove into broadcasting, stadium operations, and, above all, improving the team's image and marketing. "The Yankees will go for a friendlier image under their new leader, Mike Burke, who suspects the Bronx Bombers have been perhaps too aloof from the fans in the past," wrote *Sporting News* columnist Bob Addie, "Who knows, you may even be able to get into the Stadium Club at Yankee Stadium without wearing your tuxedo or tails."[39] Roger Kahn was blunter: "The old Yankee attitude had all the warmth and kindness of the Prussian general staff."[40]

Burke had the stadium repainted and an open house was staged. Ushers were counselled to be polite. Giveaways and autograph days proliferated. He pushed Yankee prospect Bill Robinson because he was Black and fit with the new image of relating to all of New York.[41]

When Burke came to the Yankees, all the rougher edges of Connecticut, middle-class, and Irish, had been smoothed away. He was an impeccable dresser, a presence in any room, and a man who knew how to maintain his image. "I've devoted myself to a lot of meaningful things," he modestly told the *New York Times*'s Joe Durso, who described him as a "Renaissance man in a muscle factory, one of the beautiful people in the eddies of New York Society."[42]

He hit the New York sportswriters like a tsunami. He was determined to blow away the Yankees stuffy, corporate image. He let his hair grow in a stylish shag when that was a political statement. He drove a sports car and dated models very publicly. He gave reporters his home phone number.

It was an orgy of superlatives. "Dapper and debonair," wrote *New York Times* columnist Arthur Daley.[43] "A new breed in a world that nurtures change," said Jim Ogle of the *Newark Star-News*.[44] A man of "courage, acumen and imagination," wrote *Sporting News* owner and editor C. C. Johnson Spink.[45] He fascinated them by dropping Latin phrases into his interviews, buying tailored suits from Italy, bringing in the poet Marianne Moore to throw out the first pitch, and telling them what his favorite poem was.[46] His image was crystallizing.

Following Eckert's ouster, Burke and Hoffberger were quickly dubbed the "Young Turks" by the *New York Times*'s George Vecsey and confirmed as such in a *Sporting News* editorial.[47] The name, despite protestations from Hoffberger, would stick.[48]

The so-called Old Guard was not amused. And, the rifts of age and league came to dominate the search for Eckert's successor. Hoffberger, and the New York press, lined up solidly behind Burke. Arthur Daley, the *New York Times* lead sports columnist had been touting Burke since the brouhaha over Senator Robert Kennedy's funeral.[49] He, Milton Richman, the head baseball writer for the *United Press*, and others kept pushing.[50] At one point, Richman even reported his candidate would win.[51]

The National Leaguers dubbed Burke "the circus guy"[52] and lined up behind the Giants' Chub Feeney. Feeney was actually five years younger than Burke, but, as the nephew of longtime Giants' owner Horace Stoneham, was comfortably in the National League camp. It was "the split between the American and National Leagues that helped bring baseball to its lowest point of prestige," wrote Leonard Koppett. It was "accompanied by private bitterness, political maneuvering and suicidal rivalry."[53]

For almost two months, the stalemate raged. There was a thirteen-hour meeting with nineteen ballots and no resolution. The National League remained solidly behind Feeney. The American League waffled on Burke, with some suggesting Lee MacPhail or other candidates who attracted little enthusiasm. But they would not accept Feeney. Finally, the owners looked to a compromise candidate, choosing Bowie Kuhn, the lawyer who had won the National League's 1966 case against Milwaukee over the Braves' move to Atlanta. Kuhn received a one-year contract, the title of interim commissioner, and a mandate to work on a plan to reorganize baseball's central administration.

The idea of a more centralized governing body for organized baseball had been around since the death of baseball's first commissioner, Kenesaw Mountain

Landis, in 1944. After becoming commissioner, Happy Chandler had proposed a more central administrative organization. He noted that while his office was in Cincinnati, the National League's was in New York, the American League's in Chicago, and the National Association, the minor leagues governing body, kept their headquarters in Durham, North Carolina.

"In our joint association, the normal transaction of business is too often delayed because of the distance we are apart. If all of our offices were under one roof, then all of the records would be at the finger-tips of those concerned," Chandler said.[54] At the same time, a committee of owners produced a report sharply critical of organized baseball's organization and administration. The report was killed because of the objections of other owners and the minors.[55] Both leagues hated Chandler's suggestion and it went nowhere. Periodically, over the next decades, it was suggested that the umpiring staffs of the two leagues be combined for efficiency.[56] Again, the idea did not take root.

Old Guard owners in both leagues pushed for reorganization. The Dodgers' Walter O'Malley revived Chandler's idea of centralized offices in 1963, while the White Sox's Arthur Allyn went further, suggesting that separate league presidencies be abolished.[57] That was too far for O'Malley and other National League owners, and another reorganization push retreated for the moment.[58]

In 1964, with his retirement approaching, Chandler's successor Ford Frick suggested the new commissioner be given broader powers and the search became enmeshed in a discussion of organizational reform. The idea that the commissioner would not be a "baseball man" began to move to the front. With that idea came proposals for a staff experienced in baseball operations to deal with administration. That led to Lee MacPhail as chief of staff when Eckert was finally chosen.

Eckert's ineffectiveness soon revived talk of administrative reorganization. And, when Eckert was fired during the winter meetings in 1968, the owners selected a three-man committee to recommend changes.[59] Significantly, the committee was head by the Orioles' Jerold Hoffberger, who had spearheaded Eckert's beheading. He was joined by two other younger executives, Richard Meyer of the Cardinals and John Holland of the Cubs, both representing their owners. By February 1969, the Giants' Chub Feeney and the Yankees' Mike Burke would be added. It was a group dominated by the Young Turks.

Baseball bubbled with ideas that year.[60] The group commissioned a study by the University of Pennsylvania's Wharton School, which, after revisions from the baseball executives, suggested widespread changes in how baseball was run. The league and minor league offices would be housed in the same building with the commissioner; the league presidents would report to the commissioner rather than the owners in their league; the executive council would be expanded to eleven people, from five; and the majorities needed in joint meetings would be reduced.[61]

In 1966, the owners embraced another of the younger owners' ideas and created the Major League Promotion Corp.[62] Burke, its major sponsor, was put in charge. Complaints about the way baseball marketed itself had been percolating for years. It was personified by longtime Yankee executive George Weiss. When approached with the idea of staging a Cap Day promotion, he exclaimed, "Do you think I want every kid in the city walking around in a Yankee cap?"[63]

In 1963, *Business Week*'s marketing section headlined "Baseball Tries to Keep Its Bounce." Except for highlight films and some booklets from the commissioner's office, marketing was left to the individual teams.[64] Even the Promotion Corp. envisioned little but novelties in its first incarnation. Its first big contract was with Coca-Cola where kids collected plastic liners from Coca-Cola bottle caps and traded them for autographed photos, caps, or balls.[65]

In August 1968, the project was renamed (Major League Baseball Promotion Corp.) and Burke trotted it out as a new thing.[66] The effort essentially remained a licensing program, but it did produce a red, white, and blue logo of a batter about to hit a pitch. When the game's official centennial came around in 1969, there were lots of tie-ins.[67] That year, Commissioner Bowie Kuhn even showed up for the official rollout of the new *Macmillan Baseball Encyclopedia*, a volume that would revolutionize the study of the game.

But the Young Turks did not revolutionize the game.

The Wharton study drifted into the filing cabinets in a welter of committee meetings and further study groups. The National League elected Chub Feeney its new president even before the plan was formally presented. Significantly, Feeney had made it clear he would not take the job if the provisions to consolidate power in the commissioner's office and reduce the role of league presidents were accepted.[68] It would be three more decades before baseball's leadership was consolidated into the same office building, the league presidencies abolished, and the central bureaucracy established.

The Promotion Corp. never made as large an impact as hoped. Kuhn was viscerally attached to the image of the game he grew up with, vetoing a Burger King promotion he said was "prostituting" the game and blocking a shaving lotion company's offer to pay $1,000 a game to the batter with the season's longest hitting streak. Broader efforts were undermined by owners' image of the game. When the Promotion Corp. wanted to sign Rolaids to sponsor a relief-pitchers award, the owners asked if they couldn't find a more "classy" company.[69] "Advertising is," complained Promotion Corp. president Robert Shea, "substantially less than it should be."[70]

The surge of the Young Turks passed. Hoffberger felt so ineffective he quit attending owners' meetings "on the accurate premise that nobody was listening to him anyway."[71] When Burke left baseball a few years later, *Chicago Sun-Times* columnist Jerome Holtzman wrote, "And to think that only several years ago Burke was among the leaders of the so-called 'Young Turk' owners who were going to overthrow the Old Guard. Never did make it, did they?"[72]

All was not lost, however. The red, white, and blue logo of the batter about to hit a pitch is still around fifty years later. And, projecting a positive image for the American League was about to get harder in the maelstrom that was Charles O. Finley.

CHAPTER NINE

The Luckiest City since Hiroshima

I t had taken Charlie Finley barely eight months to make a mess in Kansas City.

He started out saying all the right things. He was committed to Kansas City. No longer would the Athletics be a farm club for anybody else—especially the Yankees. There were suspicions around baseball in that era that there were some nefarious doings in the Athletics-Yankees relationship—perhaps dating back to former Athletics' owner Arnold Johnson's purchase of Yankee Stadium, a big payday for Webb and Topping. The Yankee owners subsequent lobbying when Johnson bought the Athletics deepened the suspicions and the constant parade of Athletics prospects, such as Roger Maris, who wound up representing the Yankees in multiple All-Star games seemed to confirm them.[1]

Finley publicly appealed to the suspicion and said there would be no trades with the Yankees. Instead, he would pay the price to sign young players and develop them for the Athletics. Any profits would be poured back into making the team better. He started a large direct-mail campaign to increase the number of season ticket holders and created the first partial season ticket plans—one game against each team in the league.[2]

Two months after his approval, league president Joe Cronin saluted him as a man of vision, courage, and patriotism.[3] Finley's early enthusiasm found him directing traffic outside Municipal Stadium on Opening Day and joyfully interacting with the fans.[4] An early portrait in *Sports Illustrated* called him "the kindliest owner in baseball" and doubted if any "owner has ever been as solicitous about the comfort of the fan or the peace of mind of his players."[5]

He quickly hired Frank Lane, a veteran, if erratic, general manager and kept well-liked manager Joe Gordon. He said he put over $400,000 into improvements for city-owned Municipal Stadium. The stadium was then almost forty years old but had been substantially refurbished when the Athletics arrived for the 1955 season. He said he wanted to get rid of a clause in the team's lease with the city that made it easier for him to leave town. The clause allowed him to move if annual attendance fell below 850,000, and that threshold dropped by 50,000 every time a game was televised, as Opening Day had been. Attendance had been 775,000 in 1960. In February, he ostentatiously burned the contract. He said he did not want the clause and vowed to remain in Kansas City.[6]

But then Finley ran into Ernie Mehl. Mehl was the sports editor and lead sports columnist for the *Kansas City Star*. He had been a big booster of the city's successful effort to lure the Athletics in 1955 and was committed to keeping the team in Kansas City.

As the first summer of Finley's ownership progressed, Mehl began hearing rumors that Finley was interested in moving the team. He reported on disarray in the front office. Hank Peters, then a young executive in the minor league department and later a World Series–winning general manager with the Orioles, was fired after approving a bonus. Finley constantly hounded Lane with phone calls and "advice." He infuriated Gordon so much that the manager grabbed him by the throat in a late-night altercation at a bar in spring training. He then regularly used the dugout phone to complain about lineup decisions and game strategy. Players were nervous.[7] Mehl reported these stories and heard others that fueled his skepticism about the new owner.[8]

In August, Mehl reported that the contract-burning ceremony back in February had been a sham. Finley had set fire to some ordinary stationery. The attendance clause was still in effect and Finley was giving the city one excuse after another for not signing a new contract to eliminate it. He then topped it off by reporting, in a front-page story, that "Finley is considering a move of the franchise to Dallas."[9]

Finley, who was in Dallas attending a medical convention, denied any interest in Texas. But the *Dallas News* was reporting his visits to various local sports facilities and his declarations of his love for the Dallas market. It turned out Finley had made an earlier trip to Dallas barely two weeks after winning American League approval for his purchase, ostensibly to attend the Cotton Bowl but also to look over the market. Finley said Mehl's reporting was all rumors. Years later, Finley's niece would contend Mehl was upset that in buying the A's Finley had bested an ownership group in which Mehl had an interest.[10]

Then, Finley struck back. Three days after Mehl's front-page story, in between games of a Sunday double-header with the White Sox, he had a truck driven around the field emblazoned with a banner for "Ernie Mehl Appreciation Day." On the banner was a drawing of a man at a typewriter next to a bottle labeled "poison ink."[11] The owner soon told the team's traveling secretary not to make travel arrangements for reporters from the *Star* and its sister paper, the *Kansas City Times*, or to give those papers copies of press releases or other team materials. The next day, Commissioner Ford Frick called Mehl, apologized, and then told the Associated Press he had done so.

As he would prove over the next two decades, these kinds of rebukes fazed Charlie Finley not one little bit. The day after Frick's apology, Finley fired Frank Lane and appointed Pat Friday, an executive from his insurance company, as executive vice president.[12] Lane had been begging for this. He fumed at Finley's decree that the owner have the last word on all trades and then defied him by making a trade with the Yankees in direct defiance of Finley's pledge.[13] He was muttering to other employees. If Lane had been the only casualty, that would have been understandable. But Gordon had already been fired in June and other front office people were being let go as well. Finley was making it clear it was going to be his organization, and a very lean one. His reputation with other owners and the baseball establishment became shaky.[14]

Despite his denials to Mehl and other reporters, it was clear that, from the beginning, Finley wanted out of Kansas City. In 1961, Bill Grigsby was a young employee of the Majestic Advertising Agency and Schlitz Brewing Co. His employers held the sponsorship rights for Athletics' radio broadcasts, and he was sent to pick up Finley and Friday at the airport for their first visit to Kansas City that January. Grigsby told Finley biographers G. Michael Green and Roger Launius that, after a good visit at the brewery, Finley and Friday's backseat conversation was all about moving, especially to Dallas.[15]

It was also clear that Finley's grasp of the literal truth was elastic. Seeing that, Kansas Citians were increasingly reluctant to make the emotional and financial commitment to a team that did not perform on the field and always seemed interested in leaving. Attendance would average 680,000 in Finley's years in the city and never rise above eighth-best in the league at a time when the average American League team drew more than one million fans.

Finley also had a gift for phrasing that he thought made his points but added to the uncertainty he was creating in fans' minds. In August 1961, after dodging for months, he signed a new version of the stadium lease that removed the attendance clause he had ostentatiously not burned. Then, he said, "It is a shame when someone spends $500,000 of his own money on a city-owned stadium, works night and day and sacrifices, and then is criticized as I have been criticized. It makes me sick enough to want to take the club out of Kansas City."[16] Thus, he blamed the critics of his veiled efforts to leave as a righteous reason for leaving.[17]

There would always seem to be some new story about Finley's desire to leave or his subsequent denial. As the 1961 winter meetings approached, the *Sporting News* reported Finley "expressed dissatisfaction with the situation in Kaycee and said he would request league permission to move if things got worse."[18] He kept muddying the waters. In May 1962, he told a Baltimore audience he was committed to Kansas City, but then a couple of weeks later asked his fellow owners to allow him to relocate to Dallas–Fort Worth.[19] When the owners met that September, Finley's reading of the room told him he would lose any vote, probably unanimously. He dropped his request.[20]

Finley's desire to move was a spur to the continuing and confused discussion of expansion after the motley process of the early 1960s.

The expansions of 1961 and 1962 had raised appetites. Even before the Angels or Senators started their first spring training, eyes were being raised to the horizon. "You know how these baseball fellows are," said Commissioner Ford Frick in 1960, "It takes them a long time to get moving, but when they do, they want to keep moving. The only thing I fear is they'll move too fast." Belying his last thought, Frick suggested the majors could expand to twenty-four teams by 1962.[21]

The National League was much more in tune with Frick's cautionary notes. "We're still assimilating from the expansion of 1962," said New York Mets executive Bing Devine in 1966.[22] "Baseball rushed into expansion to accommodate Congress," argued the Dodgers' Walter O'Malley in 1961, "We were not— and are not now—ready for it. A big mistake has been made."[23] While this argument downplayed the American League's desire to get into the Southern California market, and the National's wish to return to New York, it was not without basis. In 1965, a group of U.S. congressmen sent Commissioner Frick a letter suggesting expansion to Buffalo and Dallas–Fort Worth, plus a franchise to replace the Braves who were about to leave Milwaukee.[24] As always when congressmen suggested, owners feared a threat to their treasured antitrust exemption.

Caution led to greater efforts at coordination between the leagues. The American League did not want the National League snapping up the better markets, as they had in 1958 and 1960. The National League feared the American League's tendency to jump into major moves without study or much forethought. At the annual winter meetings in 1962, both leagues agreed that "before either loop makes any commitment to expand again, it must disclose its plans to the other league at a joint meeting."[25]

The waters were muddied further in late 1964. After a summer of rumors and a premature story in the *Sporting News*, the National League's Milwaukee Braves announced they were moving to Atlanta, another promising market outside the Northeast quadrant.[26] Barely two weeks later, faced with a lawsuit by Milwaukee County to enforce a lease agreement for County Stadium, the National League leaders told Braves' ownership they could not move the team until the 1966 season, ensuring the lease would be fulfilled.[27] When Milwaukee sued anyway, the National League, represented by an attorney named Bowie Kuhn, won the lawsuit.

The American League, at the time of Finley's abortive move to Dallas, had made it clear the Athletics would have to fulfill the lease, so that was not an issue. But the American League owners also knew Kansas City leaders were unhappy and Missouri senator Stuart Symington was ruminating about the antitrust exemption.

Despite American Leaguers, such as President Joe Cronin, trying to tamp down the expansion talk, the pressure continued to build. In March 1967, baseball's executive council, which included owners from both leagues, ordered Commissioner Eckert to make a plan for orderly expansion after a survey of potential markets and their stadium facilities.[28] As a trial run, in the summer of 1967, the American League floated the possibility of two-division play, ostensibly so that no team would bear the stigma of finishing tenth. National Leaguers, who feared American League owners really meant they intended to expand and did not want anybody finishing twelfth, immediately shot the idea down.[29]

While Finley thought his playing along with the other American League owners on the lease issue might build up goodwill for a future move, there was a much bigger trend in play.

Since the Dodgers and Giants had moved to California for the 1958 season, the National League had been drawing far more fans than the American League. By 1965, the average National League game drew 45 percent more people than the American League average. A combination of the more exciting brand of baseball and the better markets led to almost five million more clicks of the turnstiles, with the National League's West Coast franchises leading the way. The American League papered over its problem after the 1966 season, when, without any public acknowledgment, they ordered teams to report

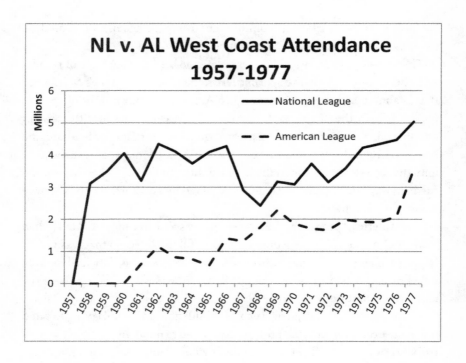

NL v. AL West Coast Attendance 1957-1977

attendance as the number of tickets sold rather than the number of people who actually attended the games. Only a query from a *Boston Globe* reporter after the 1967 season revealed the change.[30]

Changing reporting methods was cosmetic, although counting the season ticket holders who did not show certainly pumped up the number, lowering the National League's surplus over the American League from 4.8 million to 1.6 million in attendance.[31] It did not deal with the deeper issue—the league's lack of presence on the West Coast. As noted earlier, the creation of the Los Angeles Angels had not made the dent the American League had hoped for.

Even before Finley had sought permission to move, former American League president Will Harridge said, "I don't know how soon, but you'd have to say the American League needs a second club in California because of the tremendous travel expenses involved in bringing nine teams West three times each season to play only in Los Angeles." If Finley were to want to move to California, he would likely get approval quickly, Harridge added.[32] That was in 1962. Four years later, the American League was just as convinced. "We have no plan to expand at this time, but when we do make the move, we'll have to place another team on the West Coast," Cronin told the *Sporting News*.[33]

Finley's leaner organization meant significantly smaller efforts to sell season tickets and pump up the coming season each winter, and that raised further suspicions. The A's owner ignored offers by the Chamber of Commerce to help with ticket sales. Schlitz Brewing made a similar offer to help with season ticket sales. Finley not only turned them down, he turned them out as radio sponsors. He began selling ad time locally.[34] After news of Finley's 1962 request to move to Dallas surfaced, the Chamber wrote a letter to American League owners asking them for a clear-cut statement of whether the league was committed to the city.[35] American League president Joe Cronin responded that league owners had no desire for either expansion or relocation.[36] Each contradictory zig-zag had been reported in the local papers or the *Sporting News*, fueling uncertainty.

Finley tried to take a new tack. Fresh from the American League meeting where he had dropped the Dallas bid, he asked Kansas City's city council to issue bonds to build a ballpark that could seat 50,000 people and park 15,000 cars. While denying he had "ever mentioned at any time that I wanted to move the franchise," he added, "Unless Kansas City is willing to start action immediately for a new and modern stadium, its days as a major league city are numbered."[37]

Finley said he had lost $1.5 million in 1962, citing the large bonuses he had been paying for young talent. He said the team would have to cut back on expenses.[38]

Then he found another grievance. In February 1963, Lamar Hunt moved his American Football League team to Kansas City. The city council signed a seven-year lease for Municipal Stadium. The freshly renamed Chiefs would pay $1 a year in rent and half the concession profits, with escalator clauses beginning in the third year. Finley screamed that he was paying $120,000 annually in rent and not getting any heat in the team offices. The city council pointed out that the Athletics had received a deal similar to the Chiefs' when they had moved from Philadelphia nine years earlier. *Kansas City Star* reporter Joe McGuff would later determine Finley had paid between $59,030 and $71,818 in rent his first three years.[39]

Finley's unhappiness did lead to a renegotiation with the city, which produced a seven-year contract similar to the Chiefs', beginning with $1 a year rent for the first two years. The city council signed the agreement minutes before it was due to leave office, only to have the incoming council overturn the contract.

Quickly, Finley called Furman Bisher, sports editor of the *Atlanta Constitution*, and said he wanted to talk about moving to Georgia, an idea Bisher had raised with Finley earlier and before the Braves' move.[40]

It was not just Georgia. Finley continued to deny that he had asked to move the team or had any interest in doing so.[41] By late 1963, Kansas City had offered Finley a contract with the same terms as the Chiefs, but he wanted more, countering with eight different possible contracts.[42] A few months later, he asked American League owners to approve a shift to Louisville, Kentucky, where he said he had signed a contract with the city.[43]

The only support Finley got was his own. The other owners voted down the Louisville gambit nine to one and ordered him to sign a contract with Kansas City.[44] Finley threatened to sue and told American League president Joe Cronin to "keep your mouth shut." Using multiple extensions, he staved off signing a new four-year lease until February 23, 1964. Finley was by now facing other threats. His fellow American League owners had begun studying ways to force him out of the league.[45] At a February 20 owners' meeting, he felt compelled to bring nationally known attorney Louis Nizer to represent him. That seemed fair as five of the other nine owners had also taken the unusual move of bringing their team lawyers.[46] As the contract signing three days later indicated, Finley knew he had lost this round.

Tied to Municipal Stadium by the lease, Finley's search for a new home went underground. He continued to throw barbs at the city about attendance as the Athletics finished ninth or tenth in the league for the next four years. When the downtown establishment responded in the winter of 1965–66, Finley even gave them some modest support. He paid for several newspaper ads, and the Kansas City Sports Council's efforts produced over 5,000 in season ticket sales for 1966.[47] Attendance was still ninth in the league.

Despite his relative silence on the movement issue, it was clear to people around baseball that Finley already had checked out of Kansas City. In June 1967, with the Athletics only months from the end of the lease, Kansas City voters approved bonds for a $43 million complex with separate new stadiums for both the Athletics and the Chiefs. Despite having asked for something similar back in 1962, Finley stayed out of the debate over the bond measure and would only say "no comment" after it passed.[48]

He had already been talking to Milwaukee interests, but those talks fell apart over their insistence Finley would have to surrender control of the team.

After Chicago-based owners had orchestrated the departure of the Braves for Atlanta two years earlier, the Milwaukee people wanted no part of out-of-town ownership.[49]

The focus now was clearly on Oakland. Its population of 360,000 was definitely smaller than Kansas City's 1.2 million, but the broader San Francisco Bay area offered 4.2 million potential customers.[50] Since March 1962, when voters had approved bonds for constructing what became the Oakland–Alameda County Coliseum, city officials were touting their city as ripe for major league baseball.[51] A year later, San Francisco Giants owner Horace Stoneham told reporters Finley had visited the Bay Area. While there, he asked Stoneham if the Athletics could use Candlestick Park while Oakland finished the promised stadium. Stoneham said "no."[52]

Early in May 1967 even before the stadium vote, the *New York Times* and the *New York Daily News* both reported Finley was planning to move to Oakland.[53] Since both stories reflected Finley's position that Kansas City was uncooperative, it seems likely the Finley camp was the source of the stories. Soon, he was soliciting written offers from Milwaukee as well as Oakland, making a scouting trip to Seattle and giving some consideration to New Orleans.[54]

Kansas City was as sick of Charlie Finley as he was of them. While Finley played out his departure scenario, his management of the team made the local fans even sicker, despite rising young talent such as Bert Campaneris, Catfish Hunter, Sal Bando, and Rick Monday. Distressed at a report pitcher Lew Krausse had been drunk and misbehaving on an August 3 team flight, Finley ordered manager Alvin Dark to fine and suspend Krausse. Dark refused, saying nothing like Finley's description had occurred. Finley suspended Krausse on his own, then added an alcohol ban on future flights in a memo that called some players' actions "deplorable."

Finley demanded Dark's support in handling the disgruntled team. Dark refused, saying the details of what had happened on the plane remained murky. Finley fired him immediately, then minutes later rehired him for two more years with a raise. A few hours later, when Dark admitted he knew the players were working on a statement that Dark had not mentioned to Finley, the manager was fired again.

When reporters surrounded slugging first baseman Ken Harrelson seeking his opinion, he said, "The only thing I know is that Charlie Finley's actions of the last few days have been bad for baseball." A television reporter turned Harrelson's words into calling Finley "a menace to baseball."

Finley exploded and gave Harrelson his unconditional release, a move that worked out very well for Harrelson. He signed a lucrative contract with the Boston Red Sox and helped them to their first pennant in two decades that September.[55]

The two-week circus from Finley's attack on Krausse to Dark's firing to Harrelson's signing with the Red Sox, layered on top of the news of Finley's multicity bandwagon, left Kansas Citians fuming. "Kaycee's Fans Fire Blasts at Finley for 'Unbelievable Mess'" headlined the *Sporting News* over a collection of quotes from cabbies, judges, and other locals. "Don't get me wrong. I'm all for the A's, but without Finley," said Bob Raine of suburban Raytown.[56]

Others were doing something more substantive. Ewing Kauffman, who would win the expansion franchise for Kansas City after the Athletics' departure, contacted Ernie Mehl and Joe McGuff about buying the team. Alex Barket, a local banker who had been involved in baseball since the Arnold Johnson years, enquired as well. Joe Buzas, a minor league owner partnering with Ted Williams, made yet another offer.[57]

Finley was not selling and remained focused on Oakland. As the summer proceeded, he wrote the necessary letters telling the city he would not be renewing the lease on Municipal Stadium.

Despite his track record for being rejected when he wanted to move the Athletics, Finley was confident the wheel had turned in his favor. He had done what he was told, signed the new lease, and fulfilled it. This somewhat restored his standing as a member of the club and thus entitled him to the key privilege of ownership: His peers would let him do what he wanted with his team to ensure they would be allowed to do what they wanted with theirs. And, of course, lurking beyond Finley's focus on his own needs was the American League's desire for a second West Coast franchise. They might not want Finley in Dallas or Louisville, but a move that bolstered their anemic market out West was desirable.

On October 18, 1967, the other American League owners finally granted him permission to move to Oakland. On the second ballot, with Yankees changing their vote, Finley got the bare minimum for the necessary two-thirds.[58] "I sweated it out,"[59] he said.

The next day, on the floor of the Capitol, Missouri senator Stuart Symington said, "Oakland is the luckiest city since Hiroshima."[60]

While willing to let Finley go, American League leadership was not blind to the consequences. Arthur Allyn, who was believed to have made the motion to approve the move, was convinced it would have to be coupled with expansion.[61]

They knew Kansas City officials were unhappy and Senator Symington's willingness to involve himself in the issue was raising the stakes. The Kansas City people were happy to be rid of Finley but wanted to ensure that the American League would provide another team.[62] Anticipating the positive vote for Finley, Cronin had invited a delegation including Kansas City leaders and Symington to the Chicago meeting. Continuing their efforts to nip Milwaukee-like problems in the bud, the American League owners agreed on an expansion plan to approve a new team for Kansas City in three years, while making another attempt to solve their West Coast attendance deficit by adding a twelfth team in Seattle. They made their announcement at 10:30 the evening of October 18.

Cronin and the American League owners thought the Kansas City delegation would be as happy as they were. But later that evening, Mehl and McGuff encountered Boston Red Sox owner Tom Yawkey in the hotel's library. When Yawkey asked if they had gotten what they wanted, they surprised him by saying no. Yawkey immediately conveyed the message to Cronin.[63] Cronin called on the Kansas Citians and found Symington was irate that Kansas City would be without major league baseball until 1971. The senator stormed out of the meeting after threatening to introduce antitrust legislation and pointed out that while Kansas City had approved the stadium bonds, they would not be issued unless a long-term lease was signed by March 1, 1968, a bit over four months away. Kansas City mayor Ilus Davis began preparing to file an injunction the next morning.[64]

In twenty minutes, Cronin put together a meeting of five teams in his suite at the Continental Plaza hotel. Technically, it was not a quorum but the owners present approved expansion for 1969 and guaranteed an ownership group in place in time to sign the lease. It was 1 a.m. and the Missourians, still without major league baseball for 1968, grudgingly accepted.[65]

Despite Symington's threats, the American League owners had once again successfully used their cartel status to control a member of their group while also harming their supposed partners, the National League and its San Francisco franchise.

As with the 1961 expansion, the American League's owners again had acted hastily. While the American Leaguers had placated Symington and Kansas City, they had done so by breaking the 1962 agreement that neither league would expand without full discussion with the other. The National League reacted predictably.

League president Warren Giles ticked off the reasons. With Finley, the

American League was moving "into the back yard of another major league club." The Seattle move was in violation of the 1962 agreement and a major league rule that a league could claim a new territory only between October 1 and 31 of the year before they planned to operate. That meant Seattle or Kansas City could not be claimed until October 1968. And, it meant Oakland had been taken without any claim being made.[66]

American League officials chose to ignore the procedural issues, saying the National League was mad simply because the Athletics were moving into the Giants' market.[67] Because Oakland was a separate city from San Francisco, the move did not violate major league rules about invading another team's territory, they argued.

Reports circulated that the National League suggested the American League add Dallas–Fort Worth instead of Seattle, which the National League wanted to claim.[68] This was an attractive idea. The Dallas area had a population a third larger than Seattle's, and the National League, while recognizing its potential, was not going to move there. Houston owner Roy Hofheinz was not willing to give up the media revenue he received from Dallas. But, the American League owners chose the continued lure of the West Coast over the larger market size.[69]

They were aided because, even before the American League settled on Seattle, the National League had gotten the message from elsewhere in the Senate. Both Washington senators, Democrats Warren Magnuson and Henry Jackson, talked to National League people and, as with Symington, raised the possibility of changes in antitrust law if Seattle did not get a major league team.[70] On October 13, 1967, the National League owners met at Chicago's Executive House hotel and decided not to contest with the American League over Seattle. Giles cited "the interests of baseball as a whole and in the interests of not having a fight."[71]

As major league owners gathered at Mexico City's Hotel Maria Isabel for the 1967 winter meetings on November 26, the public talk was all about whether the National League would commit to expansion, which cities would get franchises if they did, and whether the National League owners really were giving up on Seattle. Milwaukee, Dallas–Fort Worth, San Diego, Denver, Buffalo, Toronto, and Montreal had delegations pressing their cases.

In private, the owners knew they would have to thrash out tangled issues that the American League had ignored in their rush to move the Athletics, pacify Kansas City, and grab another West Coast market:

- If the National League chose not to expand, and the American League, as expected, went to two six-team divisions, what would happen while the Americans played a series to choose a champion? Would that detract from the prestige (and television revenues) from the World Series?
- Baseball had a television contract that was being divided among twenty teams. Would the two, or four, expansion teams get a cut of this revenue, even though these teams would have little national appeal and weren't likely to make the World Series during the term of the contract?
- The new amateur draft process called for the leagues to alternate picks. How would that work if there were ten teams in one league and twelve in the other?
- Had anybody talked to the players' union about the inevitable dilution of the players' share of World Series receipts if 100 more jobs were added?

The last was a specious argument since the players' union was constitutionally interested in more jobs for its members. And the solution to the first three problems was glaringly obvious: The National League owners would have to swallow their irritation with the American's lack of forethought and expand, which they did.

The Nationals thought about waiting until 1971 and generally took their time, but by May 28, 1968, all had been decided. San Diego and Montreal would join Kansas City and Seattle as the expansion cities for 1969. Again, the Nationals had made better judgments about markets. Their expansion cities totaled 4.1 million in population while Kansas City and Seattle's metropolitan areas reached only 3.1 million.[72]

The relative standing of the two leagues was mirrored in the costs of getting into the game. Kansas City and Seattle would pay $175,000 apiece for thirty players to be chosen in an expansion draft plus $100,000 as a franchise fee. Total: $5.35 million each, barely over $1 million in revenue for each of the ten existing teams.

In the National League, San Diego and Montreal would pay $200,000 apiece for their thirty players. The franchise fee would be $4 million. Total: $10 million each, roughly $2 million in extra revenue for each team. The Nationals' condescending attitude about the Americans was reinforced again.

None of the four expansion teams would participate in revenues from the national television contract for three years but would have to begin contributing to the players' pension fund immediately.

The American League owners had made the decision for Seattle despite fears about finding a decent place to play while they had no clear idea who the ownership group would be. Also, they would have to wait for the results of a February 1968 ballot on public funding of a stadium in Seattle. Led by Joe Cronin, they were charging into the unknown without broad knowledge of the markets they were entering or the people who would become their partners.

Lee MacPhail, then the Yankees general manager and later president of the American League, called it "a blueprint for future trouble."[73]

CHAPTER TEN

The Nadir

L ee MacPhail knew how to read a blueprint. The American League owners' forced and hurried expansion exposed their lack of preparation. And
it would soon lead to yet another iteration with a slightly different cast
of cities and owners.

The Seattle troubles went beyond the obvious stadium problems and lack
of a strong, local ownership group. Back in 1960, Seattle and surrounding King
County had hired Stanford Research Institute to study the area's feasibility
for major league sports, particularly baseball. After visiting markets and franchises around the country, SRI gave the city a qualified "yes." The qualifications were threefold: A stadium that could seat a minimum of 25,000 people,
strong support from the city, and solid financial backing for the franchise.[1]

A stadium was the most obvious problem. The local ballpark was Sicks'
Stadium, built in 1938 by Emil Sick, owner of Rainier Brewery, for his Pacific
Coast League Seattle Rainiers. By the late 1960s, it was owned by the city. De-
pending on who was counting, it could hold between 11,000 and 16,000 seats.
It had once been considered a fine ballpark but age had done it no favors.

In 1964, when the Cleveland Indians explored moving to Seattle, concerns
about Sicks' Stadium scuttled their interest. The city's and county's inability
to come up with a viable refurbishing plan had been a central factor. More
recently, Charles Finley had chosen Oakland over Seattle almost completely
because of the stadium situation—Oakland was building and Seattle was not.
Later, Finley, who preferred Seattle's potential over Oakland's, would refer to
Sicks' Stadium as a "pigsty."[2]

When the league did approve an ownership group for Seattle, concerns
about the stadium situation led them to attach two major conditions: The
city would have to bring Sicks' Stadium up to major league standards, and a
stadium bond issue, scheduled for February 1968, would have to pass.

Baseball's supporters also assumed something that the Stanford Research report had identified as a necessity—a strong desire by Seattle-Tacoma-area fans for major league baseball. A March 1963 survey found barely 50 percent of residents were interested in major league baseball.[3] Stadium bond issues had been rejected in 1960 and 1966. While the February 1968 ballot contained a measure to fund a stadium, it was there only because the powers that be were looking for an issue to bring out the vote on rapid transit and other issues they were concerned about.[4] Mayor Dorm Braman was not enthusiastic and two (of five) city council members were adamantly opposed to spending any money on Sicks' Stadium.[5]

American League leadership, mesmerized by the idea of another West Coast franchise, managed to ignore the signals.

The third of Stanford Research's cautionary notes mandated a strong, local ownership group. And the American League blithely bypassed that with its insular predilections. With Finley eyeing Seattle, American League president Joe Cronin visited the city in August 1967 to look things over. Being a baseball guy, Cronin's first contacts were with Seattle's baseball guys—the brothers Dewey and Max Soriano. Cronin was clearly giving them the inside track. Said Max Soriano, "when Mr. Cronin came to Seattle, he was intent on meeting with Dewey and giving him the framework from which to proceed."[6]

The Soriano brothers had been born in Prince Rupert, British Columbia, sons of an immigrant Spanish fisherman and his Danish wife. Dewey was born in 1920 and Max in 1925, with the family using its halibut boat to move to Seattle when Max was six weeks old. Both boys were star high school pitchers. Dewey was headed to the University of Washington when the Pacific Coast League's Seattle Rainiers offered him $2,500. He spent the 1939 through 1942 seasons there winning eleven and losing thirteen.[7]

With World War II in progress and a low draft number, Dewey joined the Merchant Marine, Max followed. Dewey finished the war with a master mariner's ticket. After the war, Max attended, and pitched for, the University of Washington before turning down a contract offer from the Pacific Coast League's San Francisco Seals and going to law school. Keeping up the family connection, he specialized in maritime law. Three other Soriano brothers earned master mariner's tickets.

Dewey returned to baseball. He continued pitching through the 1951 season, mostly in the Pacific Coast League, but spent one spring training with the Pittsburgh Pirates.

Dewey then played for two seasons in a lower minor league, but it was a harbinger of his career as a baseball executive. With $15,000 mostly borrowed from his brothers, he bought a quarter interest in the Yakima Bears of the Western International League. He spent 1949 and most of 1950 there as a starting pitcher, president, and general manager. Attendance doubled.

In late 1951, figuring his baseball career was over, Dewey returned to the sea, first as a third mate and soon as a pilot on the waters of Puget Sound. He would continue to work as a pilot off and on for the rest of his life.[8] But in 1952, he got a call from Emil Sick. Given Dewey's experience as Yakima general manager and his Canadian roots, Sick figured he would be a good operator for the Rainiers' farm club in Vancouver, British Columbia. After the 1953 season, Sick promoted him to Seattle as general manager.

Dewey, with close ties throughout the Seattle baseball community, brought back Fred Hutchinson, his high school teammate, as manager and the Rainiers won the 1955 Pacific Coast League pennant. It was during that season that he launched a campaign to build a domed stadium for Seattle. He was ridiculed in the Seattle papers and the idea went into hibernation.

In 1959, Dewey became executive vice president of the Pacific Coast League, a move made in anticipation of the retirement of President Leslie O'Connor. When O'Connor left a year later, Dewey moved into the presidency, giving him a higher profile throughout the baseball world, a profile he used to promote Seattle as a major league city.

Dewey and Max were certainly comfortable, but they were not rich. They didn't have the kind of money that could handle the $5.35 million the new franchise would need in expansion fees, much less the estimated $2.65 million that would be needed for setting up a front office and a minor league organization, renting a stadium, paying the players, publicizing their new team and a host of other details.[9] But they had a connection. In 1964, when the Cleveland Indians had scouted Seattle, Dewey had met William Daley and made friends with Gabe Paul.

Looking for investors, Dewey talked to Paul who said Daley, no longer involved with the Indians, might be interested. He was. He took 47 percent of Pacific Northwest Sports, Inc., and his Cleveland partners took another 13 percent, with the American League limiting the out-of-towners to 60 percent of the total. The Sorianos, including a third brother, paid for 33.75 percent and the rest was spread among several local people.[10] Daley said he'd asked around Seattle for potential partners, and Max said there had been meetings with Boeing people, but those weren't successful. Later, Edward Carlson of

Western International Hotels, who would play a large role in trying to retain the Pilots, said he never heard of Daley's efforts. The money attendant to such companies as Boeing, Weyerhauser, and Nordstrom, which later joined the consortium that brought the National Football League to Seattle, was not tapped. Cronin told one potential local partner, restaurateur Dave Cohn, that he would get 25 percent of the team. Dewey later said Cohn had not been willing to come up with the money.[11]

Cronin and the American League leadership did not look too closely at the financing of the partnership. They did not read the Sorianos' inability to attract local capital as a warning sign even as they limited the Cleveland investors to 60 percent. Indicating the league's cozy approach, the official screening interview with Daley was done by Gabe Paul, once Daley's partner in the Indians.[12] Barely seven weeks after bowing to Kansas City's demands for a new team, the American League owners approved the Soriano-led group in early December 1967.[13] The decision among several competing Kansas City ownership groups, a strong indication of wider local support, would not be made until early 1968. One of the Stanford Research Institute's qualifications had gone by the wayside.

The need to go to an outside investor such as Daley should have revealed another shortcoming of the Sorianos. They had poor connections with Seattle's power brokers. The February 1968 stadium bond vote was just one part of an initiative the establishment had dubbed Forward Thrust—a measure calling for regional planning and commitment on rapid transit, more parks, better streets, a trade center, and urban redevelopment. To attract public support, Forward Thrust's proponents had included the stadium bond issue, but it was not their highest priority. The Sorianos just were not part of the downtown interests.

"We talked (with the Forward Thrust people), but not too much," Dewey said. "We sometimes weren't asked to be in meetings with the establishment."[14] Harold Parrott, who worked for the Pilots for several months in early 1969, told of trying to persuade Dewey to accept an offer of help from the downtown business community. "We don't need help from outsiders," was Dewey's response.[15]

The stadium bond issue required 60 percent of voters to approve, and the fledgling ownership group had barely two months to build support. The polls were not promising, but Cronin organized a parade of American League stars to come in and talk up baseball. The initiative squeaked through.[16]

That still left the problem of Sicks' Stadium. The American League wanted at least 30,000 seats, but never formally specified its requirements, a lapse that led to disputes throughout the life of the franchise.[17] As with residents, the mayor and city council were not committed to the idea of major league baseball in the city. By August 1968, the Sorianos were writing Mayor Braman saying the work really need to get started.[18] The city felt no urgency to conclude an agreement on the stadium and balked at the costs. In January 1969, with opening day barely three months away, work on expanding and renovating Sicks' Stadium hadn't begun.[19]

The city agreed to spend $1.175 million improving the stadium to the league's unspecified requirements but lowered the targeted capacity to 28,000. The contractors' bids came in between $1.064 and $1.2 million, but none of them contained the increased seating. The city adamantly refused to increase the budget. The targeted capacity was lowered to 25,000 and quality shortcuts were taken in the restrooms, clubhouses, concessions, and other facilities. The city eventually came up with about $1.5 million in total, but the continuing disputes made it clear the city was not as committed to major league baseball as the American League wanted.[20] The politicians who opposed the spending or were lukewarm about it were feeling no pressure from constituents. Again, Stanford Research Institute's pillars of strong local support and a major league quality stadium were not being met.

All this took time and it did not work. In attendance on Opening Day, baseball commissioner Bowie Kuhn described Sicks' Stadium as "a facility that was anything but major league."[21] Attendance was 15,014 and the *Sporting News* optimistically reported with a certain understatement that "most of the seats which had been completed for the milestone opener were occupied." Fans arriving in the new left field bleachers had to wait for carpenters to finish and hundreds watched the game for free through holes in a hastily constructed fence. [22] In right field, only the concrete footings for the bleachers had been finished. Restrooms were incomplete in the main seating bowl and bleacher fans had to do with portable toilets. Concessions were operating below capacity and the beer ran out down the third base side.[23]

The work, and the problems, continued. When the Pilots returned from their second road trip for a May 6 game, fans found the not-quite-dry paint had stained their clothes. By season's end, the city conceded that warping decks and loosening seats were "substandard."[24] As the season progressed, the toilets began backing up and the Pilots withheld rent payments. The city threatened eviction. Its contract manager was fighting with the contractor, who stopped work because he was not getting paid.

Meanwhile, the successful passage of the bond issue in February was being quickly obscured by a confusing fight over where the new domed stadium should be located. Neither the city nor the team could point to a quick escape from Sicks' Stadium. And while the team had a good radio contract from Gene Autry's Golden West Broadcasting, it could not work out a television deal. Road games required renting a transmission line from the phone company. The cost of that line forced the Pilots to quote advertising rates local advertisers were not willing to pay.

The negatives built up as the drumbeat of news kept reminding potential customers the current stadium was a dump and the potential stadium was mired in partisan squabbling. There were also the high prices. As early as the first week of the season, the *Sporting News* noted that the Pilots prices outstripped those of the three other expansion teams.[25] The sports editor of the *Seattle Times* lambasted the prices of beer and Cracker Jacks.[26]

The effect on attendance was predictable, especially in a city struggling to deal with a slump in Boeing aircraft sales. After fighting with the city to get capacity raised to 30,000, or 28,000 or 25,000, the Pilots only managed to draw two crowds over 20,000. And even those could leave fans wondering. The first came on Elks Night on May 28, when 21,679 came out to see manager Joe Schultz give the umpires the wrong lineup card, leading to an Orioles' protest, which wiped out a two-run double by Tommy Davis. The other large crowd (23,657) featured the New York Yankees and a Bat Day promotion.

Seattle Times sportswriter Hy Zimmerman, a strong advocate for major league baseball in Seattle, assigned the blame in clear capital letters. "In short truth, The Establishment—and Seattle has a strong one—has not gotten with major league baseball."[27]

In June, a worried Max Soriano asked for an accounting department projection for the season. The accountants predicted a $2.2 million shortfall. "That's when I knew we were in trouble," he said.[28] The Pilots had hoped for a million in attendance but had projected 850,000 to break even. They wound up with 677,944, leading to a loss estimated at $800,000.[29]

"The team was overleveraged and it was a substantial mistake to have done so," Max reflected a quarter century later. "We were not strong enough financially to properly promote the game in Seattle."[30]

Washington Post sports columnist Bob Addie, after an August visit to Seattle, wrote, "it makes one wonder if perhaps the American League could have been precipitous in granting Seattle a franchise."[31] It made other people wonder, too. While the American League remained positive in public, the commissioner's office was getting worried barely three months into the Pilots' existence. A June 1969 memo on a possible realignment of both leagues had Seattle replaced by Milwaukee.[32]

William Daley entered Seattle's public arena in September on a trip to inspect his investment. He was in town with Cronin to smooth the team's combative relationship with the city over Sicks' Stadium. A reporter asked him if he wanted to back away from an earlier threat that unless attendance improved, the Pilots could be a one-year team. Instead, Daley doubled down. Visibly angry, he reiterated, "Seattle has one more year to prove itself." And he blamed the situation on Seattle reporters. The reaction in the newspapers was quick and severe. "That's upside down, isn't it?" said *Seattle Times* sports editor Georg Meyers, "What we're really doing is giving Daley one more chance."[33]

Daley was not up to it. When the Sorianos asked for more investment, Daley was unwilling.[34] The rumor mill produced stories about a sale to Dallas–Fort Worth interests and then a Milwaukee group. The Dallas sale never amounted to much, but it was revealed later that the Sorianos had reached a "gentlemen's agreement" with the Milwaukee buyers in October.[35]

Local interests finally were activated. Fred Danz, who ran a theater chain, and Edward Carlson of Western International Hotels, put together a group to buy out the Sorianos and all the minority partners. Daley's holdings would drop to 30 percent (or maybe 25 percent). The cost would be $10.5 million (or maybe $10.3 million), and Danz was out raising the cash.[36]

Approval by the American League was described as a "formality," with Cronin saying, "We are happy about the transaction."[37] On December 5, the sale was approved subject to conditions, including upgrading Sicks' Stadium to American League standards by the next season.[38]

Then, the Bank of California called in a $3.5 million loan it had made to the Sorianos. Cronin and the American League owners had known nothing about the loan. Fred Danz suddenly had another $3.5 million to raise. The *Seattle Times's* Hy Zimmerman, who had covered the Pilots since day one, summed it up: "Not only had the league granted the franchise without the apparent full knowledge of the financial structure, it gave blessing to the sale of the club to Danz, again without full study of the monetary pitfalls."[39]

Danz's efforts, built around selling season tickets, faltered, and soon Daley was saying, the "Pilots are up for grabs." A Dallas group was back in the running, he said. Chicago White Sox owner John Allyn agreed. "There's no real leader there," he said of Seattle, adding that he leaned toward Milwaukee getting the team as Dallas did not have a major league stadium.[40]

Edward Carlson stepped forward with a variation—the team would be bought by a nonprofit civic group for $9 million. Carlson's delegation included Washington's governor, the state's attorney general, Seattle's mayor, and other officials to show broad, and political, support. But, the American League owners had a fundamental problem with Carlson's proposal. As Allyn expressed it: "The real hangup is that no one person, group, or firm will be committed to the financial responsibility of the club. They have a lot of fancy-dan plans, but no solidity." [41]

Nevertheless, Allyn and three other American League owners voted for the Carlson group, leaving it one vote short.[42] It was part of baseball's long-standing aversion to community-based ownership. "The non-profit factor, which is completely foreign to baseball, could not fit in," said Cronin.[43] Warren Magnuson, Washington's senior senator, again threatened an examination of baseball's immunity to antitrust law.[44] Along with the Carlson group, the American League pondered a trusteeship under which the league would operate the club or a move to force the Sorianos and Daley to keep operating despite the losses. The Milwaukee and Dallas groups still hovered on the edges.[45]

Ultimately, late on the night of February 11, the league chose a mash-up of the alternatives. It would compel the Sorianos and Daley to keep running the club but would provide them with a $650,000 loan. The cash was to tide them over through spring training and to get the most pressing creditors off their backs.

On the field, the Pilots started spring training in Tempe, Arizona. Off the field, the skirmishing continued. Edward Carlson dropped his bid despite a plea from Commissioner Bowie Kuhn to reapply. On March 16, Seattle and the State of Washington sued Major League Baseball over the move, alleging antitrust violations. There were already two restraining orders in place and the Superior Court of King County had scheduled a hearing for later that week about why the orders should not be amended into an injunction.[46] In Tampa, American League owners pondered Milwaukee and Dallas.

Then, the Sorianos blew it all up. They calculated the league's $650,000 infusion was inadequate to keep them from losing more money. On March 19, Pacific Northwest Sports, Inc., filed for bankruptcy. The American League had the Pilots ripped from their control and placed in the hands of a bankruptcy referee whose duty was to ensure the best deal for the team's many creditors.

On March 31, bankruptcy referee Sidney Volinn made his decision. He had only one viable offer for the team, $10.8 million from Milwaukee Brewers, Inc. The Seattle Pilots, seven days from the opening game of their second season, were going to Milwaukee.[47] A young car dealer there named Bud Selig burst into tears.[48]

Bill Mullins, the historian who delved most deeply into the Pilots' story, summed it up: "The American League owners, in their ardor for the Seattle market, were able to suppress a nagging awareness that they were getting themselves into a sticky situation. They had breached each of the Stanford Research Institute's three nonnegotiable criteria. They had voted a franchise to a city without a major league stadium, in an area that had not pursued a team avidly, and with an ownership group that was, at best, financed by a penny-pincher and, at worst, insufficiently capitalized."[49]

The Seattle debacle also showed the owners' reliance on their antitrust exemption had another dimension. It left them very subject to political pressure. As with Symington when Finley was allowed to leave Kansas City, the willingness of Jackson and Magnuson to support Seattle's desire for a major league team pressured the owners. The potential loss of the exemption and their cartel status was enough to limit the owners' options.

It was, said new commissioner Bowie Kuhn, "a bad chapter for baseball."[50]

More particularly, it was a bad chapter for the American League. The attempt to catch up with the National League's West Coast attendance had stumbled again. The Angels had moved from Dodger Stadium to Anaheim and changed their name from Los Angeles to California. But they had not been able to compete with the Dodgers' established fan connections. In their first decade in their new stadium, the Angels would be out-drawn by the Dodgers by over a million fans seven out of ten times.

In the Bay Area, the A's were barely surpassing the Giants in attendance, despite three straight World Series winners in Oakland and poor Giants clubs in an unattractive stadium. In two of their three World Series years in the early 1970s, the A's did not even attract a million fans. In their first ten years, the Giants had averaged 1.5 million in attendance. In their second decade, with the A's in town, the two teams together averaged under 1.6 million. As predicted by the National Leaguers, the market really was not big enough for two teams yet.

And so, the leagues kept arguing. Wrote Dick Young in the *Sporting News*:

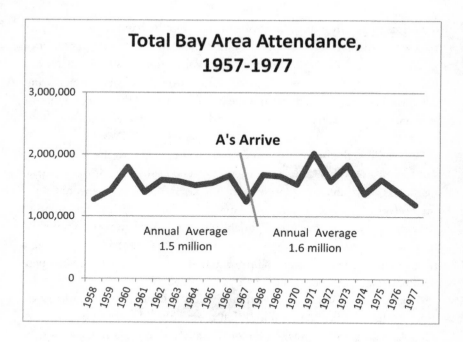

Total Bay Area Attendance, 1957-1977

"If you wonder why the N.L. and A.L. can't get together on such simple things as workable dates for their expansion draft, the answer is this: They're still feudin'. It all goes back to the A.L.'s invasion of Horace Stoneham's back yard by putting a team in Oakland. Now, two teams struggle where one prospered."[51]

And now the Pilots had been dispatched to Milwaukee by a bankruptcy referee. The National League's San Diego franchise, a reflexive move to grab the last available West Coast market when Seattle went to the Americans, had drawn even more poorly than the Pilots. But, even at a third less attendance, the more financially stable ownership chosen by the National League had managed to pay all its bills.[52]

While Milwaukee had the attractions of a well-financed ownership group and an existing major league stadium, the American League had dropped its chance to establish itself in a market with much greater growth potential. In 1970, Milwaukee was only a bit smaller than Seattle, but by 2017, the Seattle metropolitan area's population was twice Milwaukee's. And the American League had passed on Dallas–Fort Worth again.

With the Brewers came two owners who would affect the game and the American League, one for a decade and one for nearly half a century.[53]

Edmund B. Fitzgerald was the scion of a prominent Milwaukee family. His father, Edmund without the B., was all over the city's establishment, most visibly as president and chairman of the Northwestern Mutual Life Insurance Co.[54] Edmund the younger, born in 1926, joined the Marine Corps out of high school, trained as an engineer at the University of Michigan, and went back into the Marines to lead a unit in Korea. He was an impressive figure, six-foot-three and 250 pounds. After his service, he joined Cutler-Hammer, an electronic-controls manufacturing company started by his mother's family. By 1963, he was the company's chief executive officer and a prominent man in Milwaukee civic affairs.

He was also a baseball fan. As the Braves attendance slid lower in the early 1960s, Fitzgerald headed a group of businessmen who tried to pump up sales of season tickets. The Braves, owned by Chicago interests, wanted a local on their board and recruited Fitzgerald. In 1965, he joined an unsuccessful bid to buy the Braves to keep them from leaving. When the Braves moved in 1966, the partners in the bid, which included members from Schlitz Brewing, Kohl's department stores, and Oscar Mayer meatpacking, morphed into Teams, Inc., a corporate vehicle to bring baseball back to Milwaukee.

Once he joined the American League owners' meetings, Fitzgerald quickly took a role in negotiations with the Major League Baseball Players Association, serving as head of the Player Relations Committee. His moderate approach often left him isolated among more militant owners, but the battles with the union that the owners fought through the 1970s would exclude Fitzgerald from taking a lead role on other issues. He would join John Fetzer on the executive council from 1974 through 1981.

Fitzgerald's most constant companion was a man who would stay in baseball's top councils until 2015, ending as the game's commissioner. Allan H. "Bud" Selig had been born to immigrant parents in Milwaukee in 1934. His father built a successful car sales business while his mother was a schoolteacher—and baseball fan. Selig began attending games of the minor league Milwaukee Brewers in the late 1930s and soon became a diehard fan. The Braves arrived in Milwaukee when Selig was eighteen and a freshman at the University of Wisconsin. His fandom deepened through his college years and two years in the army as the Braves progressed from promise to two consecutive World Series appearances.

He moved into the family car dealership, took advantage of the season tickets, and quickly joined Fitzgerald's efforts to sell more tickets. He also joined the unsuccessful bid to buy the Braves. On April 12, 1966, the day the Braves played their first game in Atlanta, Selig pulled his car to the side of the road, tuned in a Pittsburgh radio station, and cried.[55] After the departure, he, even more than Fitzgerald, began to make the contacts and haunt the halls of major league owners' meetings seeking to bring a team to Milwaukee. He reincorporated Teams, Inc., as the Milwaukee Brewers Baseball Club to give the movement a focus.[56]

In fact, baseball consumed him. By 1976, Selig's first wife, Donna, filed for divorce after almost two decades of marriage. "From the day that Bud became involved in baseball . . . he divorced me and married baseball," she told the court. The judge granted the divorce.[57]

In the beginning of Selig's crusade, it was awkward. He made his first foray to a major league meeting at the Edgewater Beach Hotel in nearby Chicago in October 1965. Since he was not an owner entitled to the conference room, all he could do was hang around the hallways and lobby, always ready to make his pitch. "We'd look behind a potted palm, and there would be Buddy," said future Blue Jays president Peter Bavasi, then a Los Angeles Dodgers executive.[58] "I was treated like I had leprosy," Selig said.[59]

Selig, in turn, was not impressed with the group he joined around the American League owners' table. "When I first got into baseball, I was really disappointed in a lot of the people, a lot of the owners I had read about. There was a lack of unity, a lack of leadership, a lack of planning."[60]

But not John Fetzer, a man Selig deeply admired. The younger man scheduled his return flights from owners' meetings so he could soak up the Detroit owner's impressions and theories. "To me," said Selig, "John Fetzer is what this business is all about. He's everything an owner should be. Believe me, he has no peer in this game when it comes to respect."[61]

Selig's manner in this crusade would foreshadow his management methods over his decades in the game. He was incredibly persistent, a master of networks and schmoozing, confrontational with no one except the players' union, and always willing to do the committee work that other owners shunned. Within a few years, he was serving on the board of the MLB Promotion Corp. and the relocation and expansion committee.[62]

Still, Selig's ascendancy would take time. "In the 1970s," he said, "I was just another face in the hotel conference room."[63]

He was joining a new group of owners from both the 1969 expansion teams and turnover at the existing franchises, a group that would have to navigate the fallout of the Seattle fiasco.

CHAPTER ELEVEN

The New Guard — Twelve Men at a Table

T he owners who would have to deal with the fallout of letting Charlie Finley move to Oakland and botching the expansion into Seattle were coming on the scene.

If anointing the owners of the expansion franchise in Seattle was a lesson in how not to do things, choosing the new owners of the Kansas City Royals was a test case for getting it right. The American League had a city that wanted major league baseball. It had an adequate stadium and the bond issue to build a new one. And the quest to keep the A's in town had spawned four groups who either had tried to buy out Finley or were willing to fund an expansion team.

They also got the process right. They heard pitches from all four groups, examined their backgrounds, and probed their finances. And then they made the right choice.

Ewing Marion Kauffman, then fifty-one, had risen from a hardscrabble Missouri farm to a company that made him a billionaire.[1] He needed no partners to come up with the American League's $5.35 million initiation fee.

From his youth, Kauffman had an uncanny facility with numbers, a talent nurtured by his father. John Kauffman used routine farm work and automobile trips to challenge his son with increasingly complex puzzles. At eleven, Kauffman was diagnosed with endocarditis, damage to a heart valve. The only known cure at the time was total bed rest, so he spent a year on his back missing school but reading voraciously from the local library. He would read dozens of books a week and felt he had learned more from them than he would have in a classroom. More important, he formed the habits of a reader and, throughout his life, when entering a new field or encountering a challenge, he would respond by reading everything he could find on the subject.

After high school in Kansas City, Kauffman spent two years at a junior college, but family finances prevented continuing his education. He worked as a laundry delivery supervisor and stumbled in a bid to sell life insurance. When

World War II broke out, he quickly joined the navy and was trained as a quartermaster, the sailor who steers the ship. With his habit formed, Kauffman quickly read up on navigation and impressed the captain by insisting the ship's navigation officer was dangerously wrong one night. He was proven right and the captain made him an officer and encouraged his curiosity.

During his navy years, Kauffman nurtured his mathematical skills, using his appetite for competition, risk, and the availability of people less skilled at the poker table. He emerged from the war having made about $90,000 from gambling.[2] That money was spent relatively quickly on a house and a year of easy living before settling on a job selling drugs for an Illinois company.

Kauffman's selling talents were superb. "It's easy to like him and a little risky to hear him out," said a friend, "he is very persuasive." The sales skills were soon married to his relentless research on pharmaceuticals and their potential uses. The job came with no salary or benefits, simply a 20 percent commission. In less than a year, he was made a regional sales manager where he picked up 3 percent of the sales of his employees. Within two years, he was making more than the president of the company. His success led to reductions in his commissions and the size of his territories. And that led him, in 1950, to found Marion Laboratories, with several thousand dollars in savings and investments from a few people he knew around Kansas City.

The company's name reflected Kauffman's shrewdness. He was going to keep selling pharmaceuticals. Even though he would use the evocative word "Laboratories" in the company title, he was not going to involve his company in the often costly research for new drugs. He would manufacture existing formulas or modify them slightly. He chose to use his middle name as the corporate title because he felt introducing himself as Ewing Kauffman of Kauffman Laboratories or Ewing Laboratories would "have had a certain connotation of smallness."[3]

At first, it was a very small operation, as Kauffman stuffed pill bottles in his mother's basement at night, while selling during the day. He soon expanded. By 1968, Marion Laboratories maintained a 125-acre campus.[4]

Kauffman's philosophy as an owner was to recognize that all of a company's employees contributed to its success and should be rewarded for that success. Bonuses and stock options were readily available, although demands for performance were stringent. In one promotion, a sales rep's wife got a check from Kauffman for every week that she would swear he was calling on customers at 8 a.m. and still doing it at 6 p.m. Sales calls increased 20 percent.[5] Reporters found it easy to discover secretaries and janitors who had substantial retirement funds built around company stock.

When he sold Marion Laboratories to Dow Chemical in 1989, Kauffman walked away with over a billion dollars. At least 300 employees who had been able to handle Kauffman's rigorous pressure to perform became millionaires.

In baseball, he would mostly turn over management of the team to professionals. But he soon introduced wrinkles of his own. He shared his personal income statements with the players and offered them professional help with their finances.[6] He pioneered an academy where the Royals would take promising athletes with limited or nonexistent baseball experience and use innovative techniques to see if they could be developed. The system produced All-Star second baseman Frank White, but not a great deal more and was dropped after several years. Still, it indicated Kauffman's willingness to try new ideas.

On December 4, 1968, American League owners showed they had yet to absorb the lesson about weak finances that the Seattle Pilots story should have taught them. The American League still thought the Pilots' problems were with a city refusing to make promised improvements in Sicks' Stadium. So, they rather quickly approved the purchase of the Washington Senators franchise by Bob Short.

That expansion team had drifted since its birth in 1961, improving neither on the field nor at the gate. Off the field, the original ten partners had narrowed to two. Only James Johnston and James Lemon remained, each owning 50 percent. The partners remained quietly committed to propping up the team despite steady losses.[7] Then, Johnston died in late 1967 and Lemon, his longtime business partner—but not as committed to baseball as Johnston—said he was going to sell.

Short approached the American League with a strong resume. His basic business was trucking and hotels based in Minneapolis–St. Paul. But he had owned the Los Angeles Lakers, ran them successfully, and sold them to Jack Kent Cooke at a substantial profit. He had also moved the Lakers from the Twin Cities to Los Angeles, which could have been a warning sign. He had run for office, unsuccessfully, twice in Minnesota and, as a Hubert Humphrey political protégé, was the treasurer of the Democratic National Committee, all solid credentials in the nation's capital.

Short said he had the $9.4 million he needed to buy out Johnston's estate and Lemon. And the money was duly delivered. But only later was it revealed that only $1,000 of that money came out of Short's pocket. In December 1968,

American League owners unanimously approved Short's purchase.[8] A prospectus distributed to potential purchasers showed Short's cost had been the $1,000 fee to establish a corporation in Washington, D.C. All the rest had been borrowed, much of it with collateral provided by Short's other enterprises. Like all major league franchise purchases, it took tremendous advantage of the ability to depreciate the value of player contracts, and any losses in Washington could easily be used to offset the tax bills of Short's other corporations. All the transactions were legal, but they pointed to a financial structure that could not be sustained at the attendance level a team of the Senators' quality was likely to produce. In fact, one of the bank lenders had insisted that $400,000 be added to the purchase price to insure enough working capital.[9]

Bob Short could make a good first impression. Wrote one Washington columnist: "There are few sports entrepreneurs as engaging as Short. He is articulate, not above enjoying a laugh at his own expense, basically ingenuous and honest, but somehow imprisoned in a boomerang compulsion for public approval. 'By birth I like the limelight,' Short said, 'I prefer recognition to anonymity.'"[10]

Short knew he would have to prop up the Senators' finances. And he quickly unveiled that curious mix of boasting, promotions, and threats that would characterize his three years in Washington. A month after his purchase, he was pursuing a radio contract and promising a more aggressive marketing approach. "I can round up a girls' team and draw 500,000. That's what the attendance was here last year," he said. Then quickly removing the sword from the cake, he added, "If they don't want the Senators here—if there's no radio, no box-office support—then Dallas or Milwaukee or some other places do."[11]

Short set out to raise revenues with a heavy emphasis on publicity and promotions. He talked the famously irascible Ted Williams into managing, which was not that hard, and into dealing with the press, which Williams hated. With admiration for Charlie Finley, Short's promotions blossomed. He even had the Senators in white shoes. In his first year, Williams taught the woebegone Senators to hit and counselled the pitchers on how to out-think hitters. The team won more than it lost for the first time in its history and attendance rose 68 percent to 918,106.

Short did not stay with professional help in the front office, making himself the general manager, which proved disastrous. Stan Bregman, the Senators' general counsel, said Short clearly had not been following baseball. "He used to call the umpires referees and the manager the coach when he first came in.

That was his knowledge of baseball," Bregman said.[12] After the performance and attendance jump of 1969, 1970 showed declines. Short moved to gain some publicity. He paid Curt Flood $110,000 to come back from a self-imposed exile while the outfielder pursued a case against Major League Baseball to break the reserve clause. Flood managed to make it into only thirteen games.

With similar motives, but even worse results, Short traded shortstop Eddie Brinkman and third baseman Aurelio Rodriguez to the Tigers for Denny Mc-Lain, who in 1968 had won thirty-one games and dominated baseball. Flood only cost the team money, the McLain trade cost them the solid left half of the infield. McLain lost twenty-two games and was clearly washed up. The 1971 Senators fell even further in the standings. Attendance was down to 655,156. Short's reputation with Senators' fans was not improved when he acknowledged contemplating a 1970 run for governor of Minnesota.[13]

Short was another nail in the coffin of the Nationals' contempt for the Americans. At one joint meeting where Short sought help, Walter O'Malley cut him off. "When you can buy the chips, you play. When you can't, don't."[14]

As with Finley and Dewey Soriano, Short kept up running public fights with local authorities, especially the Washington, D.C., Armory Board, which operated his stadium and wanted its rent. Short was not paying and wanted concessions, if not forgiveness. And, given Short's background, he made things political, charging that a Nixon administration official in the Bureau of the Budget had killed relief from the Armory Board.[15]

And, again like Finley and Soriano, he was not much happier with the business community. At a Board of Trade luncheon, he wavered between pleas for more season-ticket sales and not so subtle threats. The Senators, he told a "sparsely attended luncheon," were "not going to leave here. But unless we get support it is going to be like Seattle. There is no way we can operate this year without community support."[16]

Short's financial position was clearly worse. He had borrowed heavily to buy the team, the cash flow was not good, and the bank was getting antsy. He claimed he was getting no help from his fellow owners, from the Armory Board, or from anyone else. In a late-night phone call to Kuhn, he insisted again and again that despite the desires of Kuhn, fellow owners, President Nixon, and others, he had the clear right to move the team if he wanted to. "Nobody can keep me in Washington, not Nixon, not Cronin, not Kuhn," Kuhn reported Short saying, "I don't give a goddamn if they stick you with the antitrust laws."[17]

Short and Kuhn agreed on his financial position. He had paid too much for the team and he was in deep financial trouble.[18] They differed on the solution. Short wanted to move the team or get back what he had paid for the team plus his losses, a figure he put at $12 million. Kuhn wanted to keep the team in Washington, where he had grown up and once spent summers working as a scoreboard boy at Griffith Stadium. He did not think Short could get the $12 million figure.

Although this was theoretically an American League issue, Kuhn got thoroughly involved. He talked to Willard Marriott of the hotel chain, which was headquartered in Washington. He talked to other local wealthy individuals. Nationally, he approached the big three automakers, plus Coca Cola, Pepsi Cola, Philip Morris, Gillette, NBC, and CBS, among others. The only possibility who stepped forward was Joseph Danzansky.[19]

Danzansky headed the Giant Supermarket chain in the Washington, D.C., area. He assured Kuhn that he and his partners could raise the $9.4 million price tag Kuhn had put on the franchise. But he could not put together a financial package that impressed the other American League owners. He said he had two possible partners but would only name one of them. When pressed for the other name, Danzansky revealed he had only met the man the previous night. That was the death knell for Washington.[20] "It was pointed out that the inadequacy of working capital and the stated unwillingness of Danzansky and his colleagues to commit additional funds made it probable that the league would be faced with the same questions one or two years from now in Washington," summarized the minutes of the September 21, 1971, meeting that turned down the local bid.[21]

At the same meeting, the American League gave in to Short's desire to move the team to Dallas–Fort Worth, where the local authorities had offered a package that made Short financially whole. Cronin, who had played for the original Senators, put aside his feelings because he knew the American League needed this market to offset the more successful National League.[22] Baltimore's Jerry Hoffberger, worried a National League team might move into Washington and compete with him for regional fans, voted against the move. So did the White Sox's John Allyn, who was upset at the financing structures, both in Washington and Texas.

Summed up by Shirley Povich, the *Washington Post*'s iconic sports columnist, "There is nothing wrong with Robert E. Short except his sense of values."[23]

Thus, in the four years from allowing the Athletics to move to Oakland to allowing the expansion Senators to become the Texas Rangers, a quarter of the American League's teams had relocated, one out of bankruptcy and another not far from it. "If baseball was going to repair its wounded image, the time had come to stop moving franchises. We had moved enough of them in the last two decades to make a troop of gypsies jealous. If the fans were going to start believing in us again, they had to be convinced we were intent upon franchise stability," said the commissioner.[24]

In Chicago, there was a quiet transition in December 1969, as Arthur Allyn Jr. sold his shares in the White Sox. "Initially, many of the owners [had] regarded him as a dynamic new personality, a definite asset," wrote *Chicago Sun-Times* baseball writer Jerome Holtzman, "Later, many of them were to indicate they wished he would go away."[25] He did not go that far. Control of the team passed to his brother, John, after Arthur Jr. despaired of ever making the White Sox a profitable venture.

After Lafayette College and a World War II stint in the navy, John had spent his career in the brokerage business, originally with his father's firm. He loved golf and played in tournaments around the country. While Arthur Jr. had butterflies, John developed a collection of muzzle-loading rifles and muskets, which he worked on in his own machine shop. To Chicago sportswriters, he had been the quiet man smoking a pipe and standing in the back at White Sox events.

Now, he had two revival projects—the White Sox and the brokerage firm, which merged with Francis I. duPont & Co. in 1970. DuPont had suffered a poor year in 1969 and John was made chairman of the board to revive the partnership.[26] By 1974, after further losses and despite a capital injection from J. Ross Perot, duPont went out of business, taking the remains of Arthur Allyn & Co. with it.[27]

The White Sox fared somewhat better, although not for long. Arthur Allyn's sale had been accelerated by a $500,000 loss in 1969 and offers from Edmund Fitzgerald and Bud Selig to buy the team for Milwaukee and from Dallas billionaire Lamar Hunt seeking a team for his city. John was determined to keep the White Sox in Chicago.[28]

In 1970, as John dealt with duPont's problems, the White Sox suffered attendance of 495,355, the worst in the American League. The second worst, the expansion Kansas City Royals, drew 40 percent more fans. There would be a revival of performance and attendance in 1972, when Wilbur Wood and Dick Allen led the team to second place, but by 1975, the White Sox attendance was back to second worst in the league and barely 13,000 ahead of the league-worst Minnesota Twins. They were the only two teams to draw less than one million fans.

Ultimately, said his general manager, Roland Hemond, he did "not have much to work with financially." He also interfered with Hemond's choices in the amateur draft, seeking to limit bonus payments.[29] John railed at the Chicago newspapers and fired announcer Harry Caray, who had the temerity to describe how badly the White Sox were playing.

Given the struggles of both the brokerage firm and the team, John Allyn could rarely raise his eyes to consider leaguewide matters, although he quickly emerged as a "forceful" presence as the Seattle Pilots situation unraveled.[30] He would irritate his fellow owners by not strictly adhering to their spring training lockout of players in 1972. He just "wasn't very vocal . . . didn't work with the majority," Hemond said.[31]

Over in Cleveland, it was a rerun of a seemingly perpetual soap opera. The Indians were struggling. Attendance averaged less than 700,000 for Vernon Stouffer's first five years of ownership, and the team had not crossed the million mark since 1959. By 1971, Stouffer said he wasn't looking to leave Cleveland but he did seize on an offer from New Orleans, which would invest $3.5 million in exchange for thirty games a year to be played in the Superdome, expected to open in 1974.[32]

In December, the American League owners, with Charlie Finley leading the charge, dashed Stouffer's hopes, arguing that such a move would alienate Cleveland fans and hurt the visitors' shares of the gate.[33] Within days, a group fronted by former Indians All-Star Al Rosen, but with most of the money provided by a shipbuilding magnate named George M. Steinbrenner, made an offer. Steinbrenner and Vernon Stouffer's son Jim, high school classmates, had negotiated a deal for $8.6 million. Vernon Stouffer nixed the deal, claiming the team was worth at least $10 million.[34]

By March 1972, Stouffer was forced to reduce his price and the Indians were sold to a partnership led by Nick Mileti for $9 million.[35] Born in 1931, Mileti had attended Bowling Green University and Ohio State University's law school. He already owned basketball's Cleveland Cavaliers, hockey's minor league Cleveland Barons, and the city's most powerful radio station. Within two days, the American League rejected Mileti's bid, focusing on the financial structure of the deal and citing their experiences with undercapitalized owners Dewey Soriano and Bob Short. They were also upset that Mileti intended to raise money through a public stock offering rather than by adding partners.[36] Mileti dropped the public sale and raised additional capital from new partners. The sale was approved two weeks later.[37]

Mileti was a short, dark promoter with a nod to Las Vegas in his speeches. "People wanted to move this team. I tell you we took over to keep the Indians here. Before us, they were going, baby, going."[38] Actually, it turned out Mileti was going as well. The American League owners had been right the first time. He had borrowed heavily to finance his share of ownership while building a new arena for his basketball and hockey teams at the same time.[39] Ted Bonda, the partner who succeeded him, said Mileti's finances were built on "marshmallows," and the banks had moved to force a change.[40]

Ted Bonda had joined Mileti owning barely 1 percent of the stock, but he was the one who stuck.[41] Born in 1917, Bonda could never afford college, although he would eventually be chair of both the Ohio Board of Regents and the Cleveland Board of Education. As a young man, he had partnered with future senator Howard Metzenbaum to develop parking lots near the Cleveland Airport. They eventually took the business to airports nationwide and added airport hotels to their developments. Both men became multimillionaires and Bonda would donate heavily to Metzenbaum's political campaigns.

As a young man, Bonda was nicknamed "Mopy" for his hangdog look. As an older man, he would show up at Cleveland's lakeside Municipal Stadium in his custom speedboat. His Metzenbaum connections would lead to donations to other Democratic candidates and a place on Richard Nixon's Enemies List.[42]

As president of the Indians, Bonda would play a major role in hiring Frank Robinson as the major leagues' first Black manager, but he would spend much of his time looking for someone to buy out his partnership. Given his relative light weight in the partnership and the Indians parlous state though the 1970s and 1980s, Bonda exercised little influence in American League councils, especially after Gabe Paul returned in 1977.

The American League's new owners tried another tactic to fan interest. Offense in major league baseball had hit a low point. Batting averages and the all-important runs-per-game measurement were at levels not seen since the

Deadball era of the early twentieth century. In 1968, games in both leagues averaged fewer than seven runs per game (total for both teams) for the first time since 1908. Bob Gibson set a record for lowest earned run average and Don Drysdale set one for consecutive shutout innings. It was the talk of baseball. Leonard Koppett did an extensive analysis in the *Sporting News* and concluded the problem was the rules change that had expanded the definition of the strike zone beginning in 1963. Offense had been sliding ever since.[43] More important to the owners was that attendance dropped for both leagues that season, something that had not happened since 1952.

"This is getting to be too much of a pitcher's game," said Minnesota Twins owner Calvin Griffith. "People don't come to see pitchers pitch. They come to see hitters hit."[44] Forgotten was that in all the high-scoring eras that the American League owners wanted to return to, the pitchers had hit for themselves. The "problem" of low scoring had clearly arisen elsewhere in the lineup.

Fans may have bemoaned the drop in runs, but for the owners, the attendance drop was the nub of the issue. The discussion of what to do included shrinking the strike zone, lowering the height of the mound from as much as fifteen inches, banning twilight games, moving the pitcher's mound further from the plate, legalizing the spitball, moving fences in, and reducing the resilience of the baseballs.

One idea that returned to the discussion was replacing the pitcher in the batting lineup with a person of greater hitting skills—a designated hitter. It was not a new idea. Henry Chadwick had discussed the idea as early as 1888 and Connie Mack had proposed a similar rule in 1906.[45] In fact, the National League had approved a similar rule in 1928 only to have the American League refuse to go along.[46]

At the winter meetings after the 1968 season, it was reversed. The National League did not want the DH rule, but both leagues agreed to return the strike zone to its 1962 definition and to mandate that mounds could not be more than ten inches higher than the surrounding infield.

It worked. The number of runs per game rose 19 percent, to above eight, in both leagues in 1969, the highest level since before the strike zone expansion. In 1970, the measure was even higher, with the National League going over nine runs per game. But then, offense in the American League started to slip again. By 1972, the metric was back under seven runs per game while the National League remained close to eight.

The National League numbers make the American League's decline seem more of a statistical blip or a phenomenon caused by circumstances beyond

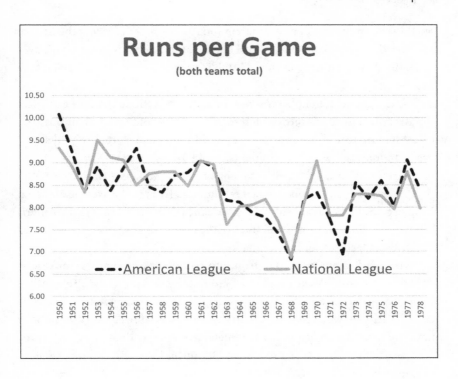

Runs per Game
(both teams total)

the rules. But the American League owners focused on their true concern. Leaguewide attendance fell by another 430,000 in 1972 and they now trailed the Nationals by more than 4 million. Pushed by the Yankees, where Lee MacPhail had been a strong proponent for years, and newcomer Bud Selig, the American League moved to adopt the designated hitter rule. The National League resisted, but in January 1973, Kuhn broke the tie and allowed the Americans to proceed with their rule change alone. It was the first significant difference between the leagues' rules in over half a century.

By 1976, the designated hitter had been in use for four seasons. *Sporting News* columnist Leonard Koppett, who was always interested in statistics, wrote: "The similarity between the American League, using the DH, and the National, without it, is astounding. It implies that the DH has surprisingly little effect" on offense.[47]

As far as the Americans were concerned, it worked. Runs-per-game surged over 8.5 in 1973 and leaguewide attendance rose by over two million. Less noticed was that the Nationals also rose to 8.3 runs-per-game and their attendance rose by 1.1 million. In 1974, despite the DH rule, the National League would score more runs per game than the American, reinforcing the idea of the Americans' reacting to statistical blips. But the rule was in place and over time, the American League would establish a steady, albeit small, advantage in scoring.

The designated hitter ploy was not the solution to the attendance gap. After the American League's 1967 switch to report seats sold rather than turnstile count had narrowed the gap, the National League had started to pull ahead again. In 1965, the National League had sold 45 percent more seats to its average game. With the statistical sleight of hand, the figure was down to 1.7 percent by the 1968 season. Then, it rebounded. By 1971, the average National League game had 41.8 percent more attendance than the average in the American League. The league was still stuck in the rut of less attractive players, older stadiums and, above all, smaller markets.

American League teams had begun to recruit and develop more African American players. "We've caught up," crowed the Indians' Gabe Paul in 1966, implicitly admitting a problem American Leaguers had been reluctant to concede.[48] Parity between the leagues on that front would really not come about until the 1970s, but at least Charlie Finley's Athletics, with exciting, high-profile stars, such as Reggie Jackson, John Odom, and Vida Blue, were changing perceptions.

Despite the new franchises, the American League still was struggling with its stadiums problem. In the period from 1965 through 1975, the American League added modern parks in Anaheim and Kansas City. The National League added six new stadia—in Houston, Atlanta, St. Louis, Pittsburgh, Cincinnati, and Philadelphia. The average American League park was over thirty-one years old. The average National League facility was thirteen years old. And while many of the new National League parks would come to be reviled justifiably as soulless, dual-purpose concrete donuts in later decades, they added a splash of modernity to the Nationals during this period.

As a *Sporting News* editorial noted in August 1966, new parks were a clear indicator of attendance success. Earlier that month, the expansion Angels, in their new Anaheim Stadium, had become the first American League franchise that season to draw one million fans. Six National League teams had already done so, and the oldest park among these teams, Candlestick Park in San Francisco, had opened in 1960.[49]

The American League's big change came in the Big Apple, but it started in Cleveland. William Paley of CBS had tired of his investment in the Yankees. CBS prided itself on being the "Tiffany Network." It had bought the Yankees because they were the "Tiffany" of baseball franchises. But what was true in 1964, was no longer true. Buying Tiffany meant buying at the top of the market. Michael Burke's work had softened the Yankees' image and would lead to significant aid from New York City for its aging stadium, but he had not produced success on the field. The team had not won a pennant since 1964 and could not see one on the horizon. Even the expansion Mets had won a World Series since then. In 1972, Yankee attendance fell below one million for the first time since World War II. The Mets drew more than twice as many.

Paley suggested to Burke that it was time to sell the team and that he was willing to sell it for a lower price to Burke. Burke began to search around for partners to provide the cash. One of the people he talked to was Gabe Paul. Paul was restless with the faltering Indians franchise and knew George Steinbrenner from the group Vernon Stouffer had rejected in December 1971.

Steinbrenner's failure to buy the Indians in late 1971 had created an itch and he jumped at the chance to scratch it. The deal was finalized in January 1973 and the price was $10 million, well under the $14 million CBS had paid for the team. Burke and CBS scrambled to explain that amortization and tax benefits meant they really had not lost money. Although records are incomplete, it would appear to be the first time a franchise had been sold for less than its purchase price since 1943, when the National League purchased the bankrupt Philadelphia Phillies.[50]

Steinbrenner's partnership included thirty-two others, with Steinbrenner as the managing partner and 15.5 percent of the shares.[51] Within a decade, after much shuffling of partners, he would own over 50 percent. Still, even in this early period, there was no question who was in charge. Said John McMullen, one of the partners, "There's nothing so limited as being a limited partner of George's."[52]

Born in 1930, George Steinbrenner came from a fifth-generation shipbuilding family in the Cleveland area.[53] While wealthy, George's father required his son run an egg-raising-and-selling business from a young age. He attended Culver Academy in Indiana and Williams College in Massachusetts, majoring in English literature. A hurdler at Williams, he was fascinated by coaching and, after two years running Air Force sports programs at a base near Columbus,

Ohio, he went to Ohio State for a master's degree in physical education. That led to coaching football at the high school and college level before his father called him home to work at Kinsman Marine Transit.

Steinbrenner could not stay away from sports. In 1960, he angered his father by selling his Kinsman stock to buy a controlling share of the Cleveland Pipers, a top semipro team that had moved into the fledgling American Basketball League. The Pipers eventually failed, but Steinbrenner established his reputation in Cleveland business circles by paying off all his partners' losses in full. He even bought an ore boat with his own money and used its profits to make the paybacks.[54]

After paying off the Pipers, Steinbrenner spent the next decade as a casual sports fan until the opportunities to buy the Indians, and then the Yankees, appeared. He devoted his energies to building up the family business, merging with American Shipbuilding, and then running the larger company. He could be a demanding, even tyrannical boss, firing many a secretary, but at times hiring them back and throwing in a bonus. He was very involved with charitable institutions around Cleveland.

In New York, the dual personality that was George Steinbrenner emerged quickly. At the news conference to announce the purchase, Steinbrenner gave strident notice he would stay away from the day-to-day operations of running the Yankees, citing the demands of American Shipbuilding. He also brought Gabe Paul with him as part of the partnership. Paul was given a vague title, but his resume implied overlap with the roles of both Burke and general manager Lee MacPhail.

Within four months, Burke was ousted, leaving baseball for good. Steinbrenner was in New York more and more and the calls from the owners' box came frequently. He complained about manager Ralph Houk's decisions, ordered haircuts for players, and forced the release of veteran outfielder Johnny Callison after he dropped a fly ball.[55]

At the end of the first season, the veteran Houk resigned as manager and the highly respected MacPhail took the job of American League president. The exodus of Yankee officials had only begun.

In Dallas–Fort Worth, Short bailed after a couple of years, or about the time the tax advantages of writing off the player contracts expired. The buyer was a coalition led by Brad Corbett, a transplanted New Yorker who had made a fortune in the plastic pipe business.

Corbett, who was born in 1937, claimed he had played briefly in the minors before working his way through Wagner College.[56] He went to work for Allied Chemical as a salesman and, within a couple of years, struck out on his own. With help from a Fort Worth suburb hungry for jobs, and loans from the Small Business Administration and local banks, he started a company called Universal Pipe and Plastics in 1967. In 1971, he merged UPPI into Robintech, a metal fabricator. By mid-1975, Robintech was reporting $97 million in sales and $11.8 million in annual profits.

Corbett's appearance invited hyperbole. He was like "Chuckles the Clown," wrote *Texas Monthly*'s Gary Cartwright.[57] A heavyset man with instant charm, the business success made Corbett's thoughts turn to baseball. His coalition contained monied men from around the Dallas–Fort Worth area but Corbett remained fully in control after the May 1974 purchase. He was an antsy presence. One reporter described a flight in Corbett's private jet as he "stands, sits, crouches, lies down, and barely stops short of rolling down the windows." Corbett said he did not play golf because he "didn't have the attention span for it."[58]

Corbett employed baseball veterans such as Eddie Robinson, Dr. Bobby Brown, and Dan O'Brien in his front office, but ultimately he was his own general manager. His trades sometimes worked and often didn't. They provided optimism each year, as did a parade of managers. There were six in Corbett's six years. Eddie Stanky lasted for a day. Billy Martin was fired after Corbett broke Short's promise that Martin could send and recall players from the minors at Martin's discretion. He was constantly on the phone. He paced his office, a long phone cord trailing. "With his bumpkin haircut, paunch and Daddy Warbucks cigar, Corbett looked something like W. C. Fields," said Cartwright.[59]

For all the tumult, the team barely broke .500 over the six years Corbett oversaw the creation of the rosters. He was consistently incapable of consistency. He consulted his teenage son on trades and celebrated with him when they came together.[60] He jousted with local reporters. His sense of humor ran to hiring a prostitute to dress as a nun and show up in the room of a hospitalized Gabe Paul. The solidly married Paul's wife had just gone downstairs when the woman arrived and Paul was able to usher her out.[61]

On the league level, he joined the newer group of owners—Jerold Hoffberger of Baltimore, George Steinbrenner of the New York Yankees, Bill Veeck of the Chicago White Sox, Gene Autry of the California Angels, and Finley.[62] He was appalled at Gussie Busch of the Cardinals because of Busch's inability to adjust to a new era. He scorned owners who were not self-made.[63]

He became involved in the first battle to fire Bowie Kuhn, while denying reports he was the "ringleader" of the group.[64] The group failed in that attempt, but his impetuosity left a bad taste. "Corbett did not stand on the bank and dip his toe into the water to judge the conditions," wrote *Dallas Time-Herald* columnist Blackie Sherrod. "He jumped in head first and thrashed around trying to prove he could swim with the big boys."[65]

As Robintech fell into financial trouble in the late 1970s, his board of directors became concerned he was spending too much Robintech time and Robintech money on Rangers' business.[66] The company had to take out large loans and give stock options to a German firm that gave it the option to take control.[67] Concerned and frustrated, Corbett started thinking about getting out. "I'm selling this team because it's killing me. They're dogs on the field and they're dogs off the field."[68]

The American League finally had its beachhead in the long-neglected, growing market of Dallas–Fort Worth, but it was not giving fans a team with performance based on consistent and sound management. As Corbett's tenure neared its end, the *Fort Worth Star-Telegram*, owned by one of the Rangers minority stockholders, editorialized: "The Rangers establishment, headed by majority owner Brad Corbett and executive vice-president Eddie Robinson, has made the Rangers look more like a circus run amok than a major league franchise. . . . The Texas Rangers have become the laughing stock of the nation."[69]

As the league moved to solve its Seattle problem, the jigsaw puzzle of franchise moves and ownership groups would be handled by these new owners.

CHAPTER TWELVE

Expansion Three

The Pilots might have become the Milwaukee Brewers, but Seattle had not gone away. That issue, its ramifications, and the fallout of earlier decisions, especially by the American League owners, would occupy a great deal of time before a new team could emerge in the Pacific Northwest.

By October 1970, the City of Seattle, the State of Washington, and King County had sued the American League. The cases moved slowly. Partly, this was tacking between state and federal courts, the accumulation of depositions and documents, the addition and removal of co-defendants, and other legal maneuvering. But it also gave the Seattle group the leverage and the time to work out a satisfactory deal with the league.

The resolution of the Seattle lawsuit would involve a swirl of conflicting desires of both leagues and of individual teams. It would be caught up in the financial difficulties and possible moves of teams in both leagues. It would bring additional focus to the problems of the overcrowded San Francisco Bay Area. It would return baseball to the thorny issues of expansion, all wrapped around Commissioner Bowie Kuhn's desire to get a team back into Washington, D.C. As such, the American League worked with less autonomy than it had in earlier expansion negotiations, which is ironic since it wound up going its own way. And, as usual, Charlie Finley's wandering eye would be part of the picture.

Hanging over all these issues were the leagues' relations with the Major League Baseball Players Association, which won the *Messersmith* arbitration case in December 1975. That raised the specter of free agency for players and occupied much of the owners' thinking time.

The complications beyond Seattle first appeared at the other end of the West Coast and in the National League. San Diego Padres owner C. Arnholt Smith had run into financial problems outside baseball. His tuna canning empire, real estate interests, and other investments were losing money, and he was using his United States National Bank to prop them up with sweetheart loans. In October 1973, the bank failed and Smith was sued by the Internal Revenue Service for $23 million in back taxes. He would eventually be convicted of embezzlement.

While the Padres were money losers, they were only indirectly involved in Smith's shenanigans. Still, they were an asset and Smith needed cash. In May 1973, Smith signed a letter of intent to sell the team to Joseph Danzansky, the Washington, D.C., supermarket executive who had failed to short-circuit Bob Short's moving the Senators to Texas. Danzansky said he intended to move the Padres to Washington.[1]

Danzansky's bid stalled over the summer, with National League owners expressing concern about San Diego's threat of a lawsuit over the stadium lease, whether a team really could succeed in Washington, D.C., and Danzansky's refusal to indemnify the league if the city's lawsuit succeeded.[2] In October, when they gathered in a second attempt to approve the sale, Smith muddied the waters by saying he had found new investors and would stay in San Diego.[3] By December, Smith announced he had agreed to sell the team to a partnership led by Marjorie Everett, the owner of Hollywood Park race track in the Los Angeles area. She planned to keep the team in San Diego and had worked out changes in the stadium lease with the city.[4]

Everett's bid would soon join Danzansky's in the discard pile. On January 9, 1974, she failed to get the nine votes needed for approval. Speculation focused on her testimony in a corruption trial of a federal judge in Chicago. Her lawyer charged the National League with not wanting either San Diego or Washington, but was aiming to move them to Seattle, Toronto, or New Orleans. National League president Chub Feeney confused things further by saying the Washington move was not dead yet.[5]

The next day, however, the head of fast-food giant McDonald's read of Everett's rejection. He decided to make a bid, and he had the funds to do it without partners. By January 25, Ray Kroc had sealed the deal with Smith and six days later he was approved by the National League owners.[6] One possibility of satisfying Seattle's lawsuit or Kuhn's desire for a team in Washington had been taken off the board.

Up the California coast, Charlie Finley and the Bay Area attendance problems were another fault line generating tremors throughout the system. On the field, the A's won their division every year from 1971 to 1975 and picked up three World Series victories in the middle of that streak. Off the field, the

American League's precipitous move to the Bay Area was not producing the financial bonanza he or his league's other owners had anticipated. In those five years, the A's broke the million mark for attendance only twice, and then barely. After two straight World Series victories, they finished eleventh of twelve American League teams in attendance.

Bay Area reporters wrote that Finley was eyeing the construction of the Kingdome in Seattle, a market he had shunned in favor of Oakland only because it lacked a stadium.[7] Finley denied that story, despite saying early in 1974 that the Athletics were for sale.[8] But his interest was well enough known in baseball that American League president Lee MacPhail wrote him six months later describing Seattle's progress and proposed terms for the stadium.[9] Finley was clearly still restless.

The other side of the Bay Area coin was Horace Stoneham and the Giants, who were doing worse than the A's, both on the field and at the gate. After the 1974 season, Stoneham told the stockholders the Giants had lost $1.7 million that year.[10] Early in the 1975 season, he was asking the National League for a loan to meet payroll and officially putting the team up for sale.[11] With all of his personal wealth tied up in the team, he was desperate to sell. His price for a local owner was $8 million.

Through the rest of 1975, he waited for a credible offer, preferably from a local group. Nothing appeared. Possibilities surfaced and then died. Minnesota banker Carl Pohlad, who would later buy the Minnesota Twins, discussed buying the Giants.[12] Pirates' owner John W. Galbreath said former General Motors president Edwin Cole was interested in buying the Giants and moving them to Washington.[13] Then, in January 1976, a Toronto group headed by brewer Labatt appeared and Stoneham announced a deal in principle had been struck.[14] It sounded like the Bay Area problem had been solved, while removing a highly attractive market from the expansion possibilities.

But, also that month, a new mayor had been inaugurated in San Francisco and George Moscone was determined to keep the Giants. He pushed the city to sue because the Giants would be breaking their thirty-five-year lease for city-owned Candlestick Park. Five days after Labatt's announcement, Moscone won an injunction preventing the transfer. He turned to Bob Lurie, a successful local developer who had been on the Giants' board of directors. Lurie said he was willing to put up half the money but was not able to find a partner. Moscone had been contacted by other potential buyers and put Lurie in touch with Bob Short, who had returned to Minneapolis after selling the

Texas Rangers. By February, Lurie and Short had worked out an agreement to buy the team and keep it in San Francisco.

Meeting late that month, the other National League owners, fully aware of Short's history in Washington, D.C., wanted no part of him. They agreed to the sale only if Lurie would be the team's sole representative and have full control. On March 1, 1976, the league's deadline for Lurie to find a partner, Short balked. "I've run baseball teams," he described as his reasoning to Lurie. "You've got the money. I'm the smart one."[15]

With the deadline looming, Lurie asked for a forty-eight-hour extension. The league gave him five hours. Optimism was in short supply when Moscone's office got a phone call from an unknown. Arthur "Bud" Herseth was a cattle and meatpacking baron from Phoenix and he said he was willing to match Lurie's investment but own only 49 percent of the shares. National League approval came quickly. The Giants would stay, the Bay Area market remained overcrowded, and another possible solution for Seattle or Washington was eliminated.[16]

Significantly, although both processes were confused and ugly, the National League had soothed its troubled markets by finding local ownership with solid finances. And, again, nothing had happened to solve the problems of Seattle, or Washington, or, indeed, the Bay Area itself.

In Minnesota, another piece of the nationwide franchise puzzle was maybe, sort of, possibly for sale. Calvin Griffith was no fan of the dawning free-agent era and thought it spelled the doom of family-owned franchises.[17] By 1975, Minnesota banker Carl Pohlad had had multiple conversations with Griffith about buying the franchise, conversations that had not gone much of anywhere, and Pohlad was one of the out-of-town interests casting his eyes at the Giants.[18] Pohlad thought Griffith's marketing and management efforts were alienating people in the Twin Cities and implied the franchise could be moved. Pohlad eventually would buy the Twins in 1984. In September, John Spellman, leading the Seattle lawsuit as King County executive, and talking with the baseball people about settlement, listed the Twins as one possibility to give his city a franchise.[19]

Spellman also noted reports that the White Sox might fill the same role. But Calvin Griffith and other American League owners made it clear the league did not want to give up on the third largest market in the country. In another indication of the two league's relative standings, one of the Seattle bidders said he would offer Horace Stoneham $15 million for the Giants, but only $10 million to Allyn for the White Sox.[20]

Spellman did not mention it, but the Cleveland Indians' ownership group was turning over as two of the original partners joined George Steinbrenner's group buying the Yankees and the original managing partner was pushed aside.[21] Possibilities for Seattle and Washington appeared and disappeared like prairie dogs scenting a coyote. In August 1975, *Washington Post* columnist Bob Addie reported five franchises were up for sale, adding the Orioles and the A's to the mix.[22]

The variations in the Seattle and Washington situations multiplied.

In late 1974, before Bob Lurie and Bud Herseth found each other, Dodgers' owner Walter O'Malley suggested the Athletics move to Seattle, with the Giants splitting their games between San Francisco and Oakland, solving baseball's problems in both areas. Finley went ballistic and called O'Malley "senile," but Kuhn was considering the idea as late as April 1975.[23] O'Malley was consistently interested in keeping the Giants, and the Dodgers' lucrative rivalry with them, in the Bay Area.

Another variation floating through the baseball world had the White Sox moving to Seattle with the Athletics switching to Chicago, a move that presumably would be more acceptable to Finley, whose insurance businesses were headquartered there.[24]

Expansion kept forcing itself into the discussion. At the summer meetings of 1974, the previously reluctant National League formed a committee to study expansion. "You want to be ready when the time is right, so you are not rushed if you are forced to expand," explained National League president Chub Feeney. "Forced" was clearly a reference to the Seattle suit and the growing pressure in Congress for a Washington franchise.[25]

While most baseball people saw Seattle and its lawsuit as the key problem, Kuhn remained focus on bringing baseball back to his boyhood home. He couched it as a necessity to keep Congress' hands off baseball's antitrust immunity, a concern shared by some other owners, especially in the American League. In the shifting whirl of possible franchise moves, he constantly looked for a team for Washington. One possibility he championed was having Baltimore and other teams play some of their home games in the capital.

In September 1975, with the Seattle lawsuit hanging over his head, and Horace Stoneham searching for a buyer, Kuhn made himself a priority list of possibilities.

First was sending the Giants to Washington, second was moving them to Toronto, and third to Seattle. The next alternatives, somewhat in parallel, were to move the Athletics to Seattle, Toronto, or Chicago with the White Sox going to Seattle. If more alternatives were needed, the White Sox could be sent to Seattle (without Chicago getting anything in return) or Toronto. The last and least alternative, he wrote, would be expansion, with the National League putting a club in Washington while the American League went to Seattle.[26] At baseball meetings during these years, the owners regularly discussed expansion and occasionally mulled the idea of buying insurance to cover litigation costs related to franchise transfers.[27] And did nothing.

Kuhn's Washington focus would founder on three rocks. The National League owners were not convinced a franchise could succeed in the nation's capital after two American League franchises had fled in the previous fifteen years. In the American League, Jerold Hoffberger of the Baltimore Orioles strongly opposed a competitor, especially an American League competitor only forty miles from his ballpark.[28]

And, Kuhn was shaky politically. He had to survive a coup attempt in the middle of the expansion debate. His original contract was up in 1975. He needed nine of the twelve votes in each league for an extension. He had all twelve in the National League, but Finley and Hoffberger found allies in Brad Corbett and George Steinbrenner. With four votes, they could block Kuhn and they gleefully announced it to the press on the eve of the crucial meeting. But, when the vote came, Corbett reversed and Kuhn survived.

It was instructive how the old guard of the National League and the "Young Turks" of the American League pursued their ends and how that reinforced the views of which league knew how to get things done. On the eve of the July 17, 1975, meeting, Finley boasted about everything to the press. He had the votes. The Nationals were running into the Americans' meeting seeking a new vote. He had them on the run.

The Nationals, guided by Walter O'Malley, kept quiet. They used a parliamentary maneuver to create a day's delay. Then, they went to Corbett, who was still early in his learning curve as an owner. They knew he had been recruited by Finley while they watched one game together. Any man who could be persuaded on so short an acquaintance could be reversed, they calculated. They were right. The overconfident Finley and Hoffberger had not sought to shore up Corbett's support overnight, bathing in their public triumph instead. Corbett's reversal came as a surprise.[29]

As the situation moved into 1976, things were getting clearer. The National League had stabilized its troubled franchises. The American League franchises that supposedly were in play either were not really available (Minnesota and Cleveland) or were taken off the table, as with Chicago.

The White Sox financial troubles were growing. Even when they made a run for the pennant in 1972, the team lost $867,000. As 1975 ended, the losses for the John Allyn years totaled $8 million.[30] One *Chicago Tribune* columnist referred to the team as "John Allyn's headache."[31] Seattle's John Spellman was not the only one seeing an opportunity. Denver and Washington were being mentioned, but none were willing to meet Allyn's price—$10 million for the franchise and $4 million for Comiskey Park.

The problem was that the man who could strike a deal with John Allyn was not a man the other American League owners wanted at their table. They thought they had bid Bill Veeck goodbye when he sold to the Allyns in 1961. But he could never stop tweaking them. *Veeck as in Wreck*, which skewered the other owners with glee while selling thousands of copies, was published in 1962. *New York Herald-Tribune* columnist Red Smith called it "380 pages of aggravated assault."[32] Other galling, derogatory books, articles, and quotations in reporters' stories continued to appear even as Veeck made attempts to buy a franchise in Washington or Baltimore.

Veeck and Allyn reached their agreement in October 1975. Veeck struck an optimistic, if snarky, note when asked about the owners' approval of the sale. "Unless you are a felon, or unsound morally, or don't have a good credit rating, you aren't likely to be turned down by the AL owners," he said.[33]

Veeck was wrong, at least in the short term. In early December, only three of the league's twelve owners were willing to approve the deal. "We considered Mr. Veeck's proposal and found the financial conditions were not satisfactory," league president Lee MacPhail announced, "We felt that under Mr. Veeck's proposal the club could not make a go of it financially." Veeck was given a week to restructure the bid.[34]

The restructuring worked, but it took a rather impassioned speech by John Fetzer to gain approval. "Gentlemen," Fetzer began, "This man has called me a son of a bitch repeatedly, and I don't like being called a son of a bitch any more than the rest of you do. But gentlemen, we gave this man our word that if he would do certain things, we would approve his purchase of the ball club. He did all that we asked, and now baseball can't go back on its word."[35] Ten, of twelve, owners agreed.

Gene Autry did not. "Bill's a fine guy. I just thought he was underfinanced."[36] Autry would be proven correct, especially in the dawning era of free agency.

Veeck would sell soon after the tax benefits wore off, and after discussions about moving the team.

Kuhn's alternatives had been eliminated and expansion was becoming inevitable.

That scenario was looking better for the American League because Seattle was rectifying the problems that had contributed to the Pilots' demise.

The leverage of the suit gave Seattle consistent opportunities to talk with baseball officials, whether Kuhn, MacPhail, or the occasional American League owner visiting Seattle. The message coming back was clear. Baseball officials wanted a modern stadium and a financially sound ownership group.

A stadium was finally being built. Spellman, unlike the earlier generation of local politicians, pushed ahead with what became the Kingdome. Although hindered by neighborhood, environmental, and financial concerns plus an underperforming contractor, Spellman got ground broken by 1972 and completion by early 1976. The Kingdome was a bare-bones project in many ways, but its suitability had been confirmed by the National Football League. In June 1974, the NFL agreed to an expansion franchise, the Seattle Seahawks, to debut with the stadium in 1976. Professional soccer had come aboard that spring although it would play its games in an older stadium for two years. Significantly, at the Sounders debut game in 1974, former *Seattle Post-Intelligencer* sports editor Royal Brougham introduced the team and then led the crowd in singing "Take Me Out to the Ballgame."

That was misleading. The crowd booed Brougham. Seattle fans reacted much more enthusiastically to both football and soccer than they had to the Pilots. The Seahawks sold 50,000 season tickets in two weeks.[37] Soccer crowds, while they could not fill the Kingdome, consistently drew better than most teams in the North American Soccer League.

An ownership group was a different issue. Johnny O'Brien, a former major league infielder and now a King County councilman, was made the region's contact with Kuhn. He asked the commissioner if Seattle should try to lure an existing team or wait for expansion. Kuhn suggested O'Brien should focus on putting together a viable ownership group.[38]

Restaurateur Dave Cohn re-emerged with a potential group and Bank of California said it represented an unnamed three-person partnership. Executives from the Pacific Coast League headed a group that said it could invest $12 million and a broker from Houston told Spellman he could put together an ownership group.[39] In the end, the winning group was assembled by radio station owner Lester Smith. He persuaded Walter Schoenfeld, owner of a fashion jeans company; jeweler Stan Golub; Jim Walsh, president of the Bon Marche department store chain; and construction magnate Jim Stillwell to join the group. But his big backer was a man who was already his partner in a string of entertainment ventures—movie star Danny Kaye. Kaye-Smith Enterprises owned radio stations, concert promoters, a recording studio, plus film production and radio syndication companies.

There was an echo of the Pilots, however. Kaye was the big money man and, like Daley in 1969, he did not live in Seattle. Unlike Daley, he was a dedicated baseball fan. He was the original co-managing partner of the team. The franchise and players cost $5.53 million with working capital bringing the total to $6.5 million, still a bit undercapitalized. In addition, the expansion teams had to forego their share of the national television contract for the first three years. With all that, the ownership lacked the financial depth to promote the team consistently and to endure the inevitable trials of building a fan base with a bad team. In 1981, as soon as the tax benefits of player-contract depreciation were used up, the group sold.[40]

George Moscone's efforts to keep the Giants had polished another expansion possibility—a well-financed ownership group had come together in Toronto, a large, attractive market with good demographics and an adequate stadium. The Toronto group had been focused on the National League because it saw a lucrative rivalry with Montreal, the existing Canadian entry in the major leagues. But spurned there, they saw their opportunity and struck up talks with MacPhail.

In January 1976, expansion finally moved to the fore. The franchise committee, formed in 1974 to deal with the questions of franchise movement and financial health, was pinning its hopes on moving one of the Bay Area teams to either Toronto or Seattle. That would still leave one of these cities and Washington out in the cold, and the committee's report "urges all of Baseball to recognize that the only way to do this is through expansion."[41] On the same day the committee report was sent to major league clubs, Stoneham announced the Giants sale to Toronto.

So, what would expansion look like? As a first idea, the committee's report suggested one league go to fourteen teams, but acknowledged that would create inequities between the leagues over contributions to the Major Leagues Central Fund, the number of players each league could take in the various drafts, and "in other ways as well."[42] So, they went to Plan B, each league would add one team. The problem was that one team would have to be idle every day or they would have to schedule interleague play, an idea that had been bandied about for decades without earning any strong support.[43]

The National League had opposed interleague play for years. With their attendance advantage, they had no incentive to accept games with opponents who were likely to be less attractive than their existing rivals. They also had studies that showed that fans preferred games against teams in their own divisions, teams they were more familiar with, rather than teams in other divisions, albeit in their own league.[44] And, quite frankly, they were contemptuous of a group of businessmen who could not seem to make good decisions, cooperate, or choose solid members for their boys' club. "Much of this was colored by the presence of Veeck and Finley. It was like, "why should we get involved with *those* people . . . riffraff," said Kuhn.[45]

In January 1976, the American League forced the pace and the National League undercut the neat solution of the Giants moving to Toronto.

American League president Lee MacPhail announced his league's decision to award a franchise to Seattle. "What the people in Seattle want is a ballclub, not a lawsuit," he said. Years later, MacPhail would add "I didn't think we were going to fare very well" in a jury trial in the State of Washington. Thus, he added, "we gave them an expansion team."[46] Seattle's mayor, Wes Uhlman, and Washington's attorney general, Slade Gorton, said they would not drop the lawsuit until they had a formal and specific offer.[47] *Seattle Times* baseball writer Hy Zimmerman reported the city was "lukewarm" to the American League offer.[48] MacPhail said any issues with the National League could be worked out at a planned meeting on January 31.

The National League's owners ducked comment on the American League's move but, with Walter O'Malley pushing hard, did agree to provide openended financial aid to Stoneham to keep the Giants in San Francisco.[49] The next day, the National League owners discussed expansion for four hours, but, concluded league president Chub Feeney, "there is just not sentiment in our league at this time to follow the American League." MacPhail became ambivalent, saying at one point that Seattle would "probably" get a team, but at another point saying the American League "would expand alone if we have to" and "I want to reiterate the definite intention of the American League to solve our problems with Seattle."[50] Kuhn said, "I will not tolerate any unilateral action."[51]

Things looked even more unilateral when the leagues met on January 31.

The American League voted to give Seattle a franchise, albeit with three conditions: the lawsuit would be dropped, the Kaye-Smith group would be accepted as the franchise owner, and a suitable lease would be worked out for the Kingdome.[52] MacPhail acknowledged a thirteen-team schedule was "impractical" but declined to discuss any further expansion.[53] Seattle worked out a stadium lease and agreed to suspend the lawsuit. But, suspicious after eight years of dealing with the American League, they said they would not drop it until a team actually played in Seattle.[54] The National League said again that it was not interested in expansion.

At least they were not interested until March. Then, after the leagues met on March 20, both groups said they were interested in expanding to Toronto. The American League held a formal vote to offer Toronto a franchise and, after hearing of that, the National League said it would actively consider doing the same. Toronto, with the largest open market in North America and Labatt's attractive ownership group, was looking like a prime candidate. The National League was familiar with Toronto and the ownership group because of the aborted Giants' sale, and the Toronto interests were more interested in the National League because of the natural rivalry with Montreal. Baseball reporters began to discuss the variables of two thirteen-team leagues and interleague play or the National League getting Toronto and accepting Washington, while the American League went into Seattle and New Orleans.[55]

The Nationals' interest lasted barely a week. The American League, which needed only 75 percent approval, awarded Toronto a franchise on Friday, March 26. The National League, whose rules required a unanimous vote, was scheduled to meet on Monday, March 29 and asked Kuhn to persuade the American League to hold off. He failed, and in the end, the Nationals voted only ten to two for expansion. Cincinnati and Philadelphia were the negatives.[56]

With Kuhn's commitment to Washington, D.C., this was not the end of the matter. On April 1, he ordered the American League to make a provision for baseball in Washington within a week or he would overrule the National's unanimity rule and allow them to expand to Toronto and Washington. There was discussion of the Baltimore Orioles or other teams playing some games in Washington, but Orioles' owner Jerold Hoffberger remained opposed. The American League made no provision for Washington and Kuhn's deadline passed.

So, on April 16, Kuhn issued yet another deadline, giving the National

League two weeks to firm up its own plans for Toronto and Washington.[57] The National League balked. On April 26, its teams' owners voted against expansion, this time seven to five, and for dropping their request to Kuhn to invalidate the American League's Toronto move.[58]

Kuhn, having been ignore by both leagues' owners, felt forced to go along and approve a unilateral move.[59]

The American League finally had begun to make up the attendance deficit and shore up their franchise values. The new Seattle and Toronto owners would pay $5.53 million for their franchises, little more than the $5.35 million the Pilots and Royals had paid in 1969, and still considerably less than the $10 million the National League had been able to charge that year.

Still, as the *Sporting News* editorialized, "For one of the few times in recent years, the American League outmaneuvered the National."[60] The American League was laying the foundations that would bring them back to parity with their rival.

CHAPTER THIRTEEN

Comeback and Irrelevance

The knife fight with the National League over Toronto, and Bowie Kuhn's Washington fixation, had muddied the 1977 expansion process. But that round had gone considerably more smoothly for the American League than it had in either 1961 or 1969. It would, in fact, set up the league's return to attendance parity with the National League. It would only delay the death of an independent American League.

A major difference was the league's new president. Lee MacPhail brought a far more thoughtful and organized executive style to the office than either of his predecessors. He was the first man at the level of commissioners and league presidents who realized the very definition of the job needed to adapt to baseball's changing priorities.

Leland Stanford MacPhail Jr. had spent his life in baseball.[1] He was born in 1917 to Leland Stanford MacPhail Sr., better known as Larry, and Inez Thompson. After college, Larry required Lee to work in a non-baseball business for a year before giving him a job. That came in late 1940, as general manager of the Brooklyn Dodgers' Reading, Pennsylvania, farm club. By 1942, he had moved to the same role in Toronto and then into the U.S. Navy during World War II.

By the time Lee was discharged in 1946, Larry was president of the New York Yankees and Lee joined as an assistant to George Weiss. From there he would go to the Orioles in the late 1950s, take a pay cut to join the commissioner's office in the mid-1960s, and go back to the Yankees in 1966. Each move brought increasing responsibilities, broader experience, and more contacts throughout the game. They also cemented a reputation as a man far removed from his father's mercurial, often alcoholic, career. In 1998, he joined his father in the Hall of Fame, the only father-son duo so honored.

As he became league president, Lee was a more contemplative man than either his father or his previous boss, George Steinbrenner. MacPhail visited at least two art galleries in every major league city and attended all their symphonies as well. He spent his time on airplanes reading at least one biography of every American president. When he retired from baseball in 1986, commissioner Peter Ueberroth called him "the best man in the game" and nobody objected, except maybe Steinbrenner.[2]

Steinbrenner had inherited MacPhail as the Yankees' general manager when he bought the team. Two weeks after the announcement of Steinbrenner's purchase, a second press conference revealed that Gabe Paul would be a member of Steinbrenner's partnership and serve as team president. Given Paul's long record as a major league general manager, the revelation made MacPhail uneasy. "As the [1973] season approached an end it became very apparent that working for the Yankees in the future would be quite different," the ever-diplomatic MacPhail said.[3] He became an early refugee from the Steinbrenner Yankees, being elected American League president on October 24, 1973, and taking office on January 1, 1974.

Replacing Joe Cronin as league president was not a smooth process. It was clear the baseball world was catching on to just how ineffective Cronin had been. "Joe made no more waves than were necessary," noted *New York Times* columnist Arthur Daley as Cronin left office.[4] In his obituary, his hometown *Boston Globe* could find nothing better to say than he "brought great dignity and poise into his executive life."[5]

Just getting control of the league meetings was difficult for MacPhail. "The meetings had pretty much gotten out of hand in Joe's latter years, primarily because some people simply enjoyed hearing themselves talk," he said. MacPhail introduced a three-minute egg timer and the talkers slowly learned to edit themselves. He also had a hard time getting the group to focus. "I had to keep the meeting from becoming a social get-together. Sometimes, I felt like an eighth-grade teacher admonishing the students to stop talking."[6]

Since the owners were equals, the style had always been to seek consensus, but MacPhail took it to a more structured level. He would often introduce a new proposal with attached background documents and perhaps comments from an expert. Then, he would go around the table seeking comment. If that round indicated agreement, he would drop into Roberts Rules of Order and gain formal acceptance. If the proposal looked wobbly, he would pull it back for revision.

MacPhail's renewed focus went beyond the meetings and found substance in a new definition of his job. In the great tradition of league presidents since Ban Johnson's retirement, Cronin had been reactive. MacPhail tried to get ahead of the story. As the possibility of expansion rose through 1975 and 1976, MacPhail was providing American League owners with the kind of materials they had never seen before. There were not merely lists of cities, but population numbers for both the cities and their metropolitan areas, data on age and income for each market, information on stadiums and possible stadiums, and background on possible ownership groups.[7] This time, as the results showed, the American League's owners had the tools for more intelligent scrutiny of the bids from Seattle, Toronto, and other candidates for expansion.

It was MacPhail delivering the consistent message to the Seattle politicians. Make sure we have a major league stadium and help us find a well-financed, stable ownership group. He was functioning as both an invaluable staff resource as well as an executive laying the groundwork for his owners. He was anticipating the business structure that would become Major League Baseball at the turn of the coming century.

MacPhail was a man who avoided getting caught up in personalities. He got along with both Charlie Finley and Bowie Kuhn. He could take a hand grenade of an issue and use research and calm logic to resolve a problem to the satisfaction of most people. Steinbrenner was another matter. On MacPhail's last day as league president, Steinbrenner called to say MacPhail was not welcome at Yankee Stadium.[8]

Why? On July 24, 1983, as the New York Yankees and the Kansas City Royals fought for a pennant, the Royals' George Brett hit a mammoth, apparently game-winning, home run off Yankee reliever Goose Gossage. As the Royals dugout celebrated, Billy Martin walked onto the field, protesting that the sticky pine tar Brett used to improve his grip extended further up the bat than the eighteen inches the rules allowed. The umpires huddled, measured Brett's bat against the seventeen-inch-wide home plate, and plate umpire Tim McClelland called Brett out, ending the game as a four to three Yankee victory. Brett's mad charge was barely contained by teammates, coaches, and the other umpires. The Royals lodged an appeal with MacPhail.

MacPhail not only studied the rule, he talked to Steinbrenner and asked the Yankees to file any points they would like to make. He did the same with the Royals. He talked to the members of the Rules Committee and examined the minutes of meetings to understand the rule's intent, he spoke with the league's umpire supervisors. In the end, he ruled that while the pine tar had crept up the bat further than the rule technically allowed, the pine tar had not hit the ball out of the stadium. "It is the strong conviction of the league that games should be won and lost on the playing field—not through technicalities of the rules," MacPhail's statement on the ruling said. The game would have to be replayed from the point where Martin had lodged the appeal.[9]

Steinbrenner tried mightily to foul up the process. He threw up objections about the replay date and the starting time. He encouraged "fans" lawsuits. He insulted MacPhail publicly. MacPhail kept his cool. When Kuhn moved to fine or suspend Steinbrenner, MacPhail recommended against that in the interests of minimizing contention.

MacPhail, meanwhile, was anticipating what the Yankees might do when the game was replayed. When it did resume on August 18, Martin immediately had his pitcher throw to second base and allege that Brett, and/or baserunner U. L. Washington, had failed to touch second base on the play. Since the replay was being officiated by a different crew of umpires, the Yankees alleged the fresh crew could not know if the bases had been properly touched. MacPhail had anticipated the protest and his assistant Bob Fishel provided the replay umpires with a notarized statement from the original crew saying the bases had been properly touched. As his parting shot at MacPhail showed, Steinbrenner remained livid, but the decision won general praise.

Outside the spotlight, MacPhail's influence for owners would show in his next job. The owners asked him to head their Player Relations Committee, the committee charged with negotiating with the players' union. Labor relations was the owners' most important issue and they wanted their best man, and best diplomat, at the helm. MacPhail negotiated the next round of contracts and was able to bring in the beginnings of drug-testing for players and an increase in the length of service before players could file for arbitration. "Find some boring, tiresome and enormously important area of the old game that's in decent working order, or headed that way, and it probably bears MacPhail's stamp," wrote *Washington Post* columnist Thomas Boswell.[10]

In a very different manner, Steinbrenner proved another major impetus for the comeback of the American League and a major influence for the end of its independence.

His early promises to focus on American Shipbuilding and leave the Yankees to the professionals were soon compromised, although the compromise was gradual. Gabe Paul put together the core of the team that would make the playoffs five times between 1976 and 1981, winning two World Series. He started with a dubious trade just weeks before he emerged as Steinbrenner's partner in New York, sending future All-Star Graig Nettles from the team he was leaving to the team he was joining. In New York, he soon added Chris Chambliss, Dick Tidrow, Lou Piniella, Willie Randolph, Mickey Rivers, and Ed Figueroa and created the Yankees' first pennant winner since Topping and Webb sold out.

But many of Paul's moves came after Steinbrenner's heavy hand was lightened. In 1974, Steinbrenner pled guilty to charges of illegal campaign contributions to Richard Nixon's 1972 re-election campaign and to obstruction of justice charges for trying to cover it up. Bowie Kuhn suspended him in 1974, a suspension that was not lifted until the Paul-constructed team was dominating the 1976 American League. It was not that Steinbrenner was completely out of the scene, getting involved in signing free agent Catfish Hunter just as his suspensions took effect. He was, however, limited to a few larger, generally financial, issues.

With the suspension over, the negatives of George Steinbrenner's involvement in team construction began to appear. After the end of that first season, manager Ralph Houk resigned and MacPhail went to the American League. It was to become a pattern. Managers, especially five-timer Billy Martin, would be hired, fired, rehired, and harassed by calls from the owner's box. Paul, seeking the autonomy he had before, went back to Cleveland after the 1977 season.

Signing Reggie Jackson for 1977 paid major dividends, contributing to three World Series appearances in his five years with the team. After Jackson, the slugging free agent outfielder/designated hitter types Steinbrenner liked to acquire did not bring pennants and Paul's acquisitions inevitably aged. After 1981, with Steinbrenner becoming more involved, the Yankees would not play another postseason game for fourteen years. The 1980s were the team's worst decade for postseason appearances since the 1910s. The 1995 appearance came after Steinbrenner's second suspension by a commissioner, this one for hiring a sleazy informer to dig up dirt on Dave Winfield, one of Steinbrenner's more successful free agent signings, but one who dared to challenge "The Boss."

In between his benchings by the commissioner, Steinbrenner managed to sandwich in the only time an owner was suspended by a league president. Inevitably, it seemed, it was MacPhail after a series of confrontations with umpires and the press, all conducted at maximum volume. "I had had it with the Yankees," MacPhail said, "and I suspended Steinbrenner for seven days." Earlier that season, Kuhn had hit the Yankee owner with a $50,000 fine when he questioned the integrity of National League umpires after decisions in an exhibition game.[11]

Steinbrenner's record as a general manager may have been mixed, but his record as a businessman was superb, especially in marketing. He loved the attention he attracted as owner of the Yankees. He could command the back pages of New York's tabloids every time he enforced a grooming code, hired/fired/rehired a manager, started a trade rumor, or lashed out at some enemy real or perceived. When he signed a free agent or took him to task for not performing, there he was again. Steinbrenner assured the headlines by off-the-record leaks, especially to reporters like Bill Madden of the *Daily News*, the largest circulation newspaper in the city.[12]

The constant signing of free agents, and the demands that they perform, demonstrated a determination to win, a determination that built a strong bond with Yankee fans. His treatment of employees was often abominable but reflected his, and the fans, overwhelming desire to win. His fight with MacPhail over the rescheduled "pine tar game" was panned nationally but mirrored a fan's almost irrational commitment to the team. Steinbrenner appealed to the "New York, New York" mystique Yankee fans loved and appropriated the images of Yankee "class" and "pride." The Yankee fans loved it even if it was no longer the dignified and lordly Yankees of Jacob Ruppert, Ed Barrow, Dan Topping, Del Webb, and George Weiss. To outsiders, it appeared more like the Bronx Zoo.

In New York, and around the league, people responded to the excitement the soap opera generated. Much of the rest of the country was still prepared to dislike New York but the frenetic publicity would draw them when the Yankees were the visiting team.

The Yankees of Steinbrenner's early years benefitted not only from Paul's roster construction but also from the political contacts and savvy of the first man Steinbrenner drove out of the organization. Mike Burke thought he had brought Steinbrenner in as the money man for a team Burke would run. He said Steinbrenner had promised that Burke would continue as the day-to-day boss of the team. Like MacPhail, he was stunned when Gabe Paul showed up unannounced as a member of Steinbrenner's partnership. With Paul's much broader baseball experience, Burke could see the future and, merely three months after the announcement of Steinbrenner's purchase, Burke quit.[13]

Later that year, the fruits of Burke's major accomplishment for the team began to flower. Construction began on a two-year project to refurbish Yankee Stadium. Burke had convinced the city of New York to finance the work. It was a mammoth project budgeted at $24 million, but came with a final price tag of $160 million for a city on the brink of bankruptcy.[14]

The Yankees, and the league as a whole, were the beneficiaries of the city's fiscal recklessness. When the rebuilt stadium opened in 1976, almost a million more fans came than the last year before the renovation. The Yankees made the playoffs and their attendance led the league, the first time either had happened since 1964. It was also the first time they had outdrawn the Mets since 1962.

Having its lead horse back in the traces was only good news for the American League. New York was still the media capital of the country. All three major television networks, most major national magazines, and twenty of the twenty-one largest advertising agencies had their headquarters in Manhattan.[15] Journalists' requests for credentials for the 1976 American League Championship Series were twice the number seeking National League credentials.[16] The media capital of America was once again interested in a baseball game and that excitement would be reflected in the coverage and where advertisers spent their dollars.

Led by the resurgent Yankees, and the racket echoing from Steinbrenner's office, the attendance gap between the two leagues began to shrink. By 1989, the American League's average attendance per game would squeeze into the lead over the National's, its first since 1955.

Beyond attendance, Steinbrenner created profound effects, good and bad, in the baseball world outside New York. The Yankees' resurgence drove attendance when they visited other cities, but Steinbrenner's competitive nature pushed up salaries. His return from his first suspension coincided with the arrival of free agency, and he began to spend. The top free agents moved at Steinbrenner-level salaries, even if they went to other teams. Marvin Miller of the players union could joke on the square that Steinbrenner was his favorite owner because of what he was doing for salaries across the game.[17]

The salaries were something the Yankees could afford because of the size of the New York market. And Steinbrenner proved adept at raising Yankee revenues with cable television, merchandising, and higher ticket prices. American League owners, led by Steinbrenner, but also including Gene Autry and others, were much more active participants in signing the annual crops of free agents. There were plenty of bad decisions involved, but as the 1970s blurred into the 1980s, more and more talent was concentrated in the American

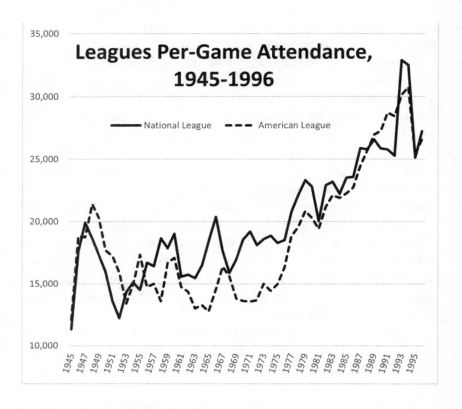

League. It showed in the All-Star games. The American League came to dominate once again.

The days of poorly capitalized owners such as Dewey Soriano, Bob Short, the Allyn Brothers, and Bill Veeck were dead. Owners such as Calvin Griffith, Horace Stoneham, and even Peter O'Malley, who had their wealth tied up in their franchises, were also being pushed out. They felt they could no longer compete with the likes of Steinbrenner, although they tended to blame this on the players. Ownership became less attractive for those raised in a more feudal time. The "benevolent father" syndrome personified by the St. Louis Cardinals' Gussie Busch or the Kansas City Royals' Ewing Kauffman was undermined as the players displayed the capitalistic drive for economic maximization that had characterized the owners for decades. Owners saw players as ungrateful, unreasonable, or just plain greedy, and it was harder for players to assume the owners' fallback mantle of claiming to preserve a community institution. Corporate ownership and broad-based partnerships became the rule.

Despite the efforts of MacPhail and Steinbrenner, the American League's hard-won attendance parity was something of an empty victory. Trends throughout baseball were conspiring to reduce the American League name to a marketing label. The National League, too. Differences remained necessary to promote the All-Star game and the World Series and earn all the connected television money. But, aside from the designated hitter rule, the leagues moved closer together as the pressure from the Players Association and its victories on free agency created a new world by 1999.

The Players Association had substantially changed the meaning of the antitrust exemption. The owners had perceived it as legal protection for the reserve clause, which they saw as the foundation of their control over players. Briefly put, the standard player contract was for one year plus an option for a second year. If the player did not sign at the salary offered for the option year, the team unilaterally could renew the contract for one year. The teams argued that renewing the contract also renewed the option clause and thus the contract became perpetual.

In 1975, Marvin Miller finally had a player who had fulfilled his contract and the option year who was willing to challenge that interpretation. Miller, with decades of experience in labor law, was confident that an arbitrator would rule that one year was indeed one year and that Andy Messersmith could be a free agent. He was right. Miller had circumvented the antitrust exemption for the players.

This changed the cartel substantially, but it did not change everything. In particular, the traditional cartel functions of controlling who owned teams, where they located, and how they did business remained. Under their antitrust exemption, the owners were limited pretty much to controlling each other.

As owners spent more time and energy fighting with the Major League Baseball Players Association and Marvin Miller, whatever disagreements they had with the other league faded into the background. Commissioner Peter Ueberroth, who succeeded Kuhn in 1984, increased the joint owners' meetings to four a year and mandated that owners, not any kind of subordinate, attend. Owners' meetings became much more important, and much longer, than league meetings.

With the emergence of ESPN and regional cable television networks, as well as the ascendancy of the sports-hungry Fox network, national television money grew into a larger portion of team income. And when some teams began broadcasting their games nationwide on superstations, the gap between the haves and the have-nots among franchises widened. "The difference between larger and smaller markets became more important than A.L. versus N.L.," summed up San Francisco Giants owner Bob Lurie.[18]

Ueberroth ramped up the quiescent Major League Baseball Promotions Corp. He also turned to one of the tactics he had used to make the 1984 Olympics profitable—sponsorships. He got equipment manufacturers, uniform makers, ticket agencies, airlines, and others to pay for the right to advertise as the official providers of their products to the major leagues. The rights, and the payouts to the teams, covered all teams equally. Ueberroth's harangues against long-term contracts, the germ of the collusion rulings that hit owners in the later 1980s, grew out of joint meetings.

For the moment, expansion was off the table. The National League was not interested and, frankly, most of the attractive markets were gone, waiting for further growth in the West and South.

Interleague play, after nearly 100 years of discussion and resistance, became a reality in 1997. The mystery that pervaded every World Series and All-Star game was reduced because these hitters and pitchers faced each other during the regular season. The two leagues' umpiring staffs, each with slightly different definitions of the strike zone, were merged, stripping the league presidents of one of their major functions. Other functions, such as scheduling, preparing for league meetings, and negotiating with the other league president faded away as the commissioner's office stepped forward.

In 1999, the idea of a centralized structure for managing baseball, an idea that dated back at least to Commissioner Albert Chandler in the late 1940s, came to fruition. The leagues ceased to exist as anything but brand labels for the World Series, All-Star games, and interleague play. Gene Budig, 1994–99, was the last American League president.[19] His remaining duties were subsumed into the entity now called Major League Baseball, generally MLB.

MLB was baseball fully revealed as an organized cartel, with a process for setting long-term priorities and a staff to help the owners and prod them toward reasoned decisions.[20] It would handle expansion, marketing, television, scheduling, umpires, relations with the minor leagues, and all the other issues that had been handled separately by the leagues. The commissioner was no longer limited to a specific list of tasks related to the reputation of the game and the enforcement of the owners' rules. He was the manager of a mature business asked to look ahead, deal with baseball-wide issues, and seek financial opportunities for the game as a whole.

The infrastructure that governed baseball in the 1950s had outlived its usefulness even then. Now, it was gone, replaced by a centralized bureaucracy with its focus on the baseball industry rather than one of its units.

Introduction

1. The first Washington Senators were a charter team of the American League in 1901. They were allowed to relocate to Minneapolis–St. Paul after the 1960 season and became the Minnesota Twins. They were replaced for the 1961 season by an expansion team also called the Senators. It was this second iteration that moved to Texas for the 1972 season.

2. The Boston Braves moved to Milwaukee for the 1953 season; the St. Louis Browns became the Baltimore Orioles for the 1954 season; and the Philadelphia Athletics moved to Kansas City for the 1955 season. The Boston Red Sox, St. Louis Cardinals, and Philadelphia Phillies stayed put.

3. From "*Good Grief, They've Done It Again!,*" an unpublished manuscript in the Bill Veeck Papers at the Chicago Historical Society, attributed to Veeck and Ed Linn. No date, but roughly late 1967.

4. Interview with Bob Lurie, May 31, 2018.

5. William Leggett, "A Success Is Killing the American League," *Sports Illustrated,* September 9, 1963: 18.

6. Harris, *The League,* 16.

7. Lyons, *On Any Given Sunday,* chapters 19–23.

Chapter One

1. Pietrusza, *Judge and Jury.*

2. Leonard Koppett column, *Sporting News,* March 27, 1965: 14.

3. Banner, *The Baseball Trust.*

4. This definition was not as ridiculous as it seems to us today. Antitrust Law was relatively new, and still evolving. At that time, insurance companies also were defined as not being involved in interstate commerce.

5. Joseph Durso, "Baseball Meetings End, Problems Don't," *New York Times,* December 12, 1976.

6. Veeck with Linn, *Veeck—As in Wreck,* 256.

7. Clifford Kachline, "'Most Progress in 15 Years' Frick Declares After Meetings," *Sporting News,* December 13, 1961: 5.

8. Dan Daniel, "A.L. Moguls Okay Ten-Club League—Keep Eye on L.A," *Sporting News,* September 7, 1960: 4. Of note, Dan Topping of the New York Yankees did

not attend the meeting despite his strident demands that the American League be allowed into the Los Angeles market, the main topic of the meeting. His partner, Del Webb, did attend.

9. Shirley Povich column, *Sporting News*, November 2, 1960: 4.

10. MacPhail, *My Nine Innings*, 169.

11. Miller, *A Whole Different Ball Game*, 309.

Chapter Two

1. For an interesting side note, look at the 1963 Topps baseball cards celebrating the previous year's home run leaders in both leagues. The National League leaders card (No. 3 in the set) feature five future Hall of Famers (four African Americans—Willie Mays, Hank Aaron, Frank Robinson, and Ernie Banks—and one dark-skinned Latino—Orlando Cepeda). All are in the Hall of Fame. The American League's six leaders featured one African American—Leon Wagner—and five white players—Harmon Killebrew, Norm Cash, Rocky Colavito, Jim Gentile, and Roger Maris. Only Killebrew made the Hall of Fame. The back of the American League card shows the next nine biggest home run hitters in the American League were also white.

2. Hall of Famer Willard Brown, inducted primarily for his play in the Negro Leagues, and Hank Thompson both had fewer than 100 plate appearances.

3. A dark-skinned Latino, Cuban Tony Oliva, had won the American League Rookie of the Year award in 1964.

4. MacPhail to Chandler, October 25, 1945, memo on "The Negro in Baseball." Giamatti Research Center, National Baseball Hall of Fame and Museum, Integration—Correspondence & Clippings: Papers 1937–1980. BA MSS 67. Correspondence and Clippings.

5. Halberstam, *October 1964*, 55. McGregor, *A Calculus of Color*, 80.

6. Wendell Smith, "The Most Prejudiced Teams in Baseball," *Ebony*, May 1953: 111.

7. McGregor, *Calculus of Color*, 55, 60.

8. The American League numbers are somewhat inflated because of the 1961 season. Due to expanding a year earlier, the American League played 31 percent more games, but stole only 23.5 percent more bases, tripled 15 percent more often, and homered 28 percent more often. In 1962, with both leagues expanded and playing an equal number of games, the National League resumed its lead in stolen bases and triples.

9. These concerns spread over the 1950s and 1960s. For a sampling, see Gerry Hern, "A Warning to A.L. Owners," *Baseball Digest*, November–December 1954: 23; Red Smith column, *New York Herald Tribune*, December 26, 1958; Paul Richards with Tim Cohane, "The American League Is Dying," *Look*, February 17, 1959: 41; William Leggett, "A Success Is Killing the American League," *Sports Illustrated*, September 9, 1963:

18; Al Hirshberg, "Is the American League *That* Bad?" *Sport*, March 1964: 26; Bill Veeck with Edward Linn, "They've Wrecked the American League," *Saturday Evening Post*, July 11, 1964: 10; Roger Kahn, "The Yankees: Descent from Olympus," *Saturday Evening Post*, September 12, 1964: 80.

10. Tom Meany, "New Minor League—the National?" *Saturday Evening Post*, March 19, 1938: 12.

11. By baseball rules, a player could not be sent out of his league until every other team in the league had passed on him, a process known as asking for waivers. Over time, this ban was softened with designated interleague trading periods, which grew longer.

12. Edgar Munzel, "N.L. Prexy Giles' Persuasion Blocked More Deals with A.L," *Sporting News*, December 31, 1966: 28.

13. Ed Prell, "More \$\$ for \$couts, Farm\$ Give N.L. Edge," *Sporting News*, July 27, 1960: 9.

14. Arthur Daley, "A Final Bit of Star-Gazing," *New York Times*, July 14, 1949.

15. Greenberg with Berkow, *Hank Greenberg*, 214–15

16. C. C. Johnson Spink column, *Sporting News*, September 9, 1967: 14.

Chapter Three

1. Frederick G. Lieb, "Inside of Browns' Near-Shift to L.A. Revealed." *The Sporting News*, January 17, 1946: 2; J.G. Taylor Spink, "Full Story of Browns Near-Shift in '41." *The Sporting News*, August 31, 1949: 3; Ray Gillespie, "Coast Missed Major Ball by Day in '41." *The Sporting News*, December 4, 1957: 5; "Major League 'Gag' Killed," *Los Angeles Times*, December 10, 1941.

2. Andy McCue, "Open Status Delusions: The PCL Attempt to Resist Major League Baseball." *Nine: A Journal of Baseball History and Social Policy Perspectives*, Spring 1997: 288.

3. "Study of Realignment Essential." The *Sporting News*, October 24, 1951: 12; "Planning Needed Before Map Changes." *The Sporting News*, July 29, 1953: 12; J.G. Taylor Spink, "Frick Calls on Game to Blueprint Reforms." *The Sporting News*, December 2, 1953: 1.

4. J.G. Taylor Spink, "Wrigley Raps Game's Hidebound Policy." *The Sporting News*, December 8, 1954: 1.

5. In the 1950s, baseball's Executive Committee consisted of the Commissioner, the two league presidents, and an owner representative from each league. Its membership would be broadened over the years, but O'Malley, who had joined the committee in 1951 would serve almost until his death in 1979.

6. McCue, *Mover & Shaker*.

7. Garratt, *Home Team*, 9-19.

Chapter Four

1. John Topping was a founder of Republic Iron and Steel while Reid speculated successfully in corn futures and became known as "The Tin Plate King."

2. Obituaries, *Sporting News*, June 1, 1974: 40.

3. "Dan Topping Dead at 61; Yankee Owner 22 Years," *New York Times*, May 20, 1974.

4. He would eventually become a colonel in the Marine Corps Reserves. "Topping Appointed Colonel in Marine Corps Reserve," *Sporting News*, July 6, 1960: 9.

5. Dick Young, "Topping One of Wheels Who Keeps Yanks Going," *New York Daily News*, July 20, 1958.

6. Red Smith, "Dan Topping: Money and Class," *New York Times*, May 22, 1974.

7. Arthur Susskind Jr, "Topping, the Tycoon Who Makes Yankees Tick," *Sporting News*, January 3, 1962: 4.

8. "Senator Official Challenges A's Shift," *Chicago Tribune*, October 14, 1954.

9. Joe David Brown, "The Webb of Mystery," *Sports Illustrated*, February 29, 1960: 68–80.

10. "Man on the Cover: Del Webb," *Time*, August 3, 1962: 49.

11. Carl T. Felker, "'Majors Now Battle of Business Giants'—Webb," *Sporting News*, June 19, 1946: 13.

12. Undated 1949 Bob Cooke column in the *New York Herald Tribune* contained in the National Baseball Hall of Fame and Museum's Del Webb file.

13. Robert Greene et al., "Barry and the Boys: Highlights of the Crime Report on the Sunbelt," *New West*, April 11, 1977: 21–30, esp. 26.

14. Veeck, *Veeck—As in Wreck*, 266–7.

15. "Sox Deal," *Time*, March 6, 1933; Thomas Rogers, "Tom Yawkey, 73, Owner of the Red Sox," *New York Times*, July 10, 1976.

16. The reported size of the inheritance varied over the years, from $4 million when he bought the Red Sox to $20 million later in his life. In any case, it was substantial. Much of the material about Yawkey is drawn from Nowlin, *Tom Yawkey*.

17. Al Hirshberg, "The Sad Case of the Red Sox," *Saturday Evening Post*, May 21, 1960: 38.

18. James S. Kunen, "The Man with the Greatest Job in Boston," *Boston Magazine*, July, 1975: 60.

19. Edgar J. Driscoll, "Tom Yawkey, Red Sox Owner, Dies," *Boston Globe*, July 10, 1976.

20. Lester Smith, "Do Red Sox Lose Money? Only Yawkey Can Answer," *Sporting News*, July 31, 1965: 17.

21. Appel, *Pinstripe Empire*, 224.

22. Nowlin, *Tom Yawkey*, 167; Arthur Sampson, "Yawkey Opposed to Gate 'Hypos,'" *Sporting News*, May 15, 1957: 13.

23. J. G. Taylor Spink, "Yawkey Tabbed True Sportsman," *Sporting News*, August 2, 1961: 7; and Dan Daniel column, *Sporting News*, July 27, 1960: 12.

24. Shirley Povich, "Yawkey, Webb Led Fight to Stymie Senators Shift," *Sporting News*, July 30, 1958: 4.

25. "Yawkey Points the Way," *Sporting News*, August 24, 1968: 14.

26. Ewald, *John Fetzer*, 50–57.

27. Watson Spoelstra, "Heat on DeWitt After Gordon Quits Bengals," *Sporting News*, October 12, 1960: 7.

28. Watson Spoelstra, "Prexy Fetzer Buys Final One-Third of Tiger Stock," *Sporting News*, November 22, 1961: 5.

29. Torry, *Endless Summers*, 60.

30. Harry Jones, "Daley Once Usher at Indians' Games," *Cleveland Plain Dealer*, February 15, 1956; Hal Lebovitz, "'Where Can You Get 6 Per Cent With as Much Fun?'" *Sporting News*, February 22, 1956: 8.

31. Hal Lebovitz, "'Staying Put,' Tribe's Chief Assures Fans," *Sporting News*, July 24, 1957: 10; John F. Lawrence, "Cleveland Businessmen Seek to Save a City Asset: The Indians," *Wall Street Journal*, August 26, 1958; Torry, *Endless Summers*, 50, 72.

32. When the A's made another trade with the Yankees that seemed to favor New York, it was Veeck and Lane who protested the trade publicly as some baseball people suggested a formal ban on trading between the two teams. The Yankees dismissed the criticism and the proposal went nowhere. Dan Daniel, "Weiss Thunders Answer to Critics of Yankee Swaps," *Sporting News*, January 13, 1960: 23.

33. Torry, *Endless Summers*, 78–83.

34. Dan Daniel, "Expansion Peace Bears Galbreath Stamp," *Sporting News*, December 21, 1960: 6.

35. Bob Addie columns, *Sporting News*, July 23, 1958: 17; October 8, 1958: 13; and November 19, 1958: 16.

36. Jessie Linthicum, "Orioles to Keep Spending—But Not on Bonus Babies," *Sporting News*, December 7, 1955: 8; Bob Addie column, *Sporting News*, December 7, 1955: 10; Jessie Linthicum, "Walsingham Bird-Watcher on Spending," *Sporting News*, December 19, 1956: 16.

37. Miller, *The Baseball Business*, 60.

38. Daniel, "Expansion Peace Bears Galbreath Stamp."

39. Eskenazi, *Bill Veeck*, xii.

40. Eskenazi, *Bill Veeck*, 140.

41. Veeck, *Veeck—As in Wreck*, 33–42.

42. Veeck, *Veeck—As in Wreck*, 59–62; Eskenazi, *Bill Veeck*, 19–21; Dickson, *Bill Veeck*, 66–68.

43. Eskenazi, *Bill Veeck*, 21–22.

44. Arch Ward column, *Chicago Tribune*, July 10, 1946.

45. Eskenazi, *Bill Veeck*, 112, 130–31.

46. Veeck, *Veeck—As in Wreck*, 257–58.

47. Bill Veeck, "What's Wrong with Baseball...What Can Be Done about It," *Look*, April 12, 1949: 94; Bill Veeck, "My Plan to Remodel the Majors," *Sport*, May 1969: 44.

48. Dickson, *Bill Veeck*, 207.

49. Dickson, *Bill Veeck*, 351.

50. Eskenzazi, *Bill Veeck*, xii.

51. Veeck, *Veeck—As in Wreck*, 356.

52. Ernest Mehl, "Carroll Sets Progressive Course for Kaycee," *Sporting News*, March 30. 1960: 5.

53. Dan Daniel, "A.L. Moguls Okay Ten-Club League—Keep Eye on L.A," *Sporting News*, September 7, 1960: 4; Joe King, "A.L. Speeds Expansion—Ten Clubs in '61," *Sporting News*, November 2, 1960: 3–4; Dan Daniel, "Fans Want Something New, Get It in 9-Club Majors, Interloop Play," *Sporting News*, November 30, 1960: 1, 2, 16.

54. This perception is most fully drawn out in Katz, *The Kansas City A's*. It has, however, been challenged. See "The 1955–60 Kansas City Athletics Gave Away Their Talent to the Yankees," in Deane, *Baseball Myths*.

55. Francis E. Stan, "Calvin Griffith, Being Coached to Head Senators, Pitches in as Farm Prexy, Pilot and Pinch-Catcher," *Sporting News*, January 25, 1940: 5; Al Costello, "Griff's Adopted Son Cal Trained to Take Over," *Sporting News*, August 13, 1952: 11; Shirley Povich, "Senators' New President Started as Batboy," *Sporting News*, November 9, 1955: 2.

56. Miller, *A Whole Different Ball Game*, 59.

57. Helyar, *Lords of the Realm*, 131.

58. Gary Smith, "A Lingering Vestige of Yesterday," *Sports Illustrated*, April 4, 1983: 104.

59. Weiner, *Stadium Games*, 106–7.

60. Herb Heft, "Cal Urges Chain Curb to Balance A.L.," *Sporting News*, November 9, 1955: 1.

61. Armour, *Joe Cronin*, 2.

62. Hirshberg, *What's the Matter*, 50.

63. Armour, *Joe Cronin*, 215–17.

64. Hirshberg, *What's the Matter*, 116.

65. Bob Addie column, *Washington Post*, March 4, 1960.

66. Armour, *Joe Cronin*, 263–64; Al Hirshberg, "Is the American League THAT Bad?" *Sport*, March 1964: 26.

Chapter Five

1. Toronto Blue Jays, 3,885,284. The Los Angeles Dodgers had continued to hold the major league record until then, breaking their 1962 mark in 1977, 1978, and 1982.

2. Dan Daniel, "National League to Discuss Plans to Invade Coast," *Sporting News*, November 17, 1954: 2.

3. Joe Trimble, "Webb Favors Major Loop Team in West," *Los Angeles Times*, July 14, 1953.

4. Miles, *Eight Busy Decades*, 47–49.

5. Joe King, "Cronin to Put 'Dash and Color' into A.L.," *Sporting News*, February 11, 1959: 9.

6. In June 1958, the other American League owners turned down a Griffith petition to move to Minneapolis–St. Paul for the 1959 season. Three months later, he tried again, giving his reasons in greater depth. Washington's offer for a new stadium was at a site "through eight miles of colored territory," he said. By 1965, Griffith predicted, the district would be "75% colored" and "the league is not drawing colored fans." This material is from handwritten notes for minutes of the American League owners' meetings of July 7, 1958, and September 8, 1958, apparently kept by American League secretary Earl Hilligan. While Hilligan's name does not appear on the notes, they include the draft of the meeting's press release, which was one of Hilligan's responsibilities. Hilligan's notes are in the Bowie Kuhn Papers at the National Baseball Hall of Fame and Museum.

7. Shirley Povich, "Calvin Hears Tinkle of Western Dollars—Plus Capital Uproar," *Sporting News*, October 17, 1956: 14.

8. Wagner's fears were misplaced. A month after the Dodgers joined the Giants in announcing the move, Wagner won the mayoralty by an even larger plurality than he had four years earlier. In 1953, he had won 46.3 percent of the votes citywide and 46.6 percent in Brooklyn. In 1957, he gained 69.2 percent of the total and 75.1 percent in Brooklyn.

9. William C. Whitney served as secretary of the navy for Grover Cleveland's first term (1885–1889) and John M. Hay was secretary of state for William McKinley and Theodore Roosevelt (1898–1905). Hay started his career as a secretary to Abraham Lincoln.

10. George Herbert Walker was the uncle of future president George Herbert Walker Bush.

11. While Rickey listed these cities, it is not clear they ever paid the $50,000 entrance fee nor was the makeup of the ownership groups fully revealed.

12. Kelley, *Baseball's Biggest Blunder*.

13. Oscar Kahan, "N.L. Approves Special Survey for Expansion," *Sporting News*, December 10, 1958: 8.

14. "Memorandum dictated by Branch Rickey re meeting with Commissioner Ford Frick at his office, starting at 10 a.m.," October 12, 1959, and "Memorandum of conversation with Ford Frick at Dorset Hotel, Monday afternoon, 2:30 p.m., November 23, 1959," Branch Rickey Papers, Library of Congress.

15. Gordon S. White Jr., "Rickey Says Setback in Senate Won't Halt Continental League," *New York Times*, June 30, 1960.

16. Jerry Holtzman, "Big Timers Clearing Decks for Expansion," *Sporting News*, August 10, 1960: 3.

17. Rickey and others had had inconclusive talks with several parties in Los Angeles, but none had been willing to pay the $50,000 fee for Continental League membership.

18. Roy Terrell, "'The Damndest Mess Baseball Has Ever Seen,'" *Sports Illustrated*, December 19, 1960: 16.

19. "A.L. Execs Wise in Refusing to Rush," *Sporting News*, September 7, 1960: 10.

20. Dan Daniel, "A.L. Moguls Okay Ten-Club League—Keep Eye on L.A.," *Sporting News*, September 7, 1960: 4.

21. Ray Gillespie, "Dallas, Fort Worth Join Hands in Major Bid," *Sporting News*, September 21, 1960: 15.

22. Shapiro, *Bottom of the Ninth*, 240–41.

23. Joe King, "N.L. Opening Door for Houston—Dallas Likely A.L. Addition," *Sporting News*, October 19, 1960: 4.

24. "Houston, N.Y. Join National League," *Los Angeles Times*, October 18, 1960.

25. "Tuesday, October, 25, 1960—11:40 a.m.," Rickey Papers. Also see last paragraph of "Memorandum of a telephone conversation with Warren Giles, President of the National Leag [*sic*] at 11 a.m. EDT, 7/22/60," also in Rickey Papers.

26. Daniel, "A.L. Moguls"; "Memorandum Sept. 1, 1960" from Lou Niss to Rickey et al., Rickey Papers.

27. Joe King, "N.L. Speeds Expansion—Ten Clubs in '62," *Sporting News*, November 2, 1960: 4.

28. Arthur Daley column, *New York Times*, October 28, 1960.

29. King, "N.L. Speeds Expansion."

30. Al Wolf, "American League Baseball Moves Here," *Los Angeles Times*, October 27, 1960.

31. Roscoe McGowen, "Majors Put Off Changes in Rule on 2-Club Cities," *New York Times*, January 26, 1958; Al Wolf, "Let's Pull Switch in All-Star Game," *Los Angeles Times*, July 19, 1959.

32. Frank Finch, "Podres, Williams Due to Pitch, so Jackson Gets All-Star Job," *Los Angeles Times*, July 9, 1960.

33. "Tuesday, October, 25, 1960—11:40 a.m.," Rickey Papers; Veeck, *Veeck—As in Wreck*, 360.

34. Dan Daniel, "A.L. Postpones Player Picks by Two New Clubs," *Sporting News*, November 30, 1960: 2.

35. Dan Daniel, "Dove of Peace Coos Over Expansion Turmoil," *Sporting News*, November 23, 1960: 11.

36. Ray Gillespie, "'A.L. Double-Crossed Us,' Claims Angry Dallas Pair," *Sporting News*, November 2, 1960: 8.

37. King, "N.L. Opening Door for Houston."

38. "Ford Frick Believes L.A. Should be Open Territory," *Los Angeles Times*, August 15, 1960; John Drebinger, "Problems Ahead, Cronin Is Warned," *New York Times*, October 28, 1960.

39. Dick Young, "Frick Threatens to Veto AL Move Here," *Los Angeles Times*, November 16, 1960.

40. Paul Zimmerman, "Promoters Find L.A. Irresistible," *Los Angeles Times*, October 27, 1960.

41. Paul Zimmerman, "Greenberg Out, L.A. Team Up for Bids," *Los Angeles Times*, November 18, 1960.

42. Bill Veeck with Ed Linn, "Walter O'Malley: Boss of Baseball," *Look*, July 3, 1962: 81; Veeck, *Veeck—As in Wreck*, 361; "November 23, 1960. Hank Greenberg called me at about 10:02 a.m. . . . ," Rickey Papers.

43. *Los Angeles Herald Express*, November 22, 1960. Several of the people expressing interest in the franchise had supported the 1958 ballot measure to overturn O'Malley's contract with the City of Los Angeles and O'Malley remembered.

44. Autry, *Back in the Saddle*, 149; Veeck, *Veeck—As in Wreck*, 369.

45. *Los Angeles Herald Express*, December 8, 1960.

46. Dan Daniel, "Expansion Peace Bears Galbreath Stamp," *Sporting News*, December 21, 1960: 6.

47. Bob Burnes, "Expansion Accord Hailed as Guidepost," *Sporting News*, December 14, 1960: 1; Daniel, "Expansion Peace." The new Rule 1(c) emerged that any interloper needed 75 percent approval from the owners of the league already established in the city, that the city must have a population of at least 2 million, and that the incoming team use a ballpark at least five air miles from that of the established team.

48. O'Malley's insistence on 1962 had been based on his projection of when Dodger Stadium would be open and his hope the American League team would be his tenant from the beginning. His vetoes included television station owner Kenyon Brown and San Diego banker and fishing magnate C. Arnholt Smith. Brown's television station had editorialized in favor of a June 1958 public referendum to overturn O'Malley's contract with the Los Angeles City Council. Smith's brother John had been a vocal supporter and financial angel to the groups opposing O'Malley.

49. Bob Burnes, "Expansion Accord"; Newhan, *Anaheim Angels*, 80.

50. Clifford Kachline, "A.L. Blocks Farm Plan for New Clubs," *Sporting News*, December 14, 1960: 2.

51. Hy Hurwitz, "'A.L. Spent Year Laying Expansion Plans'—O'Connell," *Sporting News*, November 9, 1960: 11.

52. "Expansion Expressions—How Scribes Sum Up Additions," *Sporting News*, November 9, 1960: 7.

53. Joe Williams column, *New York World-Telegram*, March 7, 1961, reported Cleveland general manager Frank Lane attributed the death of the idea, and the support for Griffith, to Cronin, his brother-in-law.

54. Bob Burnes, "Cost of New Club? A Cool $5 Million!," *Sporting News*, December 7, 1960: 1.

55. While it is a staple trivia answer that Eli Grba (Yankees to Angels) was the first player chosen in the expansion draft, that does not mean he was the most coveted player. He was simply the most coveted pitcher.

56. Tyler Kepner, "Expansion the Hard Way by 1961 Angels," *Press-Enterprise* (Riverside, CA), November 12, 1997; Dan Daniel, "A.L. Postpones Player Picks by Two New Clubs," *Sporting News*, November 30, 1960: 2.

57. Andy McCue and Eric Thompson, "Mis-Management 101: The American League Expansion for 1961," in *Endless Seasons: Baseball in Southern California* (Phoenix, AZ: Society for American Baseball Research, 2011), 42.

58. Bill Veeck and Ed Linn, "*Good Grief, They've Done It Again*," an unpublished article in the Bill Veeck Papers at the Chicago Historical Society. Undated, but probably late 1967.

Chapter Six

1. This profile draws on a number of sources, beginning with George-Warren, *Public Cowboy No. 1*; Art Detman, "A Chief Exec Named Gene Autry," *Dun's Review*, August, 1975: 57; John Barbour, "Gene Autry: The Singing Cowboy Who Became a Millionaire," *The State*, Columbia, SC, May 12, 1974; Braven Dyer, "Autry's Close Interest in Angels Spurs Morale," *Los Angeles Times*, April 10, 1962; Don Page, "Autry: Cowhand with a $ Brand," *Los Angeles Times*, October 22, 1965; Myrna Oliver, "Cowboy Tycoon Gene Autry Dies," *Los Angeles Times*, October 3, 1998; and J. G. Taylor Spink, "Crooning Cowboy Magnate Takes the Stand," *Sporting News*, May 3, 1961: 6.

2. Formally the St. Louis–San Francisco Railway.

3. WLS stood for World's Largest Store.

4. Autry, with Herskowitz, *Back in the Saddle Again*, 177–78.

5. Ron Bass, "An Old Cowpoke Finds His Pasture," *Chicago Tribune Magazine*, December 3, 1978: 43–62; Baylor, with Smith, *Nothing but the Truth*, 108.

6. Jack McDonald, "Rajah and Autry Reported Ready to Bid for Seals," *Sporting News*, October 3, 1951: 23; Oscar Ruhl, "Bob Hyland's Radio Coup," *Sporting News*, November 28, 1951: 15.

7. Mike Fessier, "It's Just Ol' Gene Autry," *Los Angeles Times West Magazine*, February 9, 1967: 25–28.

8. Dave Distel, "A Fan as Owner," *Los Angeles Times*, July 9, 1975.

9. See letters addressed to all major league owners (and others) dated July 15, 1981, and to Commissioner Bowie Kuhn dated June 13, 1984, both in the Kuhn Papers at the Baseball Hall of Fame and Museum.

10. Jeane Hoffman, "Ex-Tribe Hero Reynolds 'Three-Day Wonder' in Baseball," *Los Angeles Times*, December 28, 1960.

11. Rebecca Grant, "Quesada the Conqueror," *Air Force Magazine*, April 2003: 76–80. Quesada obituaries in *Washington Post, New York Times*, and *Los Angeles Times*, February 10, 1993.

12. Shirley Povich column, *Washington Post*, January 30, 1963.

13. Povich column, January 30, 1963.

14. Bob Addie, "Financial Wizard Johnston Serene in Nat Red-Ink Sea," *Sporting News*, January 23, 1965: 18.

15. Dave Brady, "Johnston Steps into New Role," *Washington Post*, January 31, 1963; Bob Addie, "Johnston Was Fan First, Then Owner," *Washington Post*, December 29, 1967; "James M. Johnston, Board Chairman of New Senators," *Sporting News*, January 13, 1968: 44.

16. Brady, "Johnston Steps into New Role."

17. "James Johnston, Financier and Owner of the Senators," *Washington Post*, December 30, 1967.

18. Helyar, *Lords of the Realm*, 73.

19. Durso, *All-American Dollar*, 127.

20. Rex Lardner, "Charlie Finley and Bugs Bunny in K.C.," *Sports Illustrated*, June 5, 1961: 24.

21. This profile is drawn from numerous sources, esp. Green and Launius, *Charlie Finley*; "Charlie Finley: Baseball's Barnum," *Time*, August 18, 1975: 42–51; Edwin Shrake, "A Man and a Mule in Missouri," *Sports Illustrated*, July 19, 1965: 36–46; John F. Lawrence, "Travels with Charlie: Baseball Owner Finley Moves on to Oakland with Mule, Controversy," *The Wall Street Journal*, April 8, 1968.

22. Interview with Bob Lurie, May 31, 2018.

23. In baseball, his methods could cause doubts among other owners even before he got a team. Veeck, *Veeck—As in Wreck*, 324.

24. Wells Twombly, "Charlie O., the Missouri Mule," *New York Times Magazine*, July 15, 1973: 12.

25. Tom Clark, "The Real Finley," *New York Times*, September 19, 1976.

26. "Charlie Finley: Baseball's Barnum," *Time*.

27. Armour and Levitt, *Paths to Glory*, 240.

28. Kuhn, *Hardball*, 126.

29. "Open Draft, Like Grid Pros, Rickey's Solution to Bonus," *Sporting News*, July 9, 1952: 11.

30. Allan Simpson, "The Inexact Science," in *2017 Sporting News Baseball Yearbook* (Charlotte, NC: Sporting News Yearbooks, 2017), 31.

31. Clifford Kachline, "'Socialism Threatens Game'—O'Malley," *Sporting News*, December 22, 1962: 1. The comparison with other sports is in "Draft Hasn't Erased Grid, Cage Dynasties—O'Malley," *Sporting News*, December 22, 1962: 2.

32. W. C. Madden, *Baseball's First-Year Player Draft*, 9.

33. J. G. Taylor Spink, "Uneasy Majors Eye Free-Agent Draft," *Sporting News*, June 28, 1961: 1; Dan Daniel, "Majors Hint Move Toward Free-Agent Draft," *Sporting News*, July 5, 1961: 5.

34. C. C. Johnson Spink, "'Free-Agent Draft Legal'—Antitrust Expert," *Sporting News*, December 12, 1964: 4.

35. Clifford Kachline, "Frick Lauds 'Great Progress Program,'" *Sporting News*, December 19, 1964: 1.

36. John Lawrence, "Cleveland Businessmen Seek to Save a City," *Wall Street Journal*, August 26, 1958.

37. Hal Lebovitz, "Now Indians Here for Good . . . Hal," *Cleveland Plain Dealer*, August 14, 1966. One of several articles on the sale appear in that edition.

38. "Off the Diamond," *Baseball Digest*, August 1942: 39.

39. MacPhail, *My Nine Innings*, 137.

40. The commissioner stepped in and removed some of the Reds from the starting lineup.

41. Richard Goldstein, "Gabe Paul, Ex-Yankee Official, Dies at 88," *New York Times*, April 28, 1998.

42. Goldstein, "Gabe Paul."

43. Alia Akkam, "Before It Became Synonymous with Lean Cuisine and French-Bread Pizza, the Frozen-Foods Monolith Was Just a Little Restaurant Company That Could," *Taste*, October 22, 2018. Retrieved online July 10, 2020, from https://www.tastecooking.com/stouffers-secret-history/.

44. Torry, *Endless Summers*, 105.

45. Marcus Glesser, "Stouffer Began as Lunch Counter," *Cleveland Plain Dealer*, July 24, 1990; "Stouffer Corp," in *International Directory of Company Histories* (Detroit: St. James Press, 2006). Retrieved August 14, 2019, from https://www.encyclopedia.com/books/politics-and-business-magazines/stouffer-corp.

46. "Litton Set to Buy Stouffer Foods," *New York Times*, April 3, 1967.

47. Nowlin, *Tom Yawkey*, 234, 251, 335.

48. Clifford Kachline, "Corporate Groups Control Most Major Clubs," *Sporting News*, December 13, 1961: 11.

49. Al Hirshberg, "The Sad Case of the Red Sox," *Saturday Evening Post*, May 21, 1960: 38; Hy Hurwitz, "Yawkey Calls Balk on Hub Scribes' Squawks," *Sporting News*, June 8, 1960: 7.

50. Stout and Johnson, *Red Sox Century*, 297–98, 317–18.

Chapter Seven

1. Now called Andrews University.

2. Nancy Kool, "Enlightenment and the Oldest Tiger," *Monthly Detroit*, April 1981: 32–41.

3. Fetzer, *One Man's Family* and *The Men from Wengen*.

4. Watson Spoelstra, "Boss Fetzer 'Regular Guy' to Tiger Players," *Sporting News*, October 12, 1968: 5.

5. Kool, "Enlightenment," 32–33.

6. Fetzer Institute, https://fetzer.org/. Retrieved July 12, 2019.

7. Dan Daniel, "Expansion Peace Bears Galbreath Stamp," *Sporting News*, December 21, 1960: 6.

8. "The Business of Baseball," *Newsweek*, April 26, 1965: 66.

9. Walker and Bellamy, *Center Field Shot*, 113–14.

10. "Cardinals and Cubs Will Play in NBC-TV's Opening Show," *Sporting News*, April 6, 1968: 11.

11. Holtzman, *The Commissioners*, 177.

12. Ewald, *John Fetzer*, 100.

13. Veeck, with Linn, *Hustler's Handbook*, 69.

14. This timetable is draw from a letter from Donald H. Loomis to Webb and Topping dated May 31, 1963, and a memo dated September 28, 1964, both in the Topping Papers (Box 1, Folder 16) at the National Baseball Hall of Fame and Museum. Webb and Topping's ownership was organized as a partnership rather than a corporation, which made avoiding taxes a much more difficult proposition.

15. Leonard Wallace Robinson, "What? A TV Drama," *New York Times Magazine*, November 15, 1964: 49.

16. "Wire Poll Violates A.L. Rules, Allyn Tells Cronin," *Chicago Tribune*, August 15, 1964.

17. "Cronin Turns Down AL Meeting Demand," *Chicago Tribune*, August 18, 1964.

18. "The Big Sellout," *Sports Illustrated*, August 24, 1964: 12.

19. Editorials in the *Sporting News*, "Why Wasn't CBS-Yank Deal Aired in Chicago," August 29, 1964: 14; and "Yankees Sale Demands League Discussion," September 5, 1964: 14.

20. Larry Claflin, "Cronin Rejects Allyn Request for Meeting," *Sporting News*, August 29, 1964: 2. He said both Allyn's purchase of the Comiskey holdings in the White Sox and Finley's purchase of the Athletics had been approved by telegram and telephone.

21. C. C. Johnson Spink, "Finley, Allyn Carry Fight Against Yank Sale to Justice Dept," *Sporting News*, October 10, 1964: 6.

22. "No Holds Barred as Scribes Spar with Yanks," *Sporting News*, August 29, 1964: 7.

23. Dick Young column, *Sporting News*, September 5, 1964: 16.

24. "Colts Want Action," *Chicago Tribune*, August 16, 1964.

25. "CBS Entry into Sports Causes Mixed Reactions," *Advertising Age*, August 17, 1964: 1; Robinson, "What? A TV Drama," 44; Dave Brady, "Senate Hearing Airs Support for CBS," *Sporting News*, March 6, 1965: 1.

26. William Barry Furlong, "A Sad Day for Baseball," *Sports Illustrated*, September 21, 1964: 26.

27. Surdam, *The Postwar Yankees*, 296.

28. Charles Maher, "Club Owners Indebted to Veeck," *Los Angeles Times*, November 3, 1975.

29. Veeck with Linn, *Hustler's Handbook*, 311; Rudolph Unger, "Arthur Allyn; Once Owned White Sox," *Chicago Tribune*, March 23, 1985.

30. Lindberg, *Stealing First*, 146.

31. William Barry Furlong, "The Butterfly Buff Who Ran the White Sox," *Chicago Tribune Magazine*, March 29, 1970: 20.

32. *Milwaukee Journal*, January 24, 1966.

Chapter Eight

1. C. C. Johnson Spink, "Owners Cut Commissioner List to 16 Names," *Sporting News*, August 7, 1965: 5.

2. Melvin Durslag, "An Unfair Choice for Owners," *Los Angeles Herald Examiner*, August 12, 1964.

3. Leonard Koppett, "Baseball's Biggest Crisis," *Sport*, March 1965: 22.

4. C. C. Johnson Spink, "Club Owners Act — Game Moves Forward," *Sporting News*, November 21, 1964: 8.

5. "Owners to Start Sifting Names for Frick's Post," *Sporting News*, April 10, 1965: 6; Frank Finch, "O'Malley Favors Baseball Man to Take Over Commissioner's Job," *Los Angeles Times*, July 23, 1965. This report was challenged by an unnamed baseball official. C. C. Johnson Spink, "Riled Club Owners Deny Writer's Rap of 'Foot-Dragging,'" *Sporting News*, November 13, 1965: 4.

6. Kachline, with Roewe, *Sporting News Official Baseball Guide, 1966*, 155.

7. Johnson Spink, "Owners Cut Commissioner List to 16 Names"; MacPhail, *My Nine Innings*, 95. Other names included former Florida governor LeRoy Collins, former attorney general William Rogers, Senator Philip Hart, Federal Judge Arthur Lane, and Secretary of the Air Force Eugene Zuckert. The Supreme Court justices were Potter Stewart and Byron "Whizzer" White. *The Sporting News Official Baseball Guide, 1966*, added General Maxwell Taylor; Secretary of the Army Stephen Ailes; G. Keith

Funston, head of the New York Stock Exchange; retiring New York mayor Robert Wagner; Oklahoma football coach Bud Wilkinson; American Football League president Joe Foss; Peace Corps director Sargent Shriver; Dodgers general manager Buzzie Bavasi; Pirates general manager Joe E. Brown; Giants vice president Chub Feeney; and Braves president John McHale (155).

8. "7 Candidates Still in Race for Post of Commissioner," *Sporting News*, November 6, 1965: 6.

9. William Furlong, "An Uninvited Guest Spills Baseball's Beans," *Sports Illustrated*, November 1, 1965: 62.

10. Max Nichols, "Eckert Learns Quickly Says Ex-Foe Griffith," *Sporting News*, January 28, 1967: 22. Griffith later said Finley and others had also voted against Eckert. See Holtzman, *The Commissioners*, 124.

11. Dick Young column, *Sporting News*, January 22, 1966: 14.

12. "Fetzer First to Interview Eckert, Game's New Boss," *Sporting News*, December 4, 1965: 4.

13. Holtzman, *The Commissioners*, 121.

14. Barney Kremenko, "'I'll Call the Signals,' Eckert Promises," *Sporting News*, December 4, 1965: 3.

15. C. C. Johnson Spink, "Two-Man Team to Run Game? Club Owners Will Air Proposal," *Sporting News*, July 10, 1965: 6.

16. Leonard Koppett, "Eckert's Appointment to Bring Radical Changes in Baseball Administration," *New York Times*, November 18, 1965.

17. Clifford Kachline, "Club Owners Vote Absolute Power to Baseball's Boss," *Sporting News*, December 19, 1964: 6.

18. Bob Sales, "Retired AF General to Replace Frick," *New York Herald Tribune*, November 18, 1965.

19. Leonard Koppett, "New Eckert Era—The First 275 Days," *Sporting News*, September 3, 1966: 5.

20. Dick Young column, *Sporting News*, December 11, 1965: 16.

21. "Eye on Eckert," *Sporting News*, December 25, 1965: 25.

22. Holtzman, *The Commissioners*, 121–32; Moffi, *Conscience of the Game*, 52.

23. Joe Trimble, "Mets Made Giants Observe RFK's Memory," *New York Daily News*, June 9, 1968. In that same issue, columnist Dick Young blasted Eckert as a man who could not make a decision because he wanted everyone to be happy.

24. William Leggett, "Court-Martial for a General," *Sports Illustrated*, December 16, 1968: 24.

25. Dick Young column, *New York Daily News*, April 23, 1971.

26. John Steadman, "Happy Hoffberger: Leader of Baltimore Band," *Sporting News*, October 8, 1966: 5.

27. "Orioles Sponsor Protests Ad Deal," *Baltimore Sun*, October 22, 1953.

28. Shirley Povich, "Showdown Is Near on Bidding for New Club in Washington," *Sporting News*, November 16, 1960: 4.

29. Jim Elliot, "Harris Likes Position Here," *Baltimore Sun*, September 5, 1961.

30. Various percentages were reported. See Neal Eskridge, "Hoffberger Now No. 1 Strong Man on Oriole Board," *Sporting News*, November 16, 1963: 21; Doug Brown, "Iglehart Absent from Meeting; Oriole Stockholder Rift Widens," *Sporting News*, December 28, 1963: 8; Doug Brown, "Krieger, Hoffberger Now Control Orioles," *Sporting News*, June 5, 1965: 23; Lou Hatter, "No Changes Seen Now In Orioles," *Baltimore Sun*, December 9, 1963; Bob Maisel column, *Baltimore Sun*, December 13, 1963; Lou Hatter, "Oriole Control 'Alliance' Is Disclaimed by Krieger," *Baltimore Sun*, December 15, 1963; Lou Hatter, "Orioles," *Baltimore Sun*, January 8, 1964; Lou Hatter, "Bill Veeck Not in Oriole Picture After Stock Sale," *Baltimore Sun*, May 27, 1965; and Lou Hatter, "Hoffberger Becomes Chairman of Oriole Board of Directors," *Baltimore Sun*, June 12, 1965.

31. Iglehart's presence on CBS's board was the clearest conflict, but owners and executives (including Yawkey, Allyn, Autry, Fetzer, Krieger, and MacPhail) throughout baseball owned CBS stock, a popular investment at the time. At one point, all franchises were required to submit lists of employees and their CBS holdings. It was a bureaucratic mess and another issue that was overlooked when it should have been approached thoughtfully. See C. C. Johnson Spink, "CBS Stock Inquiry—Conflict of Interest," *Sporting News*, February 6, 1965: 1; Dave Brady, "Senate Hearing Airs Support for CBS," *Sporting News*, March 6, 1965: 1–2; Doug Brown, "Owners Allow Iglehart to Keep CBS Holdings," *Sporting News*, April 10, 1965: 18; and Dick Young column, *Sporting News*, June 19, 1965: 2.

32. Mike Fuller interview with Bavasi, June 1994, posted on http://seattlepilots.com/bavasi_int.html. Retrieved October 16, 2018.

33. Helyar, *Lords of the Realm*, 190–91.

34. MacPhail, *My Nine Innings*, 76–77.

35. Cashen, *Winning in Both Leagues*, 7–9.

36. Doug Brown, "At Height of Pennant Revelry, Orioles Remembered Dick Brown," *Sporting News*, October 8, 1966: 26.

37. Miller, *Baseball Business*, 109–11.

38. Burke, *Outrageous Good Fortune*, 61.

39. Bob Addie column, *Sporting News*, December 17, 1966: 14.

40. Roger Kahn, "The Yankees: The Descent from Olympus," *Saturday Evening Post*, September 12, 1964: 80.

41. Appel, *Pinstripe Empire*, 365–68. Robinson would be a bust for the Yankees but go on to a successful career elsewhere.

42. Durso, *All-American Dollar*, 122.

43. Arthur Daley, "Cloak and Dagger Man," *Sporting News*, October 15, 1966: 11.

44. Jim Ogle, "Yanks Boast Own New Breed: Burke," *Sporting News*, June 3, 1967: 5.

45. C. C. Johnson Spink column, *Sporting News*, June 10, 1967: 14.

46. Bill Reel, "Mike Burke: The Go-Getter of Sports and Business Isn't Going to Stop Until He's Got the Yankees Playing Like Yankees Again," *New York Daily News*, July 9, 1967. The poem was William Butler Yeats's "An Irish Airman Foresees His Death," which references Kiltartan Cross, a traditional stronghold of the Burke clan.

47. "Crisis of the Old Order," *Sporting News*, December 21, 1968: 14.

48. George Vecsey, "Young Turks Picked to Shift Baseball's Stance," *New York Times*, December 7, 1968; "Crisis of the Old Order."

49. Arthur Daley column, *New York Times*, June 11, 1968.

50. Arthur Daley column, *New York Times*, December 10, 1968.

51. Milton Richman, "Yanks' Burke Reportedly Next Commissioner," *Los Angeles Times*, December 10, 1968.

52. Kuhn, *Hardball*, 32.

53. Leonard Koppett column, *Sporting News*, December 20, 1969: 6.

54. John B. Old, "Chandler Urges One Office Center for O.B.," *Sporting News*, July 31, 1946: 1.

55. Jack Walsh, "Lost MacPhail Report 'Whodunit' of Hearings," *Sporting News*, October 24, 1951: 1.

56. Edgar Munzel, "'Pool Umps and Save $$,' Short Urges," *Sporting News*, May 13, 1963: 1.

57. Bob Hunter, "Smokey Leans Again on Top-Job Jim," *Sporting News*, August 17, 1963: 7; Edgar Munzel, "'Abolish League Presidencies'—Allyn," *Sporting News*, January 23, 1965: 1.

58. Edgar Munzel, "Allyn Proposal Hit by Wrigley and O'Malley," *Sporting News*, January 30, 1965: 15.

59. John G. Griffin, "Baseball Could Be Headed for Stunning Changes Soon," *Los Angeles Times*, December 8, 1968.

60. See the *Sporting News* articles by Bob Hunter, "'Coming Changes Were Long Planned'—O'Malley," December 28, 1968: 29; C. C. Johnson Spink, "Burke's Blueprint for Bowie," March 15, 1969: 14; Edgar Munzel, "Allyn Sees Restructuring of Majors Before 1970," June 7, 1969: 21; Ralph Ray, "Sharp Changes in Store for Baseball Structure," November 8, 1969: 38; and Leonard Koppett, "Kuhn Would Have Czar Power If Planners' Ideas Win Okay," December 20, 1969: 29.

61. Koppett, "Kuhn Would Have Czar Power."

62. Clifford Kachline, "Majors Follow Pro Football Lead—Plan to Tap Novelties Market," *Sporting News*, December 17, 1966: 22.

63. Helyar, *Lords of the Realm*, 67.

64. "Baseball Tries to Keep Its Bounce," *Business Week*, April 20, 1963: 144.

65. "Coke, Majors to Be Linked by $2,000,000 Promotion," *Sporting News*, February 11, 1967: 27.

66. "Majors to Step Up Promotion Efforts," *Sporting News*, August 24, 1968: 34.

67. Martin Rossman, "Baseball Promotion: A Long Way from a Case of Wheaties," *Los Angeles Times*, December 7, 1970.

68. Leonard Koppett column, *Sporting News*, December 20, 1969: 6.

69. Helyar, *Lords of the Realm*, 309, 316.

70. Rossman, "Baseball Promotion."

71. Jerome Holtzman, "Charlie-Jerry vs. Establishment," *Sporting News*, August 2, 1975: 18.

72. Jerome Holtzman column, *Sporting News*, June 16, 1973: 10.

Chapter Nine

1. Katz, *The Kansas City A's and the Wrong Half of the Yankees*.

2. Jerry Holtzman, "Finley Rips Kaycee's 'Farm-Club' Label"; and Ernest Mehl, "'A's Will Develop Stars and Keep Them' — Finley," *Sporting News*, December 28, 1960: 7.

3. Hy Hurwirtz, "Cronin Hails 3 New Owners at Boston Dinner," *Sporting News*, February 8, 1961: 9.

4. Robinson, with Rogers, *Lucky Me*, 158.

5. Rex Lardner, "Charlie Finley and Bugs Bunny in K.C.," *Sports Illustrated*, June 5, 1961: 25–26.

6. Ernest Mehl, "Buys All of A's Stock," *Kansas City Star*, February 16, 1961; "A Ceremonial Burning . . .," *Kansas City Times*, February 18, 1961.

7. Peterson, *Kansas City Athletics*, 137–40.

8. Ernest Mehl, "A's Ills Linked to Front Office Interference," *Kansas City Star*, August 17, 1961.

9. Ernest Mehl, "Rumors of A's Move Persist," *Kansas City Times*, August 17, 1961.

10. Finley, *Finley Ball*, 17–18.

11. Ernest Mehl, "Kaycee's Future Cloudy in Swirl of Shift Rumors," *Sporting News*, August 30, 1961: 6.

12. "Athletics Dismiss Frank Lane; Owner Says He Harmed Club," *New York Times*, August 23, 1961.

13. The trade actually could have worked out well for the Athletics. Bud Daley gave the Yankees three and a half seasons of useful pitching. Art Ditmar gave the A's little over his two years, but prospect Deron Johnson would spend sixteen more years in the majors, hitting 245 home runs. Unfortunately, Finley would sell his contract to the Cincinnati Reds before Johnson blossomed. Some researchers consider the story

of the unfair trades to be untrue. See "The 1955–60 Kansas City Athletics Gave Away Their Talent to the Yankees," in Deane, *Baseball Myths*.

14. Clifford Kachline, "Smouldering Kaycee Ruckus May Blaze Up at Big-Timer Huddle," *Sporting News*, November 29, 1961: 25.

15. Green and Launius, *Charlie Finley*, 55.

16. "New contract on A's Stadium," *Kansas City Star*, August. 26, 1961.

17. Green and Launius, *Charlie Finley*, 61.

18. Kachline, "Smouldering Kaycee Ruckus May Blaze Up."

19. Ernest Mehl, "A's Fans Ask Showdown on Shift," *Sporting News*, June 2, 1962: 1.

20. Ernest Mehl, "'Build Park or Lose Franchise,' Finley Tells Kaycee City Council," *Sporting News*, September 29, 1962: 16.

21. "Expansion to 24 Major Clubs '62 Possibility, Frick Says," *Sporting News*, December 28, 1960: 12. Frick was not the only optimist. Throughout the 1960s, many issues of the *Sporting News* carried articles touting the "inevitable" next round of expansion. For examples, see Pat Harmon, "'Start Planning for 24 Clubs in 1964'—Dewitt," *Sporting News*, June 16, 1962: 1; or Bob Wolf, "McHale, Bartholomay See 12-Club League in Future," *Sporting News*, February 8, 1964: 10.

22. Harry Chandler, "Braves' Financial Picture Read into Record of Trial," *Terre Haute (Indiana) Star*, March 25, 1966. See also Dick Kaegel, "Owners Veto Early-Expansion Plans," *Sporting News*, January 29, 1966: 1.

23. *Los Angeles Examiner*, April 16, 1961.

24. Armour, *Joe Cronin*, 297.

25. Clifford Kachline, "Majors Pick Up $10 Million Tab in Minors," *Sporting News*, December 15, 1962: 5, 10.

26. C. C. Johnson Spink, "Braves' Shift Needs Only Okay by N.L.," *Sporting News*, July 11, 1964: 1; Braves ownership dodged the question until late October. See Reese Cleghorn, "Hush-Hush Atlanta Deal Sealed with Handshake," *Milwaukee Journal*, October 22, 1964.

27. Bob Wolf, "'Unpack,' N.L. Tells Itchy-Footed Braves," *Sporting News*, November 21, 1964: 7.

28. Cronin's caution is in Clifford Kachline, "Expansion 'Years Away,' Majors Insist," *Sporting News*, December 18, 1965: 1, while the orders to Eckert are in Oscar Kahan, "Exec Council Takes Steps on Expansion," *Sporting News*, April 15, 1967: 6.

29. Charles Maher, "Baseball Playoff Defeated—This Is Progress?" *Los Angeles Times*, August 12, 1967; Edgar Munzel, "N.L. Blocks Move by A.L. to Install Two-Division Play," *Sporting News*, August 19, 1967: 4.

30. "Red Sox Lead AL Attendance Mark," *Boston Globe*, November 12, 1967; the National League did not move to tickets sold rather than turnstile account until the early 1990s. Turnstile count for the A.L.'s 1967 season had actually fallen from the 1966 level.

31. By 1971, the National League's advantage would be back up, to 5.4 million.

32. *Los Angeles Herald Examiner*, April 22, 1962.

33. Edgar Munzel, "Cronin Says A.L.'s Path Leads to West Coast, Not Milwaukee," *Sporting News*, February 19, 1966: 4.

34. Peterson, *Kansas City Athletics*, 157.

35. Ernest Mehl, "A's Fans Ask Showdown on Shift," *Sporting News*, June 2, 1962: 1.

36. Ernest Mehl, "'Build Park or Lose Franchise,' Finley Tells Kaycee City Council." *Sporting News*, September 29, 1962: 16.

37. Mehl, "'Build Park or Lose Franchise."

38. "Finley Clamps Tight Budget on A's After $1.5 Million Deficit in 1962," *Sporting News*, October 20, 1962: 25.

39. McGuff, *Winning It All*, 128–30.

40. Bisher, *Miracle in Atlanta*, 13–14.

41. Ernest Mehl, "'No Plea Made to Shift A's'—Finley," *Sporting News*, August 31, 1963: 2.

42. Joe McGuff, "Kaycee and Finley Play Catch—Wild Pitches Fly All Over Lot," *Sporting News*, January 11, 1964: 6.

43. "Finley Faces League 'No' on Louisville," *Chicago Tribune*, January 7, 1964.

44. "Rebuffed Finley Vows Court Fight," *Chicago Tribune*, January 17, 1964; and Joe King, "'Ink Kaycee Pact or Lose A.L. Franchise,' Owners Tell Finley," *Sporting News*, January 25, 1964: 4.

45. Clifford Kachline, "A.L. Ready to Bid Finley Farewell," *Sporting News*, January 18, 1964: 1.

46. Associated Press, "League Meeting Starts Late, and with Review of Hassel," *Iola (Kansas) Register*, February 21, 1964.

47. Peterson, *Kansas City Athletics*, 227.

48. Joe McGuff, "Kansas City Voters Approve Bonds for Two New Stadiums," *Sporting News*, July 15, 1967: 15.

49. C. C. Johnson Spink, "Finley Dickering to Move A's to Milwaukee," *Sporting News*, July 22, 1967: 9; C. C. Johnson Spink, "Oakland Jumps Back into Finley Plans," *Sporting News*, July 29, 1967: 15.

50. All figures from 1970 census.

51. Prescott Sullivan, "A 'New' Oakland Is on the March!," *San Francisco Examiner*, March 7, 1962.

52. Bob Brachman, "A's Talk Oakland Move," *San Francisco Examiner*, July 9, 1963.

53. "Kansas City Observers Feel A's Might Move," *New York Times*, May 7, 1967.

54. C. C. Johnson Spink, "Finley Dickering to Move A's to Milwaukee," *Sporting News*, July 22, 1967: 9; C. C. Johnson Spink, "Oakland Jumps Back into Finley Plans"; Green and Launius, *Charlie Finley*, 102.

55. Green and Launius, *Charlie Finley*, 103–9.

56. Joe McGuff, "What Next? Kaycee Fans Can Only Wonder," *Sporting News*, September 2, 1967: 18.

57. Peterson, *Kansas City Athletics*, 251–55.

58. Jerome Holtzman, "A.L. Vote to Expand Marks 1967 History," in Roewe and Kahan, eds., *Sporting News Official Baseball Guide for 1968*, 176.

59. Richard Dozer, "Finley to Oakland and K.C. Burns!," *Chicago Tribune*, October 19, 1967.

60. *Congressional Record*, October 19, 1967.

61. Holtzman, "A.L. Vote to Expand Marks 1967 History," Allyn had unilaterally contacted Kansas City leaders and offered to guarantee an expansion team for 1970 if they dropped any opposition to Finley's move. While Allyn's move was disavowed by the American League, it mirrored the league's eventual first offer. Paul Mac Farlane, "Kaycee Men Kayo Allyn's Pitch to Gas Up Finley's Moving Van," *Sporting News*, October 7, 1967: 39.

62. Joe McGuff, "'See You Around,' Finley Tells K.C., Packing His Grips," *Sporting News*, October 14, 1967: 13.

63. Peterson, *Kansas City Athletics*, 260.

64. Armour, *Joe Cronin*, 298; Joe McGuff, "Finley and His Mule Take It on the Lam," *Sporting News*, November 4, 1967: 33.

65. Armour, *Joe Cronin*; Morgan, *Prescription for Success*, 239; Richard Dozer, "Finley to Oakland and K.C. Burns"; and Bordman, *An Intimate History*, 4–5.

66. Richard Dozer, "N.L.'s Leader Terms Plan 'Premature': Finley Deal Is Also Rapped," *Chicago Tribune*, October 20, 1967.

67. Richard Dozer, "Finley's Move Causes Action: Influenced League's Expansion: Allyn," *Chicago Tribune*, October 24, 1967.

68. Dick Young column, *Sporting News*, November 11, 1967: 14.

69. Montreal, Toronto, and Miami also were both available and bigger than Seattle.

70. Mullins, *Becoming Big League*, 57; Mike Fuller, "Interview with Buzzie Bavasi," June 1994, posted at http://seattlepilots.com/Bavasi_int.html. Before the October 18 meeting, Magnuson and Jackson had sent both leagues telegrams urging a team for Seattle. Richard Dozer, "Finley Requests Move of A's Today," *Chicago Tribune*, October 18, 1967.

71. Dick Young, "National League Won't Contest AL Seattle Franchise," *Los Angeles Times*, November 14, 1967.

72. Population figures are from the 1970 U.S. Census and 1971 national survey by Statistics Canada.

73. MacPhail, *My Nine Innings*, 111.

Chapter Ten

1. Duckstad and Waybur, *Feasibility of a Major Sports Stadium for King County, Washington.*

2. Mullins, *Becoming Big League,* 50.

3. Mullins, *Becoming Big League,* 34.

4. Mullins, *Becoming Big League,* 78–79.

5. Mullins, *Becoming Big League,* 134–35.

6. Max Soriano interview with Mike Fuller posted at Seattlepilots.com. Retrieved May 7, 2020.

7. The profiles of the Soriano brothers are drawn from "Wayback Machine: Dewey Soriano Story, Part I," April 16, 2013, at sportspressnw.com/2149411/2013/wayback -machine-dewey-soriano-story-part-i, and "Wayback Machine: Dewey Soriano Story, Part II," April 23, 2013, at sportspressnw.com/2149857/wayback-machine-dewey -soriano-story-part-ii; "Baseball Figure Dewey Soriano Dies at Age 78," *Seattle Times,* April 7, 1998; "Where Are They Now: Max Soriano," *Seattle Post-Intelligencer,* August 1, 2007; and "Max Soriano Was Praised and Pilloried for Bringing Pilots Baseball Team to Seattle," *Toronto Globe and Mail,* October 17, 2012.

8. Dewey would have a somewhat checkered career as a pilot. Max had to represent him three times. In 1961, a ship Dewey was piloting hit a submerged object near Smith Island (*Seattle Times,* June 20, 1961). In 1967, he hit a rock in the same area and the Coast Guard temporarily suspended his license (*Seattle Times,* April 7, 1988). And in 1982, an automobile carrier he was piloting hit a bridge in Tacoma (*Seattle Times,* April 7, 1988).

9. Joseph Durso, "A.L. Juggles Seattle: A Hot Potato," *Sporting News,* March 21, 1970: 12. Max Soriano put the total at $8 million, a figure set by the league. Max Soriano interview at seattlepilots.com.

10. Fuller, Max Soriano interview.

11. Mullins, *Becoming Big League,* 61–64.

12. Mullins, *Becoming Big League,* 62.

13. Stan Isle, "Foot-Dragging N.L. Agrees to Expand," *Sporting News,* December 16, 1967: 29. At the time, there was considerable newspaper coverage of Buzzie Bavasi's interest in heading a team in Seattle. The Dodgers' general manager, who later went with the National League's expansion team in San Diego, said he passed on Seattle because of the stadium situation (Bavasi interview with Mike Fuller at seattlepilots.com).

14. Dewey Soriano interview by Mike Fuller posted at seattlepilots.com.

15. Parrot, *Lords of Baseball,* 61–62.

16. Mullins, *Becoming Big League,* 81, 86.

17. Mullins, *Becoming Big League,* 135.

18. Fuller, Max Soriano interview.

19. Hy Zimmerman, "Will Pilots Have Place to Play? Money Crisis Looms," *Sporting News*, January 11, 1969: 34.

20. Mullins, *Becoming Big League*, 136, 141; see also Zimmerman, "Will Pilots Have Place to Play?"

21. Kuhn, *Hardball*, 91.

22. Lenny Anderson, "Clear, Smooth Sailing Greets Pilots' First Seattle Cruise," *Sporting News*, April 26, 1969: 10.

23. Mullins, *Becoming Big League*, 141.

24. Mullins, *Becoming Big League*, 143.

25. Lester Smith, "Senators Set Pace in Majors' Higher Ticket Prices," *Sporting News*, April 12, 1969: 36.

26. Hy Zimmerman, "Angry Seattle and Pilots Sitting on Powder Keg," *Sporting News*, October 18, 1969: 32.

27. Hy Zimmerman, "Skimpy Gate, Rumor Waves Jolt Pilots," *Sporting News*, September 20, 1969: 24.

28. Fuller, Max Soriano interview.

29. Joseph Durso, "A.L. Juggles Seattle: A Hot Potato," *Sporting News*, March 21, 1970: 12.

30. Fuller, Max Soriano interview.

31. Bob Addie column, *Sporting News*, August 23, 1969: 14.

32. "June 19, 1969. It is possible to devise . . ." Kuhn Papers at the Baseball Hall of Fame and Museum, Series I, Sub-series 2, Box 6, Folder 5.

33. Zimmerman, "Angry Seattle and Pilots Sitting on Powder Keg."

34. Fuller, Max Soriano interview. In later testimony at the resulting lawsuits, Oakland A's owner Charlie Finley said Daley had assured them he would put in more money if necessary. Mullins, *Becoming Big League*, 61.

35. The Dallas report was in Hy Zimmerman, "Mickey Fuentes: Pride of Pilots' Hill," *Sporting News*, September 27, 1969: 20; the Milwaukee news surfaced in Zimmerman's "Seattle's on Spot for $13,700,000," *Sporting News*, November 1, 1969: 21; and Richard Dozer, "Pilot Rumors Fly on Eve of A.L. Meeting," *Chicago Tribune*, October 21, 1969.

36. Hy Zimmerman, "Seattle Tycoons Step Forward—Block Pilot Shift," *Sporting News*, November 22, 1969: 41. The revised numbers appeared in Hy Zimmerman, "Control of Pilots Shifts to Seattle; $10.3 Million Deal," *Sporting News*, November 29, 1969: 42.

37. Zimmerman, "Control of Pilots Shifts to Seattle."

38. "Seattle Relaxing After A.L. Okays Sale to Danz," *Sporting News*, December 20, 1969: 34.

39. Hy Zimmerman, "Pilots Try No-Profit Sale to Keep Ship Afloat," *Sporting News*, February 7, 1970: 33.

40. "'Pilots Up for Grabs,'—Owner," *Chicago Tribune*, January 23, 1970; Richard Dozer, "Seattle Has No Real Leader: Allyn," *Chicago Tribune*, January 24, 1970.

41. Richard Dozer, "A.L. Votes to Keep Pilots in Seattle," *Chicago Tribune*, February 11. 1970: E1.

42. Mullins, *Becoming Big League*, 211. The other three owners were Jerold Hoffberger of the Baltimore Orioles, Charlie Finley of the Oakland Athletics, and Bob Short of the Washington Senators.

43. Richard Dozer, "Old Ownership Keeps Pilots: A.L. Will Loan Club $650,000," *Chicago Tribune*, February 12, 1970.

44. Joseph Durso, "A.L. Juggles Seattle: A Hot Potato," *Sporting News*, March 21, 1970: 12.

45. Zimmerman, "Pilots Try No-Profit Sale to Keep Ship Afloat"; Richard Dozer, "A.L. Votes to Keep Pilots in Seattle," *Chicago Tribune*, February 11, 1970.

46. *Associated Press*, "AL 'Just About Ready' for Shift," *Port Angeles Evening News*, March 17, 1970.

47. "We're Big League Again! Court OKs Sale of Pilots," *Milwaukee Journal*, April 1, 1970; "Judge OK's Pilots Sale, Baseball to Return Here," *Milwaukee Sentinel*, April 1, 1970; "Pilots Sight Beacon, Steer Right for Milwaukee," *Sporting News*, April 11, 1970: 14.

48. Zantow, *Building the Brewers*, 99.

49. Mullins, *Becoming Big League*, 63.

50. Kuhn, *Hardball*, 93.

51. Dick Young column, *Sporting News*, October 12, 1968: 14.

52. The National League's Philadelphia Phillies and the American League's Chicago White Sox and Cleveland Indians also drew less than the Pilots, and also paid their bills.

53. William Daley, like an infection that does not respond to antibiotics, remained in the franchise's ownership, with 16 percent of the stock. Jerome Holtzman. "Owners Peeved at Kuhn," *Sporting News*, October 24, 1970: 24.

54. The father was the namesake of the Great Lakes ore carrier that sank in 1975 and was eulogized by Gordon Lightfoot in "The Wreck of the Edmund Fitzgerald," *Milwaukee Journal-Sentinel*, January 10, 1986.

55. Zantow, *Building the Brewers*, 52.

56. Selig, with Rogers, *For the Good of the Game*, 50.

57. "Selig's 1 Love Is Baseball," *Kenosha (Wisconsin) News*, July 16, 1976.

58. Zantow, *Building the Brewers*, 50.

59. Selig, with Rogers, *For the Good of the Game*, 51.

60. Jim Hawkins, "Tigers' Mystery Man Fetzer: 'I've Got a Manager Down There to Run Things,'" *Detroit Free Press*, January 30, 1979.

61. Hawkins, "Tigers' Mystery Man Fetzer."

62. Selig, with Rogers, *For the Good of the Game*, 124, 149.

63. Selig, with Rogers, *For the Good of the Game*, 84.

Chapter Eleven

1. This profile draws on Anne Morgan, *Prescription for Success*; Allan T. Demaree, "Ewing Kauffman Sold Himself Rich in Kansas City," *Fortune*, October 1972: 99–103; and Daniel R. Levitt, "Ewing Kauffman," in Nowlin and Carle, eds. *Kansas City Royals*, 185–94.

2. Morgan, *Prescription for Success*, 46.

3. Demaree, "Ewing Kaufman," 99.

4. Phil Koury, "Kauffman Puts Winning Record on Line," *Kansas City Star*, January 14, 1968.

5. Demaree, "Ewing Kaufman," 101.

6. Joe McGuff, "Royals Offer Players $$$ Counsel," *Sporting News*, July 11, 1970: 20.

7. Bob Addie, "Financial Wizard Johnston Serene in Nat Red-Ink Sea," *Sporting News*, January 23, 1965: 18.

8. Merrell Whittlesey, "Safer, Cleaner Park, Short Order for Nats," *Sporting News*, December 21, 1968: 29.

9. Shelby Coffey III, "Short Wheeled $1,000 into Franchise Worth Millions," *Washington Post*, December 19, 1971. For Short's rebuttal, see Max Nichols, "Short's High Finance in Baseball: Tells His Side of Senators' Ups and Downs," *Minneapolis Star*, January 1, 1972.

10. Tom Dowling, "Bob Short: Born for the Limelight," *Washington Evening Star*, October 3, 1972.

11. "Short Takes Long Look at Lack of Radio Outlet," *Sporting News*, January 18, 1969: 41. Attendance in 1968 was 546,661.

12. Ryczek, *Baseball on the Brink*, 195.

13. "People," *Sports Illustrated*, March 9, 1970: 42.

14. Helyar, *Lords of the Realm*, 191.

15. "Bob Short 4/6/71 10:30 pm EST," in Bowie Kuhn Papers, Giamatti Research Center, National Baseball Hall of Fame and Museum. These are Kuhn's handwritten notes of a phone conversation.

16. Dave Brady, "Short Raps Business for Non-Support," *Washington Post*, March 4, 1970.

17. "Bob Short 4/6/71"; and Kuhn, *Hardball*, 94.

18. Shirley Povich, "Creditors Ease Way for Short," *Washington Post*, January 5, 1971; and "This Morning," June 14, 1971; Merrell Whittlesey, "Senators, in Financial Shorts, Seek League Lift," *Sporting News*, July 7, 1971: 27; Ron Fimrite, "Bad Case of the Short Shorts," *Sports Illustrated*, August 9, 1971: 20.

19. Kuhn, *Hardball*, 96.

20. Jerome Holtzman column, *Sporting News*, February 19, 1972: 31.

21. From a partial transcript of the American League minutes attached to a letter from Major League Baseball attorney James Fitzpatrick of the law firm of Arnold & Porter to U.S. Representatives B. F. Sisk and Frank Horton, August 9, 1976. A copy of the letter and attachment are in the Kuhn Papers.

22. Kuhn, *Hardball*, 96.

23. Shirley Povich column, *Washington Post*, October 19, 1971.

24. Kuhn, *Hardball*, 95.

25. Jerome Holtzman, "Chisox to Stay, New Boss John Allyn Promises," *Sporting News*, October 11, 1969: 15.

26. Terry Robards, "Francis I. DuPont Lists Big '69 Loss," *New York Times*, February 5, 1970; Terry Robards, "F. I. DuPont Sets a Major Merger," *New York Times*, June 4, 1970; Joseph Egelhof, "Chicago Is Big in duPont's Plan," *Chicago Tribune*, July 6, 1970; Joseph Egelhof, "Allyn New Chairman of F. I. duPont Firm," *Chicago Tribune*, December 30, 1970.

27. John H. Allan, "DuPont Walston Quitting Securities Business," *New York Times*, January 22, 1974.

28. David Condon column, *Chicago Tribune*, September 24, 1969.

29. Interview with Roland Hemond, March 3, 2017.

30. Richard Dozer, "Dreary Future for Fans of Milwaukee Baseball," *Chicago Tribune*, February 14, 1970.

31. Hemond interview.

32. David Bohmer, *Cleveland Indians Team Ownership History*, https://sabr.org/research/cleveland-indians-team-ownership-history, retrieved February 19, 2020.

33. Jerome Holtzman, "A Rude Surprise for Stouffer," *Sporting News*, December 25, 1971: 32.

34. Russell Schneider, "Director Convinced Tribe Will Stay," *Cleveland Plain Dealer*, December 8, 1971; Russell Schneider, "Stouffer Snubs Local Bid for Injuns," *Sporting News*, December 25, 1971: 33.

35. William N. Wallace, "Mileti Buys Indians; Price: $9-Million," *New York Times*, March 7, 1972.

36. Dan Coughlin, "Tribe Sale to Mileti Hits Snag," *Cleveland Plain Dealer*, March 9, 1972.

37. Hal Lebovitz, "What's Nick Mileti Buying," *Cleveland Plain Dealer*, March 23, 1972.

38. Ron Fimrite, "Whooping It Up with the Indians," *Sports Illustrated*, July 29, 1974: 23.

39. Torry, *Endless Summers*, 135–36.

40. Peter Phipps and John Kostrzewa, "The Coliseum—A Fortune Lost in a Corn-field," *Akron Beacon-Journal*, June 7, 1981.

41. "Nick Mileti: The 7.5 Pct. 'Owner,'" *Akron Beacon-Journal*, July 7, 1973. See chart attached to story.

42. Torry, *Endless Summers*, 137–39.

43. Leonard Koppett, "Hitters Scrape Bottom, Figures Show," *Sporting News*, October 19, 1968: 27; and "Larger Strike Zone Key to Batting Famine," *Sporting News*, October 26, 1968: 15.

44. Arno Goethel, "Hitters Need Help, Cal Claims," *Sporting News*, May 25, 1968: 23.

45. "Base Ball: Chadwick's Chat," *Sporting Life*, August 8, 1888: 5.

46. McKelvey, *All Bat, No Glove*, 23.

47. Leonard Koppett column, *Sporting News*, June 25, 1977: 4.

48. Russell Schneider, "'We're Even with N.L. at Last,' Paul Claims," *Sporting News*, May 7, 1966: 7.

49. "Angels Point Up A.L. Problem," *Sporting News*, August 20, 1966: 14.

50. Quirk and Fort, *Pay Dirt*, 378–408. Phillies are on 397.

51. Paul, with Smith, *Yankee Princess*, 45–48.

52. There are many renderings of this quotation with slightly different wording. The earliest rendering I could find is the Dave Anderson column in the *New York Times*, May 23, 1982.

53. For much of this profile, see Madden, *Steinbrenner*.

54. Dick Schaap, *Steinbrenner*! (New York: G. P. Putnam's, 1982), 79–80.

55. The haircut order came after Steinbrenner attended Opening Day ceremonies and watched the player introductions. However, he didn't know who the players were, so he gave a list of uniform numbers to Houk, who read out the number list deadpan in the clubhouse the next day, acting as if he did not know to whom each number belonged.

56. There must be some doubt about his claim of a minor league career. Corbett said he played in Statesville, North Carolina, and Fargo, North Dakota, under the name Bob Taylor before he went to Wagner. Since Corbett was born in 1937, these appearances would have had to be in the mid-1950s. An incomplete roster for Statesville in 1953 (https://www.baseball-reference.com/register/team.cgi?id=829924c7) shows no mention of a Taylor or a Corbett. There was not another team in Statesville until 1960. There was no team in Fargo between 1922 and 2009. Corbett's claim appears most specifically in Mark Whicker, "The Man Who Runs the Rangers," *Dallas Times Herald Sunday Magazine*, April 17, 1977, 11.

57. Gary Cartwright, "Pennant Wise, Dollar Foolish," *Texas Monthly*, May 1978: 170.

58. Whicker, "Man Who Runs the Rangers," 8.

59. Cartwright, "Pennant Wise," 170.

60. Kent Hannon, "Huffing and Puffing in Texas," *Sports Illustrated*, August 7, 1978: 41.

61. Robinson, with Rogers, *Lucky Me*, 190.

62. Whicker, "Man Who Runs the Rangers," 7.

63. Blackie Sherrod column, *Dallas Times-Herald*, July 8, 1977.

64. "Corbett No 'Ringleader': Owner Denies Leading Move for Kuhn Ouster," *Dallas Times-Herald*, February 23, 1978.

65. Blackie Sherrod, "Corbett Blowing His Own Horn," *Dallas Times-Herald*, March 22, 1978.

66. Steve Mott, "Corbett: Back to Pipe Dream," *Dallas Times-Herald*, July 6, 1977.

67. "Robintech Sets Plans That Could Change Control of the Firm," *Wall Street Journal*, March 1, 1979.

68. Hannon, "Huffing and Puffing," 41.

69. Quoted in Kent Biffle, "Rangers' Owner Corbett: 'I Let Fans Down,'" *Dallas Morning News*, July 9, 1977. The editorial ran in the *Star-Telegram* on June 30.

Chapter Twelve

1. "Padres en Route to Capital with Record 12 Million Tag," *Sporting News*, June 9, 1973: 22.

2. Jerome Holtzman, "'More Study Time' N.L.'s Answer to Padres' Move Bid," *Sporting News*, October 6, 1973: 10; Phil Collier, "Padres' Fate Still Up in Air with New Prospect as a Buyer," *Sporting News*, January 26, 1974: 30.

3. Phil Collier, "New Money Grants Padres 11th-Hour Stay," *Sporting News*, October 20, 1973: 12.

4. Phil Collier, "Padres Cancel Flight Plans, Start to Unpack," *Sporting News*, December 8, 1973: 50.

5. Phil Collier, "Padres' Fate Still Up in Air"; Phil Collier, "City Comes to Aid of Poverty-Stricken Padres," *Sporting News*, February 2, 1974: 30. The confusion was such that the first series of Topps' 1974 baseball cards had the Padres' players listed as Washington NL.

6. "San Diego Gets a Break Today; Kroc Buys the Padres," *Los Angeles Times*, January 26, 1974; Phil Collier, "Padres Get Break They Deserve, From Big Mac," *Sporting News*, February 9, 1974: 29.

7. Wells Twombly, "Baseball Eyes Seattle's Domed Stadium," *San Francisco Sunday Examiner*, June 16, 1974.

8. The sale announcement was in Ron Bergman, "Letter from Finley Helps to Fog A's Future," *Sporting News*, February 9, 1974: 47. The denial was in Glenn Schwarz, "Furious Finley Calls O'Malley Senile," *San Francisco Sunday Examiner*, December 8, 1974.

9. MacPhail to Finley, June 6, 1975, in Bowie Kuhn Papers, National Baseball Hall of Fame and Museum.

10. "Stoneham's Giants in Financial Bind," *Los Angeles Times*, April 30, 1975.

11. Garratt, *Home Team*, 73–90; Pat Frizzell, "Money-Plagued Giants Placed on Block," *Sporting News*, May 24, 1975: 34.

12. "File Memorandum, July 24, 1975, AHH to BBK" [*sic*], Kuhn Papers. BBK, which should have been BKK, was Kuhn. AHH was Sandy Hadden, Kuhn's main assistant.

13. *Washington Star*, December 13, 1975.

14. Garratt, *Home Team*, 97–98.

15. Interview with Bob Lurie, May 31, 2018.

16. Garratt, *Home Team*, 96–106.

17. Bob Fowler, "Griffiths' Family Ownership in Danger," *Sporting News*, April 3, 1976: 28.

18. "File Memorandum, July 24, 1975."

19. Spellman to Lee MacPhail, September 5, 1975, Kuhn Papers.

20. Richard Dozer, "Owners Give Allyn Time," *Chicago Tribune*, September 25, 1975.

21. David Bohmer, https://sabr.org/research/cleveland-indians-team-ownership -history, retrieved March 30, 2019.

22. Bob Addie, "Players Should Heed Mantle," *Sporting News*, August 9, 1975: 13.

23. Glenn Schwarz, "Furious Finley Calls O'Malley Senile"; "Draft—April 25, 1975," Press release, Kuhn Papers.

24. Jerome Holtzman, "Finley Still Holds a Trump Card," *Sporting News*, August 16, 1975: 40; C. C. Johnson Spink, "Ailing Teams Next on Owners' Agenda," *Sporting News*, September 27, 1975: 3, 6.

25. Jack Lang, "Big Time Expansion to 28 Clubs Likely By '76," *Sporting News*, August 24, 1974: 11; and, editorial, "Expansion in the Cards," *Sporting News*, August 24, 1974: 16.

26. "FC, 9/24/1975," Kuhn Papers. FC stood for franchise committee an owners' committee designated to deal with Seattle and other issues of franchise movement and sale. It was chaired by the Mets' Donald Grant and included the Royals' Ewing Kauffman, the Brewers' Bud Selig, and the Expos' John McHale.

27. "Minutes of Executive Council Meetings," March 21, 1974, July 15, 1975, and August 15, 1978, Kuhn Papers.

28. Kuhn, *Hardball*, 193.

29. Jerome Holtzman, "Charlie-Harry vs. Establishment," *Sporting News*, August 2, 1975: 18.

30. Lindberg, *Who's on 3rd?*, 157.

31. Rick Talley, "White Sox Sale Rumors Alive," *Chicago Tribune*, November 1, 1975.

32. Red Smith column, *Washington Post*, February 3, 1963.

33. David Condon, "Veeck's 'Last Hurrah,'" *Chicago Tribune*, October 4, 1975.

34. David Condon, "AL Rejects Veeck Offer," *Chicago Tribune*, December 4, 1975.

35. Nancy Kool, "Enlightenment and the Oldest Tiger," *Detroit Monthly*, April 1981: 37–38.

36. Dick Young, "Bonds, Veeck, Other Baseball Characters," *Santa Ana (California) Register*, December 17, 1975.

37. Mullins, *Becoming Big League*, 269.

38. Mullins, *Becoming Big League*, 267.

39. "Memorandum, July 2, 1975, To: Franchise Committee, From: BKK"; see also Mullins, *Becoming Big League*, 279.

40. Mullins, *Becoming Big League*, 280–81.

41. "*Franchise Committee Report*, Draft 1/8/76," and "*Final*, January 9, 1976," Kuhn Papers.

42. The leagues had divided many issues on a per-franchise basis. Each team, at that point, got 1/24th of national television revenues, meaning each league got 50 percent. When the American League went to fourteen teams, would the money be divided into twenty-six shares or would the money be divided equally between leagues and then parceled out between teams? The leagues delayed this issue by keeping the Mariners and Royals out of the TV revenue package for several years. There were similar issues with revenue from the World Series and All-Star games. There was also a question about access to amateur talent. If the current system of each team picking in order was retained, the American League would get fourteen first-round choices while the National League received only twelve. Over time, this could direct more talent to the American League.

43. *Franchise Committee Report*.

44. Leonard Koppett column, *Sporting News*, May 15, 1976: 4. This has been borne out since interleague play was instituted in 1997. While games against "natural rivals," such as Mets-Yankees or A's-Giants, draw extremely well, those against other non-league opponents generally attract fewer fans.

45. Helyar, *Lords of the Realm*, 199.

46. MacPhail, *My Nine Innings*, 132–33.

47. "Seattle Rejoins AL Next Year," *Los Angeles Times*, January 15, 1976.

48. Neil MacCarl, "N.L. Is Impressed by Toronto Group," *Sporting News*, January 31, 1976: 34.

49. MacCarl, "N.L. Is Impressed by Toronto Group."

50. "MacPhail Vows Seattle Will Get Team," *Los Angeles Times*, January 16, 1976.

51. Ed Prell, "Majors Split on Expansion—Kuhn's Hot Potato," *Sporting News*, January 31, 1976: 33.

52. "American League Votes Seattle '77 Franchise," *Los Angeles Times*, February 1, 1976.

53. C. C. Johnson Spink, "What Happened to Unity?," *Sporting News*, February. 21, 1976: 12.

54. Mullins, *Becoming Big League*, 279–80.

55. "Toronto to Get a Team . . . One Way or the Other," *Los Angeles Times*, March 21, 1976; Leonard Koppett, "Drastic Changes Seen for Baseball," *New York Times*, February 18, 1976; Murray Chass, "Baseball Leagues Both Eye Toronto," *New York Times*, March 21, 1976.

56. "A.L. Moves First, Gives Toronto Expansion Team for 1977," *Los Angeles Times*, March 27, 1976; "N.L. Votes Down Expansion in '77," *Los Angeles Times*, March 30, 1976.

57. "*Decision Re: Major League Expansion Plans*," April 1, 1976, and April 16, 1976, Kuhn Papers. See also Steve Cady, "Kuhn Urges National League Expand," *New York Times*, April 17, 1976.

58. Leonard Koppett, "National League Bars Expansion," *New York Times*, April 27, 1976.

59. Kuhn, *Hardball*, 194.

60. "N.L. Asleep at Switch?," *Sporting News*, April 17, 1976: 12.

Chapter Thirteen

1. MacPhail, *My Nine Innings*; Harold Rosenthal, "New World Opens to Bird Boss MacPhail," *Sporting News*, November 12, 1958: 7; Doug Brown, "MacPhail: 'Vast Capacity for Work,'" *Sporting News*, December 18, 1965: 5; Leonard Koppett, "'Be Yourself'— Lee MacPhail's Credo," *Sporting News*, December 3, 1966: 4; Richard Goldstein, "Lee MacPhail, Executive Who Led American League, Dies at 95," *New York Times*, November 9, 2012; and Mark Armour, *Lee MacPhail* on the BioProject website of the Society for American Baseball Research, https://sabr.org/bioproj/person/641271d3, retrieved April 16, 2020.

2. Thomas Boswell, "MacPhail an All-Star in Any League," *Washington Post*, March 6, 1986.

3. MacPhail, *My Nine Innings*, 125–26.

4. Arthur Daley column, *New York Times*, October 25, 1973.

5. Edgar J. Driscoll Jr., "Baseball's Joe Cronin dead at 77," *Boston Globe*, September 8, 1984. Cronin was born and raised in San Francisco, but at the time of his death had lived almost half a century in the Boston area.

6. MacPhail, *My Nine Innings*, 131.

7. MacPhail's reports are in Bowie Kuhn's papers at the Giamatti Research Center of the National Baseball Hall of Fame and Museum.

8. MacPhail, *My Nine Innings*, 158.

9. MacPhail, *My Nine Innings*, 155, 178.

10. Boswell, "An All Star in Any League."

11. MacPhail, *My Nine Innings*, 152.

12. Madden, *Steinbrenner: The Last Lion of Baseball* is an excellent biography of the Yankee owner and a shrewd assessment of how he handled Madden and other reporters.

13. Burke, *Outrageous Good Fortune*.

14. Responsibility for the payments were eventually passed to the State of New York, which is still paying off the bonds as of 2020. For details of this misbegotten civic subsidy, see Sullivan, *The Diamond in the Bronx*, or Auletta, *The Streets Were Paved with Gold*.

15. Leonard Koppett column, *Sporting News*, August 16, 1975: 4.

16. Pennington, *Billy Martin*, 236.

17. Interview with Marvin Miller, April 18, 2001.

18. Interview with Bob Lurie, May 31, 2018.

19. Over the same years, Leonard Coleman served as the last National League president.

20. Just because the owners had this, didn't mean they would use it consistently.

BIBLIOGRAPHY

Archives and Websites

Baltimore Public Library

The Burton Historical Collection at the Detroit Public Library

Chicago Public Library

The Dallas History and Archives section of the Dallas Public Library

Bowie Kuhn Papers, Giamatti Research Center, National Baseball Hall of Fame and Museum

LA84 Library

Los Angeles Public Library

The Newspaper Archive Room at the New York Public Library

Owner and Executive Biographical files, Giamatti Research Center, National Baseball Hall of Fame and Museum

Branch Rickey Papers, Library of Congress

San Francisco History Center, San Francisco Public Library.

Seattle Pilots Baseball Team website: www.SeattlePilots.com, especially Mike Fuller's interviews with Max Soriano, Dewey Soriano, and Buzzie Bavasi

The Sports Research Center at Cleveland Public Library

Bill Veeck Papers, Chicago Historical Society

The Frank P. Zeidler Humanities Room at the Milwaukee Public Library

Books

Anderson, David. *Quotations from Chairman Calvin.* Stillwater, MN: Brick Alley Books Press, 1984.

Appel, Marty. *Pinstripe Empire: The New York Yankees from Before the Babe to After the Boss.* New York: Bloomsbury, 2012.

Armour, Mark. *Joe Cronin: A Life in Baseball.* Lincoln: University of Nebraska Press, 2010.

Armour, Mark L., and Daniel R. Levitt. *Paths to Glory: How Great Baseball Teams Got That Way.* Washington, DC: Brassey's, 2003.

Auletta, Ken. *The Streets Were Paved with Gold.* New York: Random House, 1979.

Autry, Gene, with Mickey Herskowitz. *Back in the Saddle Again.* Garden City, NY: Doubleday, 1978.

Banner, Stuart. *The Baseball Trust: A History of Baseball's Antitrust Exemption*. New York: Oxford University Press, 2013.

Baylor, Don, with Claire Smith. *Nothing but the Truth: A Baseball Life*. New York: St. Martin's Press, 1989.

Bisher, Furman. *Miracle in Atlanta*. Cleveland, OH: World Publishing, 1966.

Blair, Jeff. *Full Count: Four Decades of Blue Jays*. Toronto: Random House, 2013.

Bohmer, David. *Cleveland Indians Team Ownership History*. Phoenix, AZ: Society for American Baseball Research, https://sabr.org/research/cleveland-indians -team-ownership-history.

Bordman, Sid. *An Intimate History of the Kansas City Royals*. Kansas City, MO: Walsworth Publishing, 1981.

Bouton, Jim. *Ball Four: My Life and Hard Times Throwing the Knuckleball*. Edited by Leonard Schechter. New York: World Publishing, 1970.

Boxerman, Burton A., and Benita W. Boxerman. *George Weiss: Architect of the Golden Age Yankees*. Jefferson, NC: McFarland, 2016.

Brunt, Stephen. *Diamond Dreams: Twenty Years of Blue Jays Baseball*. Toronto: Viking/Penguin, 1996.

Buhite, Russell D. *The Continental League: A Personal Memoir*. Lincoln: University of Nebraska Press, 2014.

Burk, Robert F. *Marvin Miller: Baseball Revolutionary*. Champaign: University of Illinois Press, 2015.

Burke, Michael. *Outrageous Good Fortune*. Boston: Little, Brown, 1984.

Cashen, J. Frank. *Winning in Both Leagues: Reflections from Baseball's Front Office*. Lincoln: University of Nebraska Press, 2014.

Deane, Bill. *Baseball Myths*. Lanham, MD: Scarecrow Press, 2012.

Dickson, Paul. *Bill Veeck: Baseball's Greatest Maverick*. New York: Walker, 2012.

Duckstad, Eric E., and Bruce Waybur. *Feasibility of a Major Sports Stadium for King County, Washington*. Menlo Park, CA: Stanford Research Institute, 1960.

Durso, Joseph. *The All-American Dollar: The Big Business of Sports*. Boston: Houghton Mifflin, 1971.

Eskenazi, Gerald. *Bill Veeck, a Baseball Legend*. New York: McGraw-Hill, 1988.

Ewald, Dan. *John Fetzer: On a Handshake: The Times and Triumphs of a Tiger Owner*. Champaign, IL: Sagamore Publishing, 1997.

Fetter, Henry. *Taking on the Yankees: Winning and Losing in the Business of Baseball*. New York: W.W. Norton, 2003.

Fetzer, John E. *The Men from Wengen and America's Agony*. Kalamazoo, MI: John E. Fetzer Foundation, 1971.

———. *One Man's Family: A History and Genealogy of the Fetzer Family*. Ann Arbor, MI: Ann Arbor Press, 1964

Finley, Nancy. *Finley Ball: How Two Outsiders Turned the Oakland A's into a Dynasty and Changed the Game Forever*. Washington, DC: Regnery History, 2016.

Finnerty, Margaret. *Del Webb: A Man, a Company*, with second edition text by Tara Blanc and Jessica McCann. Phoenix, AZ: Heritage Publishers, 1999.

Florio, John, and Ouisie Shapiro. *One Nation Under Baseball: How the 1960s Collided with the National Pastime*. Lincoln: University of Nebraska Press, 2017.

Frick, Ford C. *Games, Asterisks and People: Memoirs of a Lucky Fan*. New York: Crown Publishers, 1973.

Garratt, Robert F. *Home Team: The Turbulent History of the San Francisco Giants*. Lincoln: University of Nebraska Press, 2017.

George-Warren, Holly. *Public Cowboy No. 1: The Life and Times of Gene Autry*. New York: Oxford University Press, 2007.

Golenbock, Peter. *George: The Poor Little Rich Boy Who Built the Yankee Empire*. New York: John Wiley & Sons, 2009.

Graham, Frank. *The New York Yankees: An Informal History*. New York: G.P. Putnam's, 1951.

Green, G. Michael, and Roger D. Launius. *Charlie Finley: The Outrageous Story of Baseball's Super Showman*. New York: Walker, 2010.

Greenberg, Hank, edited with an Introduction by Ira Berkow. *Hank Greenberg: The Story of My Life*. New York: TimesBooks, 1989.

Halberstam, David. *October 1964*. New York: Villard, 1994.

Hammarstrom, David. *Big Top Boss: John Ringling North and the Circus*. Champaign: University of Illinois Press, 1992.

Harris, David. *The League: The Rise and Decline of the NFL*. New York: Bantam Books, 1986.

Helyar, John. *Lords of the Realm: The Real History of Baseball*. New York: Villard Books, 1994.

Hensler, Paul. *The American League in Transition, 1965–1975: How Competition Thrived When the Yankees Didn't*. Jefferson, NC: McFarland, 2013.

———. *The New Boys of Summer*. Lanham, MD: Rowman & Littlefield, 2017.

Hirshberg, Al. *The Red Sox: The Bean and the Cod*. Boston: Waverly House, 1947.

———. *What's the Matter with the Red Sox*. New York: Dodd, Mead, 1973.

Hogan, Kenneth. *The 1969 Seattle Pilots: Major League Baseball's One-Year Team*. Jefferson, NC: McFarland, 2007.

Holtzman, Jerome. "A.L. Vote to Expand Marks 1967 History." In *The Sporting News Official Baseball Guide for 1968*, edited by Chris Roewe and Oscar Kahan, 175–82. St. Louis: The Sporting News, 1968.

———. *The Commissioners: Baseball's Midlife Crisis*. New York: Total Sports, 1998.

Houk, Ralph. *Ballplayers Are Human, Too*. Edited by Charles Dexter. New York: G.P. Putnam's, 1962.

Kachline, Clifford, with Chris Roewe, eds. *The Sporting News Official Baseball Guide for 1966*. St. Louis: Charles C. Spink & Son, 1966.

Katz, Jeff. *The Kansas City A's and the Wrong Half of the Yankees: How the Yankees Controlled Two of the Eight American League Franchises during the 1950s*. Hingham, MA: Maple Street Press, 2007.

———. *Split Season, 1981: Fernandomania, the Bronx Zoo, and the Strike That Saved Baseball*. New York: Thomas Dunne Books, 2015.

Kelley, Brent. *Baseball's Biggest Blunder: The Bonus Rule of 1953–1957*. Lanham, MD: Scarecrow Press, 1997.

Kerr, Jon. *Calvin: Baseball's Last Dinosaur*. Dubuque, IA: Wm. C. Brown, 1990.

Korr, Charles P. *The End of Baseball as We Knew It: The Players Union, 1960–1981*. Urbana: University of Illinois Press, 2002.

Kuhn, Bowie. *Hardball: The Education of a Baseball Commissioner*. New York: Times Books, 1987.

Leavengood, Ted. *Clark Griffith: The Old Fox of Washington Baseball*. Jefferson, NC: McFarland, 2011.

Lindberg, Richard C. *Stealing First in a Two-Team Town: The White Sox from Comiskey to Reinsdorf*. Champaign, IL: Sagamore Publishing, 1994.

———. *Who's on 3rd?: The Chicago White Sox Story*. South Bend, IN: Icarus Press, 1983.

Luke, Bob. *Integrating the Orioles: Baseball and Race in Baltimore*. Jefferson, NC: McFarland, 2016.

Lyons, Robert S. *On Any Given Sunday: A Life of Bert Bell*. Philadelphia: Temple University Press, 2009.

MacPhail, Lee. *My Nine Innings: An Autobiography of 50 Years in Baseball*. Westport, CT: Meckler Books, 1989.

Madden, Bill. *Steinbrenner: The Last Lion of Baseball*. New York: HarperCollins, 2010.

Madden, W. C. *Baseball's First-Year Player Draft*. Jefferson, NC: McFarland, 2001.

McCue, Andy. *Mover and Shaker: Walter O'Malley, the Dodgers, and Baseball's Westward Expansion*. Lincoln: University of Nebraska Press, 2014.

McGregor, Robert Kuhn. *A Calculus of Color: The Integration of Baseball's American League*. Jefferson, NC: McFarland, 2015.

McGuff, Joe. *Winning It All: The Chiefs of the AFL*. New York: Doubleday, 1970.

McKelvey, G. Richard. *All Bat, No Glove: A History of the Designated Hitter*. Jefferson, NC: McFarland, 2004.

Mead, William B. *The Explosive Sixties*. Alexandria, VA: Redefinition, 1989.

Meany, Tom. *The Yankee Story*. New York: E. F. Dutton, 1960.

Mehl, Ernest. *The Kansas City Athletics*. New York: Henry Holt, 1956.

Metz, Robert. *CBS: Reflections in a Bloodshot Eye*. Chicago: Playboy Press, 1975.

Miles, Clarence W. *Eight Busy Decades: The Life and Times of Clarence W. Miles*. Edited by Jacques Kelly. Queenstown, MD: White Banks, 1986.

Miller, James Edward. *The Baseball Business: Pursuing Pennants and Profits in Baltimore*. Chapel Hill: University of North Carolina Press, 1990.

Miller, Marvin. *A Whole Different Ball Game*. New York: Birch Lane Press, 1991.

Millson, Larry. *Ballpark Figures: The Blue Jays and the Business of Baseball*. Toronto: McClelland and Stewart, 1987.

Moffi, Larry. *The Conscience of the Game: Baseball's Commissioners from Landis to Selig*. Lincoln: University of Nebraska Press, 2006.

Morgan, Anne. *Prescription for Success: The Life and Values of Ewing Marion Kauffman*. Kansas City, MO: Andrews and McMeel, 1995.

Mullins, Bill. *Becoming Big League: Seattle, the Pilots, and Stadium Politics*. Seattle: University of Washington Press, 2013.

Newhan, Ross. *The Anaheim Angels: A Complete History*. New York: Hyperion, 2000.

Nowlin, Bill. *Tom Yawkey: Patriarch of the Boston Red Sox*. Lincoln: University of Nebraska Press, 2018.

Nowlin, Bill, and Bill Carle, eds. *Kansas City Royals: A Royal Tradition*. Phoenix, AZ: The Society for American Baseball Research, 2019.

Paley, William S. *As It Happened: A Memoir by William S. Paley, Founder and Chairman of CBS*. Garden City, NY: Doubleday, 1979.

Paper, Lewis J. *Empire: William S. Paley and the Making of CBS*. New York: St. Martin's Press, 1987.

Parrott, Harold. *The Lords of Baseball*. New York: Praeger, 1976.

Paul, Jennie, with Jody Lynn Smith. *The Yankee Princess: Why Dad and I Were in a League of Our Own*. Columbia, MD: Silloway Press, 2011.

Pennington, Bill. *Billy Martin: Baseball's Flawed Genius*. Boston: Houghton Mifflin Harcourt, 2015.

Pessah, Jon. *The Game: Inside the Secret World of Major League Baseball's Power Brokers*. New York: Little, Brown, 2015.

Peterson, John E. *The Kansas City Athletics: A Baseball History, 1954–1967*. Jefferson, NC: McFarland, 2003.

Pietrusza, David. *Judge and Jury: The Life and Times of Judge Kenesaw Mountain Landis*. South Bend, IN: Diamond Communications, 1998.

Preston, Joseph G. *Major League Baseball in the 1970s: A Modern Game Emerges*. Jefferson, NC: McFarland, 2004.

Quirk, James, and Rodney D. Fort. *Pay Dirt: The Business of Professional Team Sports*. Princeton, NJ: Princeton University Press, 1992.

Robinson, Eddie, with C. Paul Rogers III. *Lucky Me: My Sixty-Five Years in Baseball*. Lincoln: University of Nebraska Press, 2015.

Roewe, Chris, and Oscar Kahan, eds. *The Sporting News Official Baseball Guide for 1968*. St. Louis, MO: The Sporting News, 1968.

Ryczek, William J. *Baseball on the Brink: The Crisis of 1968*. Jefferson, NC: McFarland, 2009.

Schaap, Dick. *Steinbrenner!* New York: G.P. Putnam's, 1982.

Selig, Bud, with Phil Rogers. *For the Good of the Game*. New York: William Morrow, 2019.

Shapiro, Michael. *Bottom of the Ninth*. New York: Times Books, 2009.

Smith, Sally Bedell. *In All His Glory: The Life of William S. Paley, the Legendary Tycoon and His Brilliant Circle*. New York: Simon and Schuster, 1990.

Sobel, Robert. *The Rise and Fall of the Conglomerate Kings*. New York: Stein and Day, 1984.

Stout, Glenn, and Richard A. Johnson. *Red Sox Century: One Hundred Years of Red Sox Baseball*. Boston: Houghton Mifflin, 2000.

Sullivan, Neil J. *The Diamond in the Bronx: Yankee Stadium and the Politics of New York*. New York: Oxford University Press, 2001.

———. *The Diamond Revolution: The Prospects for Baseball After the Collapse of Its Ruling Class*. New York: St. Martin's Press, 1992.

Surdam, David G. *The Postwar Yankees: Baseball's Golden Age Revisited*. Lincoln: University of Nebraska Press, 2008.

Thomas, Evan. *The Man to See: Edward Bennett Williams, Ultimate Insider; Legendary Trial Lawyer*. New York: Simon & Schuster, 1991.

Torry, Jack. *Endless Summers: The Fall and Rise of the Cleveland Indians*, updated ed. South Bend, IN: Diamond Communications, 1996.

Ueberroth, Peter, with Richard Levin and Amy Quinn. *Made in America: His Own Story*. New York: William Morrow, 1985.

Van Lindt, Carson. *The Seattle Pilots Story*. New York: Marabou Publishing, 1993.

Van Rjndt, Philippe, and Patrick Blednick. *Fungo Blues: The Inside Story of Canada's Most Popular Baseball Team*. Toronto: Seal Books, 1985.

Veeck, Bill, with Ed Linn. *The Hustler's Handbook*. New York: G.P. Putnam's, 1965.

———. *Thirty Tons a Day: The Rough-riding Education of a Neophyte Race Track Operator*. New York: Viking, 1972.

———. *Veeck—As in Wreck*. New York: G.P. Putnam's, 1962.

Veve, Thomas D. "Before the Boss: Mike Burke and the CBS Yankees." In *Baseball/Literature/Culture: Essays, 2006–2007*, edited by Ronald E. Kates and Warren Tormey, 150–159. Jefferson, NC: McFarland, 2008.

Vincent, Fay. *The Last Commissioner: A Baseball Valentine*. New York: Simon & Schuster, 2002.

Walker, James R., and Robert V. Bellamy, Jr. *Center Field Shot: A History of Baseball on Television*. Lincoln: University of Nebraska Press, 2008.

Weiner, Jay. *Stadium Games: Fifty Years of Big League Greed and Bush League Boondoggles*. Minneapolis: University of Minnesota Press, 2000.

Weingarden, Steve, and Bill Nowlin, eds. *Baseball's Business: The Winter Meetings, Volume 2, 1958–2016*. Phoenix, AZ: The Society for American Baseball Research, 2017.

Whitfield, Shelby. *Kiss It Good-Bye*. New York: Abelard-Schuman, 1973.

Zantow, Chris. *Building the Brewers: Bud Selig and the Return of Major League Baseball to Milwaukee*. Jefferson, NC: McFarland, 2019.

Zimbalist, Andrew. *Baseball and Billions: A Probing Look Inside the Big Business of Our National Pastime*. New York: Basic Books, 1992.

———. *In the Best Interests of Baseball?* Hoboken, NJ: John Wiley, 2006.

Zimniuch, Fran. *Baseball's New Frontier: A History of Expansion, 1961–1998*. Lincoln: University of Nebraska Press, 2013.

Interviews

Roland Hemond, March 3, 2017

Bob Lurie, May 31, 2018

Marvin Miller, April 18, 2001

Aaron, Hank, 6
ABC, 56
Adams, Bud, 31, 32
Addie, Bob, 28, 70, 94, 121
Agee, Tommy, 7
Allen, Dick, 108
Allied Chemical, 115
Allyn, Arthur, Jr., 58, 59–61, 64, 72, 88, 96, 106, 107, 136
Allyn, Arthur, Sr., 60
Allyn, John, 60, 107, 120–21, 123, 136
Amateur draft, 50–1
American Football League, 32
American League, 9, 55, 58, 62, 72, 89, 97, 99, 107, 112, 117, 122, 124, 137–38, 142n8; All-Star games, 56; attendance, xi, 8, 29, 79–80, 110–12, 137; attitude toward NL, xii, 87, 126; presidents, 28, 130, 138
American Record Corp., 44–45
American Shipbuilding, 114, 132
Anaheim, 41
Antitrust exemption, 2–3, 59, 63, 78, 97, 121, 137–38, 141n4
Astrodome, 39
Atlanta Braves, 65, 79, 112
Armour, Mark, 27
Atlanta, Ga, 81
Atlanta Constitution, 81
Attendance, 8, 10, 13, 29, 40–41, 79–80, 97, 110–12, 118, 135–6, 137; charts 80, 98, 136, 147n1, 159n30
Austin, Thomas, 18
Automatic Canteen Corp. of America, 16

Autry, Gene, 37, 41, 42, 44–46, 48, 58, 94, 115, 123, 135

Baltimore Orioles, 11, 22, 34, 121–22, 127, 129
Bank of California, 95
Banks, Ernie, 6
Barket, Alex, 84
Barnes, Donald, 10, 29
Barrow, Ed, 134
Bavasi, Buzzie, 68
Bavasi, Peter, 100
Bell, Bert, xiii
Bisher, Furman, 81
Blue, Vida, 112
Boeing Co., 91
Bohemian Beer, 67
Bonda, Ted, 109–10
Bonus Rule, 32
Boston Braves, 10; move to Milwaukee, 11, 141n2
Boston Globe, 80, 130
Boston Red Sox, 7, 18–20, 27, 53, 84; segregationist attitudes, 19, 27
Boswell, Thomas, 132
Bowling Green University, 108
Braman, Dorm, 90, 93
Bregman, Stan, 104–5
Brett, George, 131–32
Brinkman, Eddie, 105
Broeg, Bob, 39
Bronfman, Charles, v
Brooklyn Dodgers, 6, 9; move to Los Angeles, 12, 16, 29, 65, 147n8, 149n43
Brooklyn Dodgers (football), 15

Brougham, Royal, 124
Brown Brothers Harriman, 31
Brown, Dr. Bobby, 115
Brown, Kenyon, 20
Budig, Gene, 138
Buffalo, NY, 78, 86
Bunker, George, 47
Burger King, 73–74
Burke, Michael, 69–71, 72, 73–74, 113–14, 134–35
Busch, Gussie, 64, 116, 136
Business Week, 73
Buzas, Joe, 84

California Angels. *See* Los Angeles Angels
Callison, Johnny, 114
Campanella, Roy, 6
Candlestick Park, 29, 83, 119
Cannon, Billy, 32
Cannon, Robert, 64
Caray, Harry, 108
Carlson, Edward, 91, 95, 96
Carroll, Louis, 64
Carroll, Parke, 25, 26
Cartwright, Gary, 115
Cashen, Frank, 68
CBS, 55, 70, 106; as television broadcaster, 55, 56; as Yankees owner, 57–59, 67, 113–15
Celler, Congressman Emanuel, 11
Central Intelligence Agency, 69
Chadwick, Henry, 110
Chambliss, Chris, 133
Chandler, Albert "Happy," 7, 17, 19, 62, 72, 138
Chance, Dean, 43
Charlotte, NC, 26
Chattanooga, TN, 26
Chicago Cubs, 6, 9, 23

Chicago Sun-Times, 107
Chicago Tribune, 57, 123
Cleveland Barons, 109
Cleveland Cavaliers, 109
Chicago White Sox, 21, 24, 25, 48, 58, 96, 107–8, 120–21, 123
Cincinnati Reds, 9, 10, 20, 30, 51, 112, 127
Cleveland Indians, 6, 20–22, 24, 123, 133; potential moves, 21, 34, 51, 89, 91, 108
Cleveland Pipers, 114
Cleveland Stadium, 109
Cobb, Ty, 18
Coca-Cola Corp., 73, 106
Cohn, Dave, 92, 125
Cole, Edwin, 119
Comiskey Park, 123
Commissioner's Office, 1, 62–5, 71–74, 129, 143n5, 154n7
Conrad, Frank, 54
Continental League, 18, 30–33, 147n11
Cooke, Jack Kent, 31, 103
Corbett, Brad, 114–16, 122, 167n56
Cronin, Joe, 27–28, 30, 33, 37, 42–43, 49, 58–59, 61, 64, 66, 75, 79, 81, 85, 88, 90, 92, 95, 105, 130, 171n5
Cullinan, Craig, 31, 33
Culver Academy, 113
Cutler-Hammer Inc., 99

Daily News (New York), 66, 83, 134
Daley, Arthur, 34, 71, 130
Daley, William, 20–22, 51, 52, 91–92, 95, 125, 164n53
Dallas-Ft. Worth, xi, 35, 39–40, 51, 78, 86, 95–96, 104, 107, 115, 116
Dallas News, 76
Dallas Times-Herald, 116
Daniel, Dan, 35
Danz, Fred, 95
Danzansky, Joseph, xi, 106, 118

Dark, Alvin, 83–84
Davis, Dwight, Jr., 31
Davis, Ilus, 85
Davis, Tommy, 9, 94
Dayton-Hudson Co., 31
Designated hitter rule, 109–12; chart, 111
Dean, Dizzy, 56
Del E. Webb Construction Co., 16–18
Democratic National Committee, 103
Denver, CO, 86
Detroit Lions, 46
Detroit News, 55
Detroit Tigers, 7, 18, 20, 48, 54, 67
Devine, Bing, 64, 78
DeWitt, Bill, 20
DiMaggio, Dominic, 19
Doby, Larry, 6
Dodger Stadium, 29, 36, 37
Doherty, Ed, 42
Dolin, Nate, 20–22, 47, 60
Dominican Republic, 65
Donovan, William, 69
Drysdale, Don, 110
DuPont, Francis I., & Co., 107
Durso, Joe, 70

Eaton, Cyrus, 21
Ebbets Field, 12, 15
Ebony, 7
Eckert, William, 62, 64–67, 71, 79, 155n23
Emmanuel College, 54, 153n1
ESPN, 137
Everett, Marjorie, 118
Ewald, Dan, 6,
Executive Council,
Expansion (1961–62), 16, 22, 29–43, 55, 78
Expansion (1969), xii, 78–79, 84–88, 159n21
Expansion (1977), 117–28
Expansion draft (1960), 36, 41–43, 150n55

Feeney, Chub, 71, 72, 73, 118, 121, 126
Fenway Park, 19
Fetzer, John, 20, 38, 48, 54–57, 58, 62, 63, 99, 100, 123
Fetzer Institute, 55
Figueroa, Ed, 133
Finley, Charles O., 25, 48–51, 58, 61, 74, 75–88, 89, 90, 97, 101, 104, 105, 108, 112, 117, 118–19, 121, 122, 126, 131
Finley, Nancy, 76
Fishel, Bob, 132
Fitzgerald, Edmund, 99, 107
Fitzgerald, Edmund B., 99, 164n54
Flood, Curt, 104
Forbes (magazine), 70
Fort Worth Star-Telegram, 116
Forward Thrust, 90, 92
Fox, Larry, 64
Fox Television, 138
Franklin, Pete, 52
Frick, Ford, 1–2, 4, 12, 16, 18, 29, 32, 36, 37, 55, 61, 62, 63–65, 72, 77, 78
Friday, Pat, 77
Frisco Railroad (St. Louis–San Francisco Railway), 44

Galbreath, John W., 38, 63, 119
General Motors, 119
George Washington University, 26
Gibson, Bob, 110
Giles, Warren, 8, 34, 51, 61, 66, 85, 86
Gillette Co., 106
Golden West Broadcasting, 45, 94
Golub, Stan, 125
Gordon, Joe, 20, 75, 76, 77
Gorton, Slade, 126
Gossage, Goose, 131
Grba, Eli, 42
Green, G. Michael, 77
Greenberg, Hank, 9, 25, 34, 37

Greenwade, Tom, 7
Grigsby, Bill, 77
Griffith, Calvin, 4, 20, 26–27, 30, 34, 35, 38,
  58, 59, 64, 110, 120, 136
Griffith, Clark, 15, 26, 27; racial attitudes,
  26
Griffith Stadium, 26, 39

Hall of Fame, 129
Hamey, Roy, 23
Hamms Brewing, 31
Haney, Fred, 42, 46
Harrelson, Ken, 83–84
Harridge, Will, 27, 80
Harvard University, 64
Haynes, Joe, 26
Haynes, Thelma, 26
Heisman Trophy, 32
Hemingway, Ernest, 69
Hemond, Roland, 108
Henie, Sonja, 14
Herrmann, August "Gary," 1,
Herseth, Arthur "Bud," 120, 121
Hicks, Joe, 43
Hiller, Jean, 19
Hirshberg, Al, 27
Hoffberger, Jerold, 64, 66, 67–8, 71, 72, 74,
  106, 115, 122, 127
Hofheinz, Roy, 31, 52, 65, 86
Holland, John, 72
Hollywood Park, 118
Holtzman, Jerome, 57, 74, 107
Hornsby, Rogers, 46
Houk, Ralph, 114, 133
Houston, Tx, 51, 86
Houston Astros (Colt .45s), 33–34, 38, 39,
  52, 112
Houston Oilers, 32
Howard, Elston, 6
Howsam, Bob, 31
Humphrey, Hubert, 103

Hunt, Lamar, 81, 107
Hunter, Jim "Catfish," 133
Hutchinson, Fred, 91

Iglehart, Joseph, 22, 38, 48, 59, 67
Integration, 6–8, 142nn1–3
Interleague play, 126, 138, 170n44
Irvin, Monte, 6
Irving School, 18

J. H. Whitney & Co., 31
Jackson, Henry, 86, 97
Jackson, Reggie, 112, 133
Japan, 65
Johnson, Arnold, 15–16, 18, 25, 34, 48, 75,
  84
Johnson, Byron "Ban," 8, 130
Johnson, Edwin, 31
Johnson, Lyndon Baines, 66
Johnston, Bruce, v
Johnston, James, 47–48, 103

Kachline, Cliff, 38
Kahn, Roger, 70
Kansas City Athletics, 11, 21, 25, 26, 34, 48,
  50, 75–88, 146n54; attendance, 77, 81;
  move to Dallas-Ft. Worth, 76–8; move
  to Louisville, 81; move to Oakland, xi,
  11, 75–88, 89, 101, 161n61
Kansas City Chiefs, 81
Kansas City Monarchs, 6
Kansas City Royals, 101, 108, 112, 131, 136
Kansas City Sports Council, 81
Kansas City Star, 76, 77, 81
Kansas City Times, 77
Kauffman, Ewing Marion, 5, 84, 101–3, 136
Kauffman Stadium, 81
Kaye, Danny, 125
Kaye-Smith Enterprises, 125, 127
KDKA, 54
Keelty, James, 22

Kefauver, Estes, 31–32
Keller, Hal, 42
Kennedy, Robert, 66, 71
King County (Wash.), 96, 117
King, Dr. Martin Luther, Jr., 65–66
Kingdome, 119, 124, 127
Kingswood School, 69
Kinsman Marine Transit, 114
Kirksey, George, 33
Klein, Richard, 52
KMPC, 45–46
Knorr, Fred, 20
Kohl's, 99
Koppett, Leonard, v, vi, 63, 65, 71, 110, 111
Krausse, Lew, 83–84
Krieger, Zanvyl, 22, 67–68
Kroc, Ray, 118
Kuhn, Bowie, vi, xi, 49, 71, 73, 79, 93, 96, 97, 105–7, 111, 116, 117, 118, 121–28, 131, 133

Labatt Brewery, 119, 125
Lafayette College, 107
Lake County Medical Society, 49
Landis, Kenesaw M., 1, 62, 71–72
Lane, Frank, 21, 75, 77, 145n32
Launius, Roger, 77
League Comparisons (AL v. NL), xiii, 9
League Park, 21
Lean Cuisine, 53
Lefevre, David, 52
Lehman Brothers, 57
LeMay, Curtis, 64
Lemon, Jim (Senators owner), 47, 103
Look, 24
Los Angeles Angels, 18, 36, 37, 39, 40–43, 48, 50, 68, 97, 112, 149n43
Los Angeles Dodgers, 29, 45, 50, 65, 68, 78, 97, 147n1
Los Angeles Lakers, 103
Los Angeles Times, 36
Lurie, Bob, 49, 119–20, 121, 138

Mack, Connie, 110
Macmillan Baseball Encyclopedia, 73
MacPhail, Larry, 7, 14, 15, 17, 129
MacPhail, Lee, v, 15, 22, 57, 64, 68, 70, 71, 72, 88, 89, 111, 114, 119, 129–32; as AL President, 123–8, 129–32; pine tar game, 131–32
Madden, Bill, 134
Magnuson, Warren, 86, 96, 97
Majestic Advertising Co., 77
Major League Baseball (MLB), xii, 131, 138
Major League Baseball Promotion Corp., 73–74, 100, 138
Major League Baseball Players Association, xiii, 46, 66, 87, 99, 117, 137
Marine Corps, 14–15, 23, 48, 99
Marion Laboratories, 102–3
Maris, Roger, 75
Mark Hopkins Hotel, 45
Marketing baseball, 63, 68, 73–74
Marriott, Willard, 106
Martin, Billy, 115, 131–32, 133
Mayo Clinic, 59
Mays, Willie, 6
McCarthy, Joe, 19
McClelland, Tim, 131
McDonald's Corp., 118
McGuff, Joe, 81, 84, 85
McLain, Denny, 105
McMullen, John, 113
Meany, Tom, 8
Medinger, George, 21
Mehl, Ernie, 76–78, 84, 85
Memorial Stadium (Baltimore), 67
Messersmith decision, 117, 137
Metzenbaum, Howard, 109
Meyer, Richard, 72
Meyers, Georg, 95
Miles, Clarence, 22
Mileti, Nick, 108–9
Miller, Marvin, xiii, 5, 46, 66, 135, 137

Milwaukee, WI, 86, 95, 96, 104, 107
Milwaukee Braves, 11; move to Atlanta, 11, 71, 78, 79, 99
Milwaukee Brewers (American Association), 23, 24, 99
Milwaukee Brewers (Major Leagues), xi, 97, 98, 99–100
Minneapolis, MN, 51
Minneapolis Lakers, 103
Minneapolis Star-Tribune, 31
Minnesota Twins, 58, 108, 110, 120, 123
Monday Night Baseball Spectacular, 56
Montreal, Que, 86
Montreal Expos, 87, 125
Moore, Marianne, 71
Moscone, George, 119–20, 125
Mullins, Bill, 97
Municipal Stadium (Kansas City), 75, 77, 81, 84
My Fair Lady, 58

National Association of Minor League Baseball Clubs, 72
National Brewing Co., 67–68
National Commission, 1,
National Football League, xiii, 55–56, 92, 124
National League, 9, 62, 72, 85, 98, 120, 126; attendance, xi, 29, 79–80, 119, 126; attitude toward AL, xii, 71, 87, 105, 126; expansion, 79; presidents, 51
NBC, 57, 106
Nettles, Graig, 132
Newark Star-News, 71
New Orleans, 83, 108, 118, 127
New York Giants, move to San Francisco, 12, 29
New York Herald Tribune, 123
New York Journal-American, 39
New York Mets, 33–34, 38, 39, 41, 78, 113
New York Times, 6, 7, 8, 34, 64, 70, 71, 83

New York Yankees, 7, 14, 19, 24, 25, 26, 40, 50, 54, 57–59, 62, 66, 67, 70, 75, 77, 94, 113, 129, 131, 132–37
Nixon, Richard, 64, 105, 109, 133
Nizer, Louis, 81
Nordstrom's, 92
North American Soccer League, 124
North, Henry Ringling, 69
North, John Ringling, 70
Northwestern Mutual Life Insurance, 99

Oakland Athletics, xi, 97–98, 118–19, 121
Oakland-Alameda County Coliseum, 83
O'Brien, Dan, 115
O'Brien, Johnny, 124
O'Connor, Leslie, 91
Odom, John "Blue Moon," 112
Office of Strategic Services (U.S.), 69
Ogle, Jim, 71
Ohio State University, 108, 114
O'Malley, Peter, 136
O'Malley, Walter, 4, 12, 29, 32–38, 41, 42, 50, 57, 63, 68, 72, 78, 105, 121, 122, 126, 149n43
Organizing/Re-organizing baseball, 71–74
Oscar Mayer, 99
Otis & Co., 21

Pacific Coast League, 11, 91
Pacific Northwest Sports, Inc., 91, 96
Paige, Satchel, 7
Paley, William, 57, 113
Parrott, Harold, 92
Paul, Gabe, 51–2, 64, 65, 91, 92, 109, 113, 114, 115, 130, 132, 133
Payson, Joan, 31, 147n9
Pepsi Cola Co., 106
Perot, Ross, 107
Peters, Hank, 76
Philadelphia Athletics, 7, 10, 15, 19, 36; move to Kansas City, 11, 15, 18, 76, 141n2

Philadelphia Eagles, xiii, 69
Philadelphia Phillies, 9, 30, 56, 112, 113, 127
Philip Morris Co., 106
Phoenix, AZ,
Pillsbury Corp., 31
Piniella, Lou, 133
Pittsburgh Pirates, 9, 10, 30, 50, 90, 112
Player Relations Committee, 99, 132
Pohlad, Carl, 119, 120
Polo Grounds, 39, 41
Porter, Paul, 50
Povich, Shirley, 20, 106
Purdue University, 54

Quesada, Elwood "Pete", 36, 47

Rainier Brewery, 89
Randolph, Willie, 133
Reading, Pa, 129
Reichler, Joe, 65
Reid, Daniel, 14, 144n1
Republic Pictures, 45
Reserve clause, 3,
Reynolds, Robert, 37, 45, 46
Ribble, Fred, 54–55
Richards, G.A., 46
Richards, Paul, 65
Richman, Milton, 71
Rickey, Branch, 6, 9, 30, 32, 33, 50
Rigney, Bill, 42, 46
Ringling Bros. Barnum and Bailey Circus,
    69–70
Rivers, Mickey, 133
Robertson, Billy, 26
Robertson, Calvin, 26
Robertson, Jimmy, 26
Robertson, Mildred, 27
Robertson, Sherry, 26
Robinson, Bill, 70, 156n41
Robinson, Eddie, 115, 116
Robinson, Frank, 6, 8, 109

Robinson, Jackie, 6
Robinson, Murray, 39
Robintech, 115, 116
Rodriguez, Aurelio, 105
Rogers, Will, 44
Rolaids, 74
Rosen, Al, 108
Rozelle, Pete, xiii, 56
Rudolph the Red-Nosed Reindeer, 45
Ruppert, Jacob, 14, 134

San Diego, CA, 86
San Diego Padres, 68, 87, 98, 117–18
San Francisco Giants, 29, 83, 85, 97–98, 113,
    119, 121; possible moves, 119–20, 126
San Francisco Seals, 46, 90
Saturday Evening Post, 8
Schlitz Brewing, 77, 81, 99
Schoenfeld, Walter, 125
Sears, Roebuck, 44
Seattle, WA, 86, 88, 89–90, 117–18, 120–21,
    124, 131
Seattle Mariners, 125–28
Seattle Pilots, 89–98, 97, 98, 101, 103, 108,
    161n70; attendance, 93–95; move to
    Milwaukee, xi, 98; organization, 90–92
Seattle Rainiers, 89, 90
Seattle Seahawks, 124
Seattle Sounders, 124
Seattle Times, 94, 95, 126
Seaver, Tom, 65
Selig, Allan H. "Bud," 97, 99–100, 107, 111
Selig, Donna, 100
Shea, Robert, 74
Shea, William, 30, 32, 64
Sheffield Scientific School, 18
Sherrod, Blackie, 116
Short, Bob, vi, xi, 103–6, 109, 114, 118,
    119–20, 136
Sick, Emil, 89, 91
Sicks' Stadium, 89–90, 93, 95, 101

Siegel, Bugsy, 17

Smith, C. Arnholt, 117–8

Smith, Lester, 125

Smith, R.E. "Bob," 31

Smith, Red, 15, 123

Smith, Wendell, 7

Soriano, Dewey, 90–92, 93, 95, 105, 109, 136, 161n8

Soriano, Max, 90–92, 94, 95

Spellman, John, 120–21, 123, 124

Spink, C. C. Johnson, 9, 71

Spink, J. G. Taylor, 12

Spoelstra, Watson, 55

Sport, 24

Sporting News, 9, 12, 20, 33, 34, 35, 38, 39, 41, 51, 58, 59, 63, 70, 71, 78, 81, 84, 94, 97, 110, 111, 113

Sports Illustrated, xiii, 17, 75

St. Louis Browns, 7, 10, 24; move to Baltimore, 11, 24, 141n2; move to Los Angeles, 10, 18, 29, 36

St. Louis Cardinals, 9, 21, 51, 112, 116, 136

St. Louis Post-Dispatch, 39

St. Louis-San Francisco Railway, 44

Stadiums, 112–13

Stanford Research Institute, 89, 92, 97

Stanford University, 46

Stanky, Eddie, 115

Stanton, Frank, 59, 70

Staub, Rusty, 66

Steinbrenner, George, 108, 113–14, 115, 121, 122, 129–30, 131–37, 167n55

Stengel, Casey, 15, 34, 42, 46

Stillwell, Jim, 125

Stoneham, Horace, 4, 12, 29, 83, 98, 119, 121, 136

Stouffer Foods, 52–53

Stouffer, Jim, 108

Stouffer, Lena, 52–53

Stouffer, Vernon, 52–53, 108, 113

Sukeforth, Clyde, 6

Symington, Stuart, 79, 84–88, 97

Teams, Inc., 99

Television policy, 55–57, 62

Texaco, 31

Texas Monthly, 115

Texas Rangers, xi, 114–16, 120

Thompson, Inez, 129

Tidrow, Dick, 133

Toolson v. New York Yankees, 3

Topping, Dan, 14–16, 24, 25, 34, 37, 57, 68–69, 75, 133, 134, 141n8, 153n14

Topping, John A., 14, 144n1

Toronto, Ont, 51, 86, 118–20, 125–28, 131

Toronto Blue Jays, 128, 147n1

Trimble, Joe, 66

Ueberroth, Peter, 130, 137–38

Uhlman, Wes, 126

United Press (UPI), 71

Universal Pipe and Plastics, 115

University of Illinois, 47

University of Michigan, 99

University of North Carolina, 47

University of Pennsylvania, 52, 69, 72

University of Virginia, 67

University of Washington, 90

University of Wisconsin, 99

U.S. National Bank, 118

Veal, Coot, 42

Vecsey, George, 71

Veeck As In Wreck, 123

Veeck, Bill, vi, xii, 4, 6, 18, 21, 22–25, 35, 37, 38, 43, 47,48, 49, 56, 59–60, 67, 115, 123, 124, 126, 136, 145n32

Venezuela, 65

Vernon, Mickey, 42

Volinn, Sidney, 97

Wagner, Robert, 30, 147n8
Wagner College, 115
Walker, George Herbert, 31, 147n10
Wall Street Journal, 48
Walsh, Jim, 125
Ward, Arch, 24
Washington (state), 117
Washington, D.C., attempt to get a 3rd team, 117, 121–2, 126–8
Washington, D.C. Armory Board, 105
Washington Post, 47, 94, 106, 121, 132
Washington Senators (1901–60), 7, 10, 26, 27, 29, 30, 41–43; move to Minneapolis-St. Paul, 20, 27, 30, 33, 34, 35, 40, 141n1, 147n6, 150n53
Washington Senators (1961–71), 35, 39, 47, 50, 66, 67, 103, 105–7; move to Arlington, TX, xi, 106–7, 118, 141n1
Washington, U. L., 132
Webb, Del, 9, 14, 15, 16–18, 20, 24, 25, 29, 33, 34, 35, 38, 57, 62, 75, 133, 134, 153n14
Weiss, George, 7, 14, 15, 24, 34, 57, 73, 129, 134
Western International Hotels, 92
Western International League, 91

Weyerhauser Corp., 92
Wharton School, 72
White, Frank, 103
Whitney, Wheelock, 31
Williams College, 113
Williams, Ted, 84, 104
Wills, Maury, 9, 66
Winfield, Dave, 133
WKZO, 54
WLS, 44
Wood, Wilbur, 108
Wrigley Field (Chicago), 23
Wrigley Field (Los Angeles), 38–39
Wrigley, Phil, 12, 32, 36

Yakima Bears, 91
Yale University, 18
Yankee Stadium, 15, 25, 57, 70, 134–35
Yawkey, Tom, 18–20, 25, 27, 30, 38, 53, 59, 85, 144n16
Yawkey, William, 18
Young, Dick, 65, 66–67, 97–98

Zimmerman, Hy, 94, 95, 126
Zimmerman, Paul (LA), 36
Zimmerman, Paul (NY), 22